The Aesthetics of Fantasy Literature and Art

edited by
Roger C. Schlobin

Copublished by

UNIVERSITY OF NOTRE DAME PRESS

and

THE HARVESTER PRESS

Notre Dame, Indiana 46556

First published in Great Britain 1982 by
The Harvester Press Limited
Publisher: John Spiers
16 Ship Street, Brighton, Sussex
ISBN 0-7108-0379-6

Grateful acknowledgment is made to the following sources:

The article "On the Nature of Fantasy" by C. N. Manlove is a revision of the "Introduction" to his *Modern Fantasy: Five Studies*. Cambridge, London, New York, and Melbourne: Cambridge University Press, 1975, pp. 1-12.

The article "Realms of Literary Fantasy: And the World Became Strange" by George P. Landow appeared in the *Georgia Review* (Spring 1979) and serves as a contributory essay to the exhibition catalog, *Fantastic Illustration and Design in Britain, 1850-1930,* © 1979, the Museum of Art, Rhode Island School of Design.

Illustrations by Henry J. Ford from *The Arabian Nights Entertainments,* ed. Andrew Lang, are used by permission of Longman.

Illustrations by John Batten from *Fairy Tales from the Arabian Nights,* ed. E. Dixon, are used by permission of J. M. Dent & Sons Ltd.

Illustrations by Edmund Dulac are published by Hodder & Stoughton Ltd. Copyright Edmund Dulac Estate.

Library of Congress Cataloging in Publication Data

Main entry under title:

The Aesthetics of fantasy literature and art.

Includes index.

1. Fantastic literature–History and criticism–Addresses, essays, lectures. 2. Fantasy in art–Addresses, essays, lectures. I. Schlobin, Roger C.

PN56.F34A35 809'.915 81-40446
ISBN 0-268-00598-2 AACR2
ISBN 0-268-00600-8 (pbk.)

Manufactured in the United States of America

THE AESTHETICS OF FANTASY LITERATURE AND ART

To Melody

For being there at the beginning,
For raccoons,
For Joshua,
For memories.

Contents

Preface

IT IS NOT so surprising or mysterious that this should be the first anthology of critical essays to examine the aesthetics of fantasy literature and art. Certainly it is true that in recent years a number of single-author, book-length studies have demonstrated a growing interest in fantasy within the scholarly community. The most notable of these are Tzvetan Todorov's *The Fantastic: A Structural Approach to a Literary Genre* (1970), C. N. Manlove's *Modern Fantasy: Five Studies* (1975), W. R. Irwin's *The Game of the Impossible: A Rhetoric of Fantasy* (1976), Eric S. Rabkin's *The Fantastic in Literature* (1976), Stephen Prickett's *Victorian Fantasy* (1979), this editor's *The Literature of Fantasy: A Comprehensive, Annotated Bibliography of Modern Fantasy Fiction* (1979), Brian Attebery's *The Fantasy Tradition in American Literature from Irving to Le Guin* (1980), and Rosemary Jackson's *Fantasy: The Literature of Subversion* (1981).[1]

Prior to 1970, however, examples of fantasy scholarship were scattered, infrequent, and often focused on so-called juvenile authors and works. Only E. M. Forster's essay, "Fantasy," in *Aspects of the Novel and Related Writings* (1927) and J. R. R. Tolkien's "On Fairy-Stories" (which first appeared in *Essays Presented to Charles Williams,* ed. C. S. Lewis [1947]) gained significant attention from the general scholarly community. In fact, were it not for various studies of individual nineteenth-century authors of "juvenile" fiction and nonsense verse—particularly George MacDonald, Charles Kingsley, William Morris, Lewis Carroll, and Edward Lear—modern fantasy scholarship would have little or no parentage.

A number of factors have contributed to this historical neglect and to the recent, seemingly "overnight" flurry of scholarly activity. The most obvious positive influence has been the Tolkien phenomenon and the dramatic popular and financial successes of fantasy art and literature both in the United States and abroad. Gradually this popular fascination has found its way into the classroom, so that it is now unusual to find a high school, college, or university that doesn't offer a course on fantasy (often allied with its young and empirical stepchild, science fiction). Still, the academic world has been slow to fully accept popular literature—or the "sub-literary," as it sometimes is smugly called. It is still rare to find fantasy, science-fiction, detective, or gothic literatures taught within existing, more traditional courses, despite the importance of these forms in the development of literary and aesthetic culture since the eighteenth century. Nonetheless, the popularity of fantasy literature has at last created within academia a community of scholars (as opposed to the vast population of informal and often knowledgeable enthusiasts, "fans," that has long existed in the popular realm) who are, out of necessity or affection, or both, deeply interested in fantasy.

One reason fantasy literature has succeeded in gaining only begrudging acceptance into mainstream, contemporary criticism is that most modern criticism emphasizes genres and specific literary aspects or tropes. Fantasy, however, is not detectible by such tools as theme, character, style, or structure. As E. M. Forster cogently points out, fantasy is "like a bar of light, that is intimately connected with them [time, character, logic, or their derivatives in the novel] at one place and patiently illumes all the problems, and at another place shoots over and through them as if they did not exist."[2]

That fantasy can be found in all types of fiction is well demonstrated in this anthology by a number of essays, particularly by Robert Crossley's comments on utopian fiction, Samuel H. Vasbinder's on lost-race adventure tales, Raymond H. Thompson's on medieval romance, and Jules Zanger's on heroic literature. Since it is unreasonable to expect that fantasy can be understood through the predominant analytical tools (although Kenneth J. Zahorski and Robert H. Boyer's contribution makes a strong case for the importance of "setting" in one subdivision of fantasy art), it is one of the goals of this volume to suggest other approaches. Central to these approaches is that fantasy, whether it be the dominant force in a work or one element of a larger concern, is characterized by a mode of thought that embraces the empirically impossible in its most elevated examples and the socially impossible in its most pedestrian ones. Yet, while successful fantasy is impossible from one perspective, which could vaguely be labelled "realistic," it must be psychologically valid, a point explored specifically in this volume by Gary K. Wolfe. A more general and more expansive approach to the same point is taken by C. N. Manlove, while William M. Schuyler, Jr.'s approach is a partially tongue-in-cheek examination of the validity of the arcane arts in fantasy literature.

This element of the impossible, central to most studies of fantasy,[3] has historically been disguised by numerous social preoccupations and critical methods. The concepts and turns of mind inherent in "religion," "myth," "romance," "chronicle," "epic," and "mysticism," among so many other systems, have frequently been rationalizations for the impossible, façades behind which fantasy has brooded unnoticed and unexplored. By way of illustration, consider the perspectives on natural law that are offered in the following quotation:

> nature was deformed by the emergence of a transcendent world, but the validity of natural laws remained fundamentally inviolate; *here,* on the other hand, *these laws are completely annulled and with them the predominance of classical conceptions of beauty is also broken.*[4] [my italics]

The italicized portion of the quotation could easily refer to the bizarre psychological and physiological machinations of David Lindsay's famous fantasy *A Voyage to Arcturus* or the impossible environments and creatures of E. R. Eddison's equally well-known *The Worm Ouroboros.* The first portion of the quotation, which comments on the "deformed" in "a transcendental world" that still conforms to natural laws, could be comparing Lindsay's and Eddison's extreme annulments of nature to the partial fantasies of Charles Dickens' *A Christmas Carol* and *Oliver Twist* or Henry Fielding's *Joseph Andrews,* all three of which present highly idealized affirmations of the degree of human goodness and innocence. As it is, the quotation is by Arnold Hauser, explaining how "the rigid geometricism [of the art] of the early Middle Ages was made fluid by the dynamism of the eleventh century" in his *The Social History of Art.*[5] Hauser's observation shows an important aspect of fantasy's contrast with actuality and demonstrates how the criterion of the impossible has been and still is used to identify and explore fantasy. albeit with different nomenclature and subject, in a variety of disciplines. The validity of this is further shown here by Terry Reece Hackford's essay on the illustrations for the *Arabian Nights* and George P. Landow's survey of nineteenth-century art and literature. More significantly, Hauser's work shows a historical and interdisciplinary application of the principles of fantasy and reveals that insights can be generated through retrospective and expansive application by scholars. The various genre essays by Crossley, Zanger, Thompson, and Vasbinder, plus Francis J. Molson's essay on juvenile literature, show the verisimilitude and pervasiveness of fantasy, illustrating that it is at home in all places and at all times.

Neither an oversimplification nor an exaggeration, this point is drawn from and supported by the arsenal of excellent essays in this volume. Most importantly, it may help open the doors to a legitimate debate over how contemporary criticism has failed to account for fantasy. This circumstance is brought about by a concentration on product in art and literature and an avoidance of the epistemological systems that generate creative products. (Fortunately, this limitation is not characteristic of the rare criticism that does penetrate through the surface of art, such as Northrop Frye's *Anatomy of Criticism* and the aforementioned *Social History of Art* by Arnold Hauser.)

Another major deterrent to the appreciation of fantasy is the rise of realism in the late eighteenth century and throughout the nineteenth century and the enormous influence of Samuel Coleridge's *Biographia Literaria*—points thoroughly examined, among others, in W. R. Irwin's essay on the intellectual evolution of "fancy" and "fantasy" in this volume.[6] George Eliot, in *Adam Bede* (1859), all too clearly articulates the predominant nineteenth-century attitude, one that is still current in the twentieth century:

> So I am content to tell my simple story, without trying to make things seem better than they were; dreading nothing, indeed, but falsity, which, in spite of one's best efforts, there is reason to dread. Falsehood is so easy, truth so difficult. The pencil is conscious of a delightful facility in drawing a griffin—the longer the claws, and the larger the wings, the better; but that marvellous facility which we mistook for genius is apt to forsake us when we want to draw a real unexaggerated lion. . . . I turn, without shrinking, from cloud-borne angels, from prophets, sibyls, and heroic

warriors, to an old woman bending over her flower-pot, or eating her solitary dinner. . . .[7]

It is challenging to speculate on the sources of Eliot's attitude that only things of external, perceivable "reality" can be important. Clearly, it echoes Aristotle's demand for unity of time, place, and action and Sir Philip Sidney's mandate in *An Apology for Poetry* that poetry must mirror or improve nature, never depart from it. More immediately, Eliot's and the nineteenth century's demand for a slavery to realism, also central to Wordsworth's "Preface to *Lyrical Ballads*" and Shelley's "Defence of Poetry," was probably spawned in the scientific revolution of the Copernican and Newtonian universe and in the growing faith (which graduated to belief and then "fact") in a cosmos filled with discoverable and manipulable phenomena.

There were dissenting voices: E. T. A. Hoffmann's *Märchen* speak for themselves as progenitors of contemporary fantasy, and George Meredith's *The Shaving of Shagpat* (1856) is still considered by many a masterpiece of nineteenth-century fantasy, although it was probably written for the period's fascination with pseudo-orientalism. George MacDonald, considered the "father" of modern fantasy because of *Phantastes* (1858), demonstrates that the fixation with the scientific, realistic, and empirical was not total:

> To inquire into what God has made is the main function of the imagination. It is aroused by facts, is nourished by facts, seeks higher and yet higher laws in those facts; but refuses to regard science as the sole interpreter of nature, or the laws of science as the only region of discovery.[8]

MacDonald's belief (tinged as it was by Christianity) and the beliefs of other nineteenth-century fantasists—notably William Morris and the Pre-Raphaelites—were not sustained into the twentieth century. This situation has led Erich Neumann to observe that, despite man's increasing ability to manipulate the physical universe, we live in a time "in which man's inability to deal with psychic nature, with the human soul, has become more appallingly obvious than ever before."[9] Thus, with the additional support of the Industrial Revolution and social Darwinism, affection for realism and aversion to fantasy have become predominant characteristics of modern aesthetic culture. Neumann's contention is pointedly supported by John A. Lester, Jr., as he describes the temper of the late Victorian and early Edwardian eras:

> . . . great confidence that empirical inductive reasoning was in plain fact the sole legitimate faculty of cognition enforced a continuing scepticism of all other faculties. Repeated proclamations that the world of force and matter was the only *real* world left no room for any higher order which might be perceived beyond phenomena.[10]

This approach to epistemology is clearly dangerous and, despite the apparent current interest in fantasy, the attitude that nothing exists beyond the phenomenal world is currently as threatening as it ever has been. It strikes at the very essence of creative thought and affirms a tyranny of rationality, which recognizes everything, except itself, as unreal and ephemeral. This antagonistic attitude will endure as long as intellectual, rational, and social conventions are considered the only sources of truth—sources that deny all existences other than their own and that relegate contrary modes to escapism and rebellion.[11]

Fortunately, a strong case can be made for fantasy works as the most creative of imaginative acts: for fantasy's reliance on the impossible and the empirically unknown requires less imitation and more invention than mimetic art. Its conception, as Northrop Frye explains, "transcends the limits both of the naturally possible and of the morally acceptable" and comes closest of all the arts to creation *ex nihilo,* creation generated by pure mind, what J. R. R. Tolkien calls the "most nearly pure form of art."[12]

Fantasy has been around for so long that to dismiss it is imprudent, and far too many major thinkers have pointed to its personal and cultural importance.[13] C. G. Jung identifies fantasy in its psychological inception and its descent into artistic media as a "self-justifying biological function" that is the "natural life of the psyche," that must be understood hermeneutically (not semiotically), that gives the will content, and is the living union of the outer and inner worlds.[14] C. S. Lewis and Jerome Singer agree that fantasy makes available insights that go beyond possible experience.[15] Harvey Cox cautions that "the survival of mankind as a species has . . . been placed in jeopardy by the repression of festivity and fantasy" and that without fantasy "a society cuts itself off from the visceral fonts of renewal." Further, Cox agrees with numerous other scholars of culture that fantasy determines what we consider true, factual, and lawful as surely as the reverse (a point well explored by Francis Molson's discussion of ethics in children's fantasy and also evident in the often highly lawful quality of adult fantasy) and that "fantasy is the richest source of human creativity."[16]

To go on citing authorities would be comforting, but redundant. Fantasy is inherent in what we call humanity and creativity: the essays in this volume affirm that fact. The loftiest goal of this anthology is to prompt a historical reexamination of works of art within the neglected perspectives introduced and examined here. A less lofty (and perhaps more realistic) goal is to elevate fantasy aesthetics from its present poverty to its proper place in the mainstream of contemporary culture and scholarship.

NOTES

1. See the secondary bibliography in this volume for citations to these works and others of recent note.

2. E. M. Forster, *Aspects of the Novel and Related Writings* (1927; rpt. London: Edward Arnold, 1974), p. 74.

3. Most of these studies are surveyed in the introduction to this editor's *The Literature of Fantasy: A Comprehensive, Annotated Bibliography of Modern Fantasy Fiction* (New York and London: Garland Publishing, 1979) and in the early pages of Gary K. Wolfe's essay in this volume.

4. Arnold Hauser, *The Social History of Art* (New York: Vintage Books, 1975), I, 189.

5. Ibid.

6. Readers interested in the nineteenth-century attitude toward fantasy will also profit from examining Stephen Prickett's *Victorian Fantasy* (Bloomington and London: Indiana University Press, 1979), pp. 1–37 et passim; Jules Zanger's "Goblins, Morlocks, and Weasels: Classic Fantasy and the Industrial Revolution," *Literature in Education,* 8 (Winter 1977), 154–62; and John A. Lester, Jr.'s *Journey through Despair 1880-1914: Transformations in British Literary Culture* (Princeton: Princeton University Press, 1968), pp. 111 ff.

7. George Eliot, *Adam Bede* (New York: Signet, 1961), p. 176 (chap. 17).

8. George MacDonald, "The Imagination. Its Functions and Other Essays," in *The Imagination and Other Essays* (Boston: Lothrop, [1883]), p. 2.

9. Erich Neumann, *Depth Psychology and a New Ethic,* trans. Eugene Wolfe (1949; rpt. New York: Harper & Row, 1973), p. 25.

10. Lester, p. 102.

11. For additional amplification on this point, see Herbert Fingarette's *The Self in Transformation: Psychoanalysis, Philosophy, and the Life of the Spirit* (1963; rpt. New York: Harper & Row, 1965), pp. 190 ff.

12. Northrop Frye, *The Anatomy of Criticism: Four Essays* (Princeton: Princeton University Press, 1971), p. 127. J. R. R. Tolkien, "On Fairy-Stories," rev. ed. in *The Tolkien Reader* (New York: Ballantine, 1966), p. 47.

13. For a more comprehensive discussion of fantasy as "creation *ex nihilo*" and for additional "testimonials" to the importance of fantasy, see the introduction to the editor's aforementioned *The Literature of Fantasy.*

14. C. G. Jung as follows: "Forward to Wickes: 'Von der inneren Welt des Menschen,'" 1953; rpt. in *The Symbolic Life: Miscellaneous Writings,* trans. R. F. C. Hull (Princeton: Princeton University Press, 1966), p. 527; *Two Essays on Analytical Psychology,* trans. R. F. C. Hull, 2nd ed. (Princeton: Princeton University Press, 1966), p. 291; *Psychological Types,* trans. H. G. Baynes, rev. R. F. C. Hull (Princeton: Princeton University Press, 1971), pp. 433, 52. Readers will also benefit from exploring Ravenna Helson's numerous surveys and studies, which appear to prove the accuracy of Jung's principles as they are used by fantasy authors and in fantasy literature: "The Creative Spectrum of Authors of Fantasy," *Journal of Psychology,* 45 (1977), 310–26; Experiences of Authors in Writing Fantasy: Two Relationships Between Creative Process and Product," *Journal of Altered States of Consciousness,* 3 (1977–78), 235–48; "From Magical Woman to Wizard: Comparisons of Literary Fantasy in the Nineteenth and Twentieth Centuries," in *Proceedings, XVIIth International Congress of Applied Psychology, Liège, Belgium, 25th–30th July 1971* (Brussels: Editest, 1972), II, 1515–19; "Heroic and Tender Modes in Women Authors of Fantasy," *Journal of Personality,* 41 (1973), 493–512; "The Heroic, the Comic, and the Tender: Patterns of Literary Fantasy and Their Authors," *Journal of Psychology,* 41 (1973), 163–84; "The Imaginative Process in Children's Literature: A Quantitative Approach," *Poetics,* 7 (1978), 135–53.

15. C. S. Lewis, "On Science Fiction," in *Of Other Worlds: Essays and Stories,* ed. Walter Hooper (New York: Harcourt, Brace & World, 1966), p. 70; Jerome L. Singer, *The Inner World of Daydreaming* (New York: Harper & Row, 1976), p. 185.

16. Harvey Cox, *The Feast of Fools: A Theological Essay on Festivity and Fantasy* (Cambridge: Harvard University Press, 1969), pp. 12, 69, 79, 59, et passim.

The Encounter with Fantasy

Gary K. Wolfe

IF THERE IS ONE thing the still-embryonic body of literary scholarship devoted to fantasy has made clear, it is that whatever we are to call "fantasy" must first and foremost deal with the impossible. In a 1978 survey of several scholarly works on the subject, S. C. Fredericks noted that "there is general agreement among the critics that Fantasy constitutes what Irwin calls 'the literature of the impossible' . . ." and that fantasy writers "take as *their point of departure* the deliberate violation of norms and facts we regard as essential to our conventional conception of 'reality,' in order to create an imaginary counter-structure or counter-norm."[1] W. R. Irwin, to whom Fredericks refers, goes so far as to characterize fantasy as "antireal" and defines it as "a story based on and controlled by an overt violation of what is generally accepted as possibility; it is the narrative result of transforming the condition contrary to fact into 'fact' itself."[2] Eric S. Rabkin, in *The Fantastic in Literature,* makes "a direct reversal of ground rules" a condition of the fantastic and says of fantasy that "its polar opposite is Reality."[3] C. N. Manlove agrees that "a substantial and irreducible element of supernatural or impossible worlds, beings, or objects" is needed for fantasy, explaining that supernatural or impossible means "of another order of reality from that in which we exist and form our notions of possibility."[4] And in explaining his principle of inclusion for his bibliography *The Literature of Fantasy,* Roger C. Schlobin identifies the literature of fantasy as "that corpus in which the impossible is primary in its quantity or centrality."[5]

The criterion of the impossible, then, seems firmly in place in the academic study of fantasy literature; it may indeed be the first principle generally agreed upon for the study of fantasy. Nor will the academic critics find much disagreement from fantasy authors themselves. Ray Bradbury, whose reputation as a science-fiction writer often seems to overshadow his own avowed first love for fantasy, wrote that "each fantasy assaults and breaks a particular law" and "attempts to disrupt the physical world in order to bring change to the heart and mind."[6] C. S. Lewis, a literary scholar as well as a fantasist, defined literary fantasy (as opposed to psychological fantasy) as "any narrative that deals with impossibles and preternaturals."[7] And as long ago as 1890, two of the great Victorian masters of the fantastic tale, H. Rider Haggard and Andrew Lang, prefaced their ambitious fantasy sequel to the *Odyssey, The World's Desire,* with a poem that included the following lines:

> Come with us, ye whose hearts are set
> On this, the Present to forget;
> Come read the things whereof ye know
> They were not, and could not be so![8]

Almost word for word, the modern author Samuel R. Delany echoes Haggard and Lang when he defines the "level of subjunctivity" of fantasy as "*could not have happened.*"[9]

While it would seem fatuous to dispute the importance of this criterion in discussions of fantasy, the notion of the impossible itself raises a number of intriguing questions, not all of which can be adequately addressed by the resources of literary scholarship. What, for example, are the psychological and cultural limits of what we conceive to be possible? How do we recognize the impossible when we encounter it in a work of art, and how do we decide that a particular impossible event or being signals an individual aesthetic structure rather than a private psychosis or a culturally accepted myth? What of a passage such as the following?

> The Kingdom of Yr had a kind of neutral place which was called the Fourth Level. It was achieved only by accident and could not be reached by formula or an act of will. At the Fourth Level there was no emotion to endure, no past or future to grind against. There was no memory or possession of any self, nothing except dead facts which came unbidden

when she needed them and which had no feeling attached to them.[10]

The passage is from Joanne Greenberg's autobiographical account of her own schizophrenia, and while the passage clearly describes an "impossible" place and an at least unlikely state of being, the context in which it appears in the novel makes it clear that the novel itself is not a work of fantasy. Had Greenberg presented such schizophrenic fantasies unadorned by the essentially realistic account of hospitalization and psychotherapy that surrounds them, would she have written a fantasy? The obvious answer would seem to be no, despite such a work's clear realization of the criterion of impossibility. As Fredericks observes, literary fantasy must serve a "reality-oriented function" and be deliberate and purposeful in the ways in which it diverges from cognitive reality.[11]

But the idea of a social or rhetorical motive for fantastic events also proves to be inadequate; otherwise, we would have to admit all sorts of myth systems and metaphorical conceits into the realm of fantasy. We cannot comfortably dismiss a Blackfoot creation myth as fantasy simply because its events and beings are "impossible" according to our cosmology, nor can we protest the "impossibilities" of Dante's *Divine Comedy* on the same grounds. Such works are certainly "reality-oriented," even to the extent that they stand at the opposite end of the scale from the visions of an isolated psychotic: these are the great public fantasies of other times and cultures, and what is "impossible" in them now was once accepted as possible. The notion of impossibility in fantasy, then, must lie somewhere toward the middle of this scale; it must be more public than the schizophrenic's hallucination, yet less public than myth and religion. It must, in fact, be part of an implied compact between author and reader—an agreement that whatever impossibilities we encounter will be made significant to us, but will retain enough of their idiosyncratic nature that we still recognize them to be impossible.

Even as we so locate the nature of the impossible in fantasy, however, new complications arise. We might dismiss dream literature and surrealism—works such as Robert Coates' *The Eater of Darkness* (1926) or Raymond Roussel's *Impressions d'Afrique* (1910)—as being too void of meaningful referents, too much like the heavily unconscious fantasies of the schizophrenic, to qualify for this middle ground of the impossible. But what are we to do with works such as Mervyn Peake's Gormenghast Trilogy (1946–1959) or Peter Dickinson's *The Blue Hawk* (1976)—works which, except for their bizarre and unfamiliar settings and unusual characters, contain little or nothing that contravenes what we know to be possible? In the Gormenghast Trilogy, notes Manlove, "Nothing 'supernatural' or magical by our standards is in fact present."[12] Manlove argues that the quality of "otherness" in such a work, the construction of its narrative without any direct referent to our own world, is sufficient that we may call it impossible; and the argument is persuasive, since these works certainly *feel* like fantasies and one comes away from them with the strong impression that one has been traveling in some impossible realm. But already one important factor in our criterion of impossibility is beginning to show signs of weakness, and that factor is what we might term the purely cognitive element. Cognition, at least as Darko Suvin uses the term in his characterization of science fiction,[13] may be sufficient to enable us to recognize the limits of what is possible in a work of science fiction or historical fiction, but we may find that it often fails in aiding us to recognize the impossible that is fantasy.

If the delineation of the cognitive element in science fiction has been one of the strengths of criticism in that field, it is a fallacy to assume with apparent logic that fantasy merely employs the same cognitive principle in reverse—that is, if science fiction deals with what we recognize as empirically possible, then fantasy must be what we recognize as empirically impossible. Such an approach ignores the strong affective element that accompanies and sometimes overpowers the cognitive in fantasy, and it fails to account for the ways in which fantasy narratives are carried forward. Cognitive recognition of specific impossibilities may serve to signal us that a given work is a fantasy, but it will not sustain us through multiple volumes of narrative—and in some cases, as with the Gormenghast Trilogy, it is difficult to pinpoint any such cognitive impossibility at all.

When do we decide, in a work such as that, that we are reading something impossible? There are no ghosts, dragons, hobbits, or magical transitions between worlds, and even if there were, we would devoutly hope that the author could keep them under control. A work that sustains a constant level of invention, piling impossibility upon impossibility, would be both extremely taxing on the reader and in the end probably unsatisfactory. Even a work which is remarkably rich in invention and in which the limits of impossibility in the fantastic world are not made clear until late in the narrative—a work such as David Lindsay's *A Voyage to Arcturus* (1920)—is apt to be exhausting for most readers. On the other hand, a work in which the *limits* of the impossible are clearly laid out early on can provide a convenient framework for the simplest adventure story. Phyllis Eisenstein's *Born to Exile* (1978) maintains a tightly controlled level of cognitive impossibility; its hero can, in science-fictional terms, teleport. With no more in the way of cognitive impossibility than this, Eisenstein constructs a highly satisfying series of fantasy narratives. Our sense of being in a fantastic realm arises, it would seem, from some affective apprehension of the impossible rather than from this simple cognitive device—which by itself might even allow us to categorize the work as science fiction.

An interesting principle begins to emerge: we cannot, it is apparent, use our recognition of cognitive impossibility to "test" for fantasy, at least not in the same way that we can use our recognition of what is possible to test our acceptance of a work of science fiction. Recognition of the possible can and often does sustain a reader throughout a work of science fiction, and part of the thrill of reading what is often referred to as "hard" science fiction arises from discovering just how far our concepts of the possible can be stretched. In many works of science fiction, a glaring impossibility may burst the balloon of the narrative and substantially weaken the whole work, but a glaring "possibility" in fantasy disturbs us not at all. In fact, the further we progress in a fantasy narrative, the less we expect in the way of new impossible marvels; once the ground rules have been laid, a *deus ex machina* in fantasy is as intrusive as in any other kind of fiction. Nor can a standard adventure novel be made into a true fantasy by informing us at the outset that we are in a mythic world or time, no more than a fantasy can be transformed into realistic fiction by tacking on to the ending a phrase like "And then I awoke in my room."

Does this mean that the criterion of impossibility lacks significant power as a means of identifying works of fantasy? After all, by the time we begin the second volume of Tolkien's Lord of the Rings or the third or fourth volume of Roger Zelazny's "Amber" Series, we are well located in the author's symbolic universe and do not expect many new "impossibilities" to occur. Yet it would be absurd to suggest that only the first volume of these or other fantasy series qualify as true fantasies simply because it is in those inaugural volumes that our primary dislocation of what we take to be possible occurs. Once a dragon takes flight in a work of fantasy, or a unicorn talks, or a wardrobe becomes a forest, we are not apt to be much impressed to witness the same thing for a second or third time. But in an effective fantasy work, we do not lose our sense of the wondrous or impossible even long after all the marvels have been introduced and the magic has become commonplace. To account for such works, we must move beyond the simple criterion of cognitive impossibility and examine such elements as tone and setting—elements that help to construct what we might call the affective sense of the impossible.

To use a term that has been explored by both Freud and Gaston Bachelard, fantasy is in many ways closer to daydreaming or reverie than to cognitive thought, and as Bachelard observes, "Dreaming reveries and thinking thoughts are certainly two disciplines which are hard to reconcile."[14] The reason Bachelard gives for this is that cognitive thought is based in what he calls our "reality function":

> The demands of our *reality function* require that we adapt to reality, that we constitute ourselves as a reality and that we manufacture works which are realities. But doesn't reverie, by its very essence, liberate us from the reality function? From the moment it is considered in all its simplicity, it is perfectly evident that reverie bears witness to a normal, useful *irreality function* which keeps the human psyche on the fringe of all the brutality of a hostile and foreign non-self.[15]

Bachelard's "irreality function," which he explores in greater depth using the resources of phenomenology and Jungian theory, approaches closely what I have called the affective sense of the impossible. And since reality, in the words of Peter L. Berger and Thomas Luckmann, is socially constructed, it follows that the irreality of fantasy must gain some of its power from socially determined notions of what is possible and impossible. "Finite provinces of meaning" is the term Berger and Luckmann employ to describe the alternate realities of art, religion, and myth; and the term might well be applied in a more limited sense to describe the impossible worlds of artistic fantasy.[16]

Meaning is an essential factor in the irreality function of fantasy; it is what lends the fantasy something resembling Clive

Bell's "significant form" and what sustains our interest in the impossible long after our cognitive apprehension of impossibilities has passed, long after we have resolved the momentary hesitation or irresolution that Todorov calls "the fantastic."[17] This is hardly a revolutionary thought; any work of art must hold out the promise of some significant meaning and form if we are to retain interest in it, especially in the face of manifest impossibilities. But in fantasy, the sources of meaning, the ideational structures of the narrative, are essential in molding our attitude toward the impossible and in controlling the depth of our response to it. In some kinds of fantasy, the ideational structure is very close to what we might expect from more conventional kinds of fiction. What is commonly (and often surprisingly accurately) called "sword-and-sorcery" fiction—a genre most closely associated with authors such as Fritz Leiber (who is said to have coined the term) and Robert E. Howard—seems to me in many ways closer to historical fiction and science fiction than to certain other kinds of fantasy. Its ideational structure is primarily technological and political, as the very term "sword-and-sorcery" suggests. A sword, after all, is a tool, and however primitive it is an implement of technological weaponry. Sorcery is a causal system analogous to science, its rules often so circumscribed that this genre of fiction has managed to give birth to a series of popular games that thoroughly reverse the process of discovery we ordinarily associate with fantasy: instead of discovering the limits of the impossible inductively, by following the action of a fantasy narrative, many of these sword-and-sorcery war-gamers seem to prefer to work deductively, learning the rules of the game at the outset and reducing the narrative itself literally to the level of play. It is not surprising that sword-and-sorcery tends on the one hand toward historical fiction (as with Poul Anderson's *The Last Viking*) and on the other toward science fiction (as with Anne McCaffrey's Dragonrider Series). Meaning, in all these cases, arises from the same sort of fundamental concerns.

Other kinds of fantasy deal with issues more commonly associated with fairy tales and *Bildungsroman*—issues such as education, personality, morality, duty, social relations, and other aspects of human development. Protagonists in these fantasies more often achieve control over self than over environment (though the self may take many forms in a fantastic world), and the ideational structure is psychological. As Bachelard observes of reveries, "They situate us in a world and not in a society."[18] And the objects, events, and beings that we encounter in this fantastic world—however impossible—must exist in a fullness of affect that enables us to respond to them as though they were real. A contrast with science fiction may be helpful here. In much science fiction, the fantastic environment is subordinated to a rationalized purpose, and the elements of that environment relate to the science-fiction reader in much the same way that elements of reality relate to the scientist. They are, to use Ernest Schachtel's phrase, "objects-of-use": "The scientist, in these cases, looks at the object with one or more hypotheses and with the purpose of his research in mind and thus 'uses' the object to corroborate or disprove a hypothesis, but does not encounter the object as such, in its own fullness."[19] The perceptual world of science fiction, then, is significant in that its objects are subject to manipulation and control. If the furnishings of our room begin to disappear, as they are apt to do in a Philip K. Dick novel, we will soon learn that it is not really the impossible that is happening but rather some sort of sophisticated yet understandable manipulation of these objects for some equally understandable end. In science fiction, objects, landscapes, and even characters are often stripped of all but those qualities which will eventually serve some cognitive purpose; this is why many readers who do not like science fiction sometimes complain of its "flatness," "coldness," or "lack of affect" (though it is by no means true that such accusations are always justified).

In fantasy, another kind of "stripping" often takes place, and we may encounter objects reduced not to their usefulness, but rather to their affective significance. It is at first a little disconcerting to read through five volumes of Roger Zelazny's "Amber" Series and learn so little about Amber itself. We are told early in the series that "Amber was the greatest city which had ever existed or ever would exist" and that "every other city, everywhere, every other city that existed was but a reflection of a shadow of some phase of Amber."[20] But Amber itself often seems to have no population other than its royal family and their hired minions, no streets, no economy, no network of social organization. For Zelazny's purposes, such aspects of the city are not only nonessential but might even be distracting. Amber exists not like cities in science fiction, which may function to show us the problems and promises of technology or population control or some other such issue; rather it exists to recreate for us the emotional archetype of the city. All we need really know of Amber are its power, its order, and its beauty, and what does not tend to this primary affective response can be dispensed with. Similarly, we do not need to know much about the history, design, or function of the magic wardrobe in C. S. Lewis's *The Lion, the Witch, and the Wardrobe* (1950), since it is primarily an emblem of curiosity and mystery, a place to be explored. Nor do we look for an account of the biology of the Nazgul in Tolkien's Lord of the Rings, since the fearfulness of this creation is quite sufficient to account for its presence in a fantasy.

At this point we might be tempted to conclude that our original problems concerning the criterion of the impossible in fantasy have been pretty much resolved, and that fantasy manages to sustain our interest in impossible worlds simply by making these worlds emotionally meaningful to us. This is indeed true of some kinds of fantasy, but it does not enable us to distinguish serious fantasy from the purely sensational kinds of narratives that are sometimes allied to it, such as pornography, whimsy, or horror. It may be that a single affective attitude controls a fantastic narrative to the extent that it maintains our interest, but in the most successful serious fantasies, a whole range of emotional experience is apt to be present, and we cannot depend on a particular affective construct to sustain our acceptance of the impossible. When a particular affective construct so dominates a work of fantastic literature that we find ourselves waiting for the same emotional sensation to be repeated in different guises, we are no longer in a fully realized fantastic world. The objects and events in this world are apt to become again "objects-of-use," repeatedly manipulated by the author in the service of a single dominant emotional tone. Thorne Smith's delightful *The Night Life of the Gods* (1931) is full of impossible happenings and mythological figures, but all are subordinated to a slapstick comic tone that controls the whole work. H. P. Lovecraft's "shuggoths" and "Cthulhus" may be impressive creations in their own right, but once they have served Lovecraft's primary purpose of giving us a thrill of horror or disgust, they must be hauled offstage or, equally characteristic of Lovecraft, the story must end. Just as Smith's work can be more aptly labeled comedy than fantasy, so might Lovecraft's work be more aptly labeled horror fiction.

Comedy and horror may of course be elements in any fantasy, but we cannot depend on their being controlling elements. Here another distinction may be helpful, one that is made by Manlove:

> Two broad classes of fantasy may be distinguished: 'comic' or 'escapist', and 'imaginative' fantasy. The line of division

> is simple enough: it is between fancy versus imagination, where 'fanciful' works are those carrying either no deeper meaning or one lacking in vitality. . . . Any number of Waste Lands, broken lances, grails, eucharistic or baptismal symbols may appear in a story without that story having any *potent* meaning.[21]

Manlove may be borrowing the terms "fancy" and "imagination" from one of the authors he discusses in his study, George MacDonald, who drew much the same distinction more than eighty years earlier. Of the creation of fantastic worlds and beings, MacDonald wrote:

> When such forms are new embodiments of old truths, we call them products of the Imagination; when they are mere inventions, however lovely, I should call them the work of the Fancy. . . .
>
> . . . you may, if you will, call Imagination the tailor that cuts her [Truth's] garments to fit her, and Fancy his journeyman that puts the pieces of them together, or perhaps at most embroiders their button-holes.[22]

Such a distinction between fancy and imagination suggests that in works of true imagination we can expect an ideational structure that goes far deeper than the controlling tone of the work, that is in fact based in what Manlove calls "deeper meaning" and MacDonald "old truths."

What these deeper meanings and old truths are may vary widely from one author to another, ranging from the Christian Platonism of C. S. Lewis to the blend of gnosticism and Teutonic philosophy that underlies the work of David Lindsay. What gives credence to such systems in fantasy is the manner in which the fantasist forges a unity between them and the affective structures we have already discussed. This does not mean that fantasy is necessarily didactic or allegorical, but it does imply that at the center of these works of imagination (as opposed to fancy) there must be a core of what might best be called *belief*. Belief in fantasy—what Tolkien calls "Secondary Belief" to distinguish it from the primary belief in experiential reality—arises from the conjunction of psychological affect and ideational structure, and as Tolkien notes, it is quite a different thing from Coleridge's "willing suspension of disbelief."[23] Put another way, belief is what enables genuine emotions to be aroused from impossible circumstances, not unlike Marianne Moore's familiar description of poetry as "imaginary gardens with real toads in them." Moore's poetic comment that one is not free until one is "made captive by supreme belief" is also apt here.[24]

Fantasy indeed tries to set us free by making us captive to belief, but since the kind of belief that is peculiar to fantasy arises as much from affect as from cognition, it is not necessary for us to share an author's philosophies or beliefs that are external to the work for us to accept and "believe in" their embodiment in the narrative. We need not be Christians to be impressed by the strength and kindness of C. S. Lewis's Aslan; we need not be in agreement with Jesse Weston's sometimes shaky hypotheses about hero myths to enjoy their embodiment in Roger Zelazny's "Amber" Series.[25] In Patricia A. McKillip's *The Forgotten Beasts of Eld* (1974), we can accept the final transformation of the hideous monster Blammor into the beautiful Liralen bird without necessarily agreeing with the identity of creative and destructive passions that such a metaphor implies. In all these narratives, affect and tone transform such ideational constructs into events and beings that seem fully consistent with the author's created universe.

Fantasy authors who are most successful at creating this kind of belief attempt neither to allegorize their own systems of belief nor to subordinate those systems to sensation. Instead, they achieve a balanced tension—perhaps more properly a dialectic—between cognition and affect, between moralism and passion, between the impossible and the inevitable. They do not merely construct metaphors for a preconceived reality, or if they do, the power of the metaphors is apt to transform the nature of those preconceptions into something new. At their most ambitious, these fantasists resemble the painter Peter Copping in David Lindsay's *Devil's Tor*:

> Only, what every painter worth his salt is trying to present—probably without knowing it—is neither beauty, nor life, nor truth (charming words, all of them!) . . . but . . . *the whole universe*—at one stroke. By means, necessarily, of *action*. That is symbolism in a nutshell. Nothing exists apart, but only the universe exists. Whatever individual person or thing I paint must stand, not for itself, but for the entire scheme.[26]

The notion of symbolism that Lindsay introduces here (for I believe it likely that the character Copping in this case is speaking with Lindsay's voice) provides us with the final clue as to how to deal with the impossible in fantasy. Underlying the belief in the fantastic world itself, which as we have found arises from the union of idea and affect, is a deeper belief in the fundamental reality that this world expresses. I use the term "expresses" rather than "represents" because many of the finest fantasy writers have correctly rejected the notion that their work is in any sense mere allegory or apologue—"a wall decoration with a label attached," in the words of Lindsay's Peter Copping.[27] For these writers, the fantasy world does not symbolize the experiential world but rather co-exists with it; each world, in the words of George MacDonald, is "the human being turned inside out," "a sensuous analysis of humanity."[28] C. S. Lewis, in *The Allegory of Love*, calls this attitude "sacramentalism or symbolism" and describes it as "almost the opposite of allegory":

> The allegorist leaves the given—his own passions—to talk of that which is confessedly less real, which is a fiction. The symbolist leaves the given to find that which is more real. To put the difference in another way, for the symbolist it is we who are the allegory.[29]

One might object to the apologetic for idealism that is implied in Lewis' formulation and thinly disguised in his own fiction, but if the fantasy author successfully integrates idea and affect to achieve a primary level of belief in the work, this deeper level of belief will emerge naturally, without constricting the work or reducing it to overt didacticism. When the primary level of belief falters (as I believe it does from time to time both in Lewis' *Perelandra* and in his *That Hideous Strength*), the deeper belief overpowers it, and we have at best a very entertaining homiletic. But in the best works of fantasy, ranging from the rigorous intellectuality of Lindsay's *A Voyage to Arcturus* to the delicate lyricism of Peter Beagle's *The Last Unicorn*, this deeper belief is so much of a piece with the created world that the question of "meaning" becomes a phenomenological rather than a literary one.

This discussion has of necessity been rather abstract, and has unfortunately not permitted room for detailed investigations of particular works. But our inquiry does permit us to suggest a kind of structure for the reading of fantasy that enables us to posit an answer to our original question of how fantasy not only sustains our interest in the impossible, but finally wins our belief and reveals that the impossible is, after all, the real. Briefly summarized, this structure is as follows:

1) *cognition of the impossible,* in which we realize, usually early on in a fantasy, that the accepted ground rules of our reality are in some significant way being contravened;

2) *location of the impossible,* or the awareness that this contravention of reality lies somewhere between private psychological fantasy and culturally shared myth (though in works such as Evangeline Walton's Mabinogion novels or T. H. White's *Once and Future King* the public myths of earlier cultures may be transformed into fantasies for our time);

3) *delimitation of the impossible,* which assures us that the work is under control and that some underlying system places constraints on what may happen in this fantastic world;

4) *feeling of the impossible,* or the affective sense of "otherness" (as opposed to horror's "outsidedness") or "irreality" that assures our continued emotional investment in this world even after new marvels have ceased to appear;

5) *awareness of affective significance,* which sets the work apart from mere speculation or sensationalism by promising that this emotional investment, once made, will be rewarded by some underlying affective order;

6) *awareness of cognitive significance,* or "deeper meaning," which in effect refocuses our cognitive concerns away from the surface impossibilities of the narrative and toward an emerging ideational structure;

7) *belief* in the fantastic world, arising from the interaction between affective and cognitive significance; and

8) *deeper belief,* which permits certain fantasy works to become analogues of inner experience virtually as valid as events of the "real world," and which expresses the author's own most fundamental convictions.

Not all fantasies, of course, will successfully carry the reader through all these stages of experience, and not all will try. Some will be overwhelmed by the deeper beliefs of the author, and others may fail to cohere because of a fatal imbalance of cognition and affect. At worst, a fantasy will not carry us much beyond the initial recognition that what we are reading is impossible; at best, it will lead us to a further recognition that these surface impossibilities constitute a necessary strategy for approaching some profound and intense reality. For such works, "the impossible" may be little more than a surface structure; the works themselves concern things that could not be more real. Fantasies that successfully lead us all the way to this deeper belief are still rare, despite the illustrious history of fantastic literature; perhaps, indeed, taking us that far is the most fantasy can do. If so, that is still a great deal to ask of any literature.

NOTES

1. S. C. Fredericks, "Problems of Fantasy," *Science-Fiction Studies*, 5 (March 1978), 37.
2. W. R. Irwin, *The Game of the Impossible: A Rhetoric of Fantasy* (Urbana: University of Illinois Press, 1976), p. 4.
3. Eric S. Rabkin, *The Fantastic in Literature* (Princeton, N.J.: Princeton University Press, 1976), pp. 14–15, 227.
4. C. N. Manlove, *Modern Fantasy: Five Studies* (Cambridge: Cambridge University Press, 1975), p. 3.
5. Roger C. Schlobin, *The Literature of Fantasy: A Comprehensive, Annotated Bibliography of Modern Fantasy Fiction* (New York: Garland, 1979), p. xxvi.
6. Ray Bradbury, "Introduction," *The Circus of Dr. Lao and Other Improbable Stories*, ed. Ray Bradbury (New York: Bantam, 1956), pp. vii–viii.
7. C. S. Lewis, *An Experiment in Criticism* (Cambridge: Cambridge University Press, 1965), p. 50.
8. H. Rider Haggard and Andrew Lang, *The World's Desire* (London: Longmans, Green, and Co., 1890), p. 2.
9. Samuel R. Delany, "About 5,750 Words," in *The Jewel-Hinged Jaw: Notes on the Language of Science Fiction* (New York: Berkley, 1977), p. 32.
10. "Hannah Green," [pseud.], *I Never Promised You a Rose Garden* (New York: New American Library, 1964), p. 11.
11. Fredericks, p. 37.
12. Manlove, p. 3.
13. See Darko Suvin's *Metamorphoses of Science Fiction: On the Poetics and History of a Literary Genre* (New Haven: Yale University Press, 1979), pp. 7–9.
14. Gaston Bachelard, *The Poetics of Reverie*, trans. Daniel Russell (New York: Orion Press, 1969), p. 177.

15. Ibid., p. 13.

16. Peter L. Berger and Thomas Luckmann, *The Social Construction of Reality* (Garden City: Doubleday Anchor, 1967), p. 25.

17. Tzvetan Todorov, *The Fantastic: A Structural Approach to a Literary Genre,* trans. Richard Howard (Ithaca, N.Y.: Cornell University Press, 1975), p. 25.

18. Bachelard, p. 14.

19. Ernest Schachtel, *Metamorphosis: On the Development of Affect, Perception, Attention, and Memory* (New York: Basic Books, 1959), p. 171.

20. Roger Zelazny, *Nine Princes in Amber* (New York: Avon, 1972), p. 90.

21. Manlove, p. 11.

22. George MacDonald, "The Fantastic Imagination," in *Gifts of the Child Christ: Fairy Tales and Stories for the Childlike,* ed. Glenn Edward Sadler (1893; rpt. Grand Rapids, Mich.: Eerdmans, 1973), I, 24.

23. J. R. R. Tolkien, "On Fairy-Stories," in *The Tolkien Reader* (New York: Ballantine, 1966), pp. 37–38.

24. "Spenser's Ireland," in *A Marianne Moore Reader* (New York: Viking, 1961), pp. 33–34.

25. For a discussion of the importance of Weston's *From Ritual to Romance* to Zelazny's Amber novels, see Carl B. Yoke, *Roger Zelazny: Starmont Reader's Guide 2,* ed. Roger C. Schlobin (West Linn, Ore.: Starmont House, 1979), pp. 81–83.

26. David Lindsay, *Devil's Tor* (London: G. P. Putnam's Sons, 1932), p. 145.

27. Ibid., p. 145.

28. George MacDonald, "The Imagination: Its Functions and Culture," in *The Imagination and Other Essays* (Boston: Lothrop, [1883]), p. 9.

29. C. S. Lewis, *The Allegory of Love* (New York: Oxford University Press, 1958), p. 45.

On the Nature of Fantasy

C. N. Manlove*

IN THE INTRODUCTION to his *A Checklist of Modern Fantastic Literature* (1948), E. F. Bleiler writes,

> If anyone were to ask me what is meant by the term "fantasy," I fear that I would have to admit my ignorance. A year or so ago I would have had no difficulty answering, but the compiling and reading involved in the preparation of the *Checklist* has forced me to realise that fantasy may be almost all things to all men. I have often wished that the subject of this book were something with an objective reality, such as minerals or plants.[1]

This *caveat* has force, and the definition of "fantasy" that will be outlined here makes no claim to satisfy everyone; all that matters ultimately is the isolation of a particular kind of literature. However, though the name is relatively unimportant, that of "fantasy" is kept here because most people, Bleiler included, apply it to the books we shall be considering.

This understood, a fantasy is: *A fiction evoking wonder and containing a substantial and irreducible element of supernatural or impossible worlds, beings or objects with which the mortal*

*The following is the definition of fantasy which appeared in my *Modern Fantasy: Five Studies* (Cambridge University Press, 1975). It seemed to me best to present it more or less as it stood and then to add my further reflections in an afterword. I have added a paragraph at the end and omitted a distinction I made between what I called "imaginative" and "fanciful" fantasy.

characters in the story or the readers become on at least partly familiar terms.

A fiction. A work such as Bovet's *Pandaemonium, or The Devil's Cloyster. Being a further Blow to Modern Sadduceism, Proving the Existence of Witches and Spirits* (1684) is not a fantasy, because the book sets out to make us believe that such "authenticated" incidents as "A Remarkable passage of one named the Fairy-Boy of Leith in Scotland, given me by my worthy friend Captain George Burton, and attested under his own hand," or "A Relation of the Apparition of Fairies, their seeming to keep a Fair, and what happened to a certain man that endeavoured to put himself in amongst them,"[2] really occurred. Of the same order is the account in Bishop Leadbeater's *The Hidden Side of Things* of the hierarchies and colours of the fairies he studied with his 'inner eye' on the hillside of Slieve-na-mon in Ireland[3] or the photographs in Arthur Conan Doyle's *The Coming of the Fairies*[4] of the little people (some in contemporary dress; e.g., p. 71) found by children in the glen near the village of Cottingley, Yorkshire. The aim in these works is to produce absolute credence in the reader. Some Christian fantasies try to prove or make us come to believe in the existence of God and heaven generally (thus going as far as the aim announced in Bovet's title), but none ask us to take the particular stories or characters they present simply at face value. C. S. Lewis remarked of Conan Doyle's book:

> When Sir Arthur Conan Doyle claimed to have photographed a fairy, I did not, in fact, believe it: but the mere making of the claim—the approach of the fairy to within even that hailing distance of actuality—revealed to me at once that if the claim had succeeded it would have chilled rather than satisfied the desire which fairy literature had hitherto aroused.[5]

Thus, when J. R. R. Tolkien states that The Lord of the Rings is an expansion of the historical record in an extant Middle-earth chronicle, the Red Book of Westmarch, his object is to increase the verisimilitude, not the verity of his work—unless we are simple-minded, or Tolkien himself turns out to be an elf.[6] On the other hand, if a fantasy is powerfully presented or realized, it can produce an imprint on our imaginations deep enough to give it a measure of truth or reality, however much that truth is unverifiable. Something that we *know* at the outset to be impossible—a world like Mervyn Peake's Gormenghast, a system of angelic planetary intelligences like Lewis' Oyéresu, or a stone that is a gateway to mystic union as in Charles Williams' *Many Dimensions*—may by virtue of the strength and skill with which it is created make us feel simultaneously that it does and does not have reality.

Christian, or implicitly Christian, fantasy may also see another kind of balance of belief: here the "real" world is often not our universe, which to the writers is no less fantastic than those they have created, but is equated with the final Reality from which all worlds stem. For Tolkien, the fantasist "may actually assist in the effoliation and multiple enrichment of creation. All tales may come true; and yet, at the last, redeemed, they may be as like and unlike the forms that we give them as Man, finally redeemed, will be like and unlike the fallen that we know" (*Tree and Leaf* [1964], p. 63). Or as the formula used by Charles Williams and C. S. Lewis after him has it, "This also is Thou: neither is this Thou."[7] Here of course the distance between the fantastic world and truth is a measure of its limitation. For the Christian, only one fantasy has come true in our world without ceasing to be a fantasy—the story recounted in the Gospels.

Supernatural or impossible worlds, beings or objects (we shall come back to earlier parts of the definition). This phrase is meant to cover whatever is treated as being beyond any remotely conceivable extension of our plane of reality or thought. Peake's Gormenghast, for instance, has no connection with our sphere of possibility: the author suggests no way in which it might be reached from our world, nor does he give it any location in time or space. Nothing "supernatural" or magical by our standards is in fact present: the inhabitants of the castle are bizarre, and the ancient Ritual by which they govern their lives makes them still more odd, but none are gods, angels or fairies, and there are no miracles. Only the existence of the realm itself is impossible or wholly "other" in relation to ours, just as ours would be to it: the situation is one of two separate natures. In science fiction we find that such otherness is never present, however remote the location: for example, the planets described in Frank Herbert's *Dune* or the far galaxy in Asimov's Foundation Trilogy are possible worlds in that they are set in our universe and describe the sorts of events and civilizations that conceivably could exist, whether now or in the future.

There are fantasies that are set in the empirically known world, but the world is either juxtaposed with or transfigured by the presence of the supernatural. Some of E. Nesbit's fairy tales for children describe the appearance of strange and amusing beasts with magic powers, like the Phoenix or the Psammead, who turn up in contemporary England; the fantasies of Charles Williams portray what happens when such objects or forces as the Holy Grail, the original Tarot Pack, a stone made of the First Matter of Creation, or the archetypes of the forces sustaining life appear in our society.

Supernatural or impossible means, therefore, "of another order of reality from that in which we exist and form our notions of possibility." Charles Kingsley set out in *The Water-Babies* to show "that there is a quite miraculous and divine element underlying all physical nature,"[8] but he knew well enough that whatever apologetics may do, they still rightly leave the need for the final leap of faith—the leap from nature to supernature.[9] As soon as the "supernatural" has become possible, we are no longer dealing with fantasy but with science fiction. Consider, for example, Theodore Cogswell's short story, "The Wall Around the World." This describes a pastoral society of people who use flying broomsticks as their mode of transport. They cannot, however, fly high enough to get over a thousand-foot wall that surrounds their country, until one Porgie builds the first broomstick-assisted glider. On the other side of the wall, he finds a machine-based society. One member of it explains to him how, years previously, when men saw how increasing technology led to neglect of the development of spiritual power, they resolved to train a number of people in habits of superstition and then set them in a world that would foster these habits. Thus, the growth of the mind's power over matter would prosper. Porgie is told that when such power eventually becomes

> "simply a matter of training and method, then the ritual, the mumbo-jumbo, the deeply ingrained belief in the existence of supernatural forces will be no longer necessary."
>
> "These phenomena will be only tools that anybody can be trained to use, and the crutches can be thrown away. Then the Wall will come tumbling down."

And a little later, " 'Mind and Nature . . . magic and science . . . they'll get together eventually.' "[10] In this story broomsticks and levitation have become another tool of technological advance.

Even stories that explore possibility in the form of "might-have-been" worlds remain on our terms science fiction. The notion that the form of our world and universe is, in every instant, one among an infinity of possibles is behind H. Beam Piper's "He Walked Around the Horses," the story of an English envoy, en route in 1809 "to the court of what Napoleon had left of the Austrian Empire," who suddenly disappears while examining a change of horses in a Prussian inn-yard, never to be seen again—"At least, not in this continuum . . .":[11] he proceeds, minus his horses and servants, in what otherwise appears to be the same inn-yard, and only gradually finds that he is now living in a world where neither the American nor the French Revolution has succeeded and Napoleon is a little-known royalist colonel in the French army. Similar to this story is Robert Sheckley's "The Store of the Worlds" and a variation of it, found in Frederick Pohl's "Let the Ants Try" or "Target One," Arthur Porges' "The Rescuer" or Ray Bradbury's "A Sound of Thunder": what might happen to the present if time travel enabled us to tamper with the past?[12] On a formal level at least, none of these stories is any less probable, as speculation about what the past or the present might have become, than predictions concerning the future like *Brave New World* or *Nineteen Eighty-Four*. All of them are based on the idea of an infinity of possible worlds, but their possibility has reference only to our actualized world. A common medium of possibility for our world and those of fantasy, however, would only be found by referring back to an original Creator in whom all worlds would share their reality—and comparative unreality.

A substantial or irreducible element. Take *substantial* first. In part this refers quite simply to the sheer amount of the impact of the supernatural on the story. E. H. Visiak's *Medusa*, where the awful fascination of the monster of the abyss is reached only at the end of a book primarily engaged in description of an eighteenth-century voyage to Pernambuc, is arguably no fantasy. But the use of the term *substantial* here also relates to what is the true subject of a book. Virginia Woolf's *Orlando*, for instance, because it simply uses Orlando's reincarnations as a machine or device by which he may enact the cultural history which is the book's real concern, does not come under our heading either. The *Iliad*, the Ithacan section of the *Odyssey*, the *Aeneid*: despite the impact of the gods on the affairs of men, these epics are all primarily concerned with the working out of human destiny:

unlike *Paradise Lost*, they are not *about* the gods as well. Chaucer's Knight's and Franklin's tales, Henryson's *Testament of Cresseid, Hamlet*—the supernatural here is never more than a postulate, a backcloth to the portrayal of this mortal estate.

Irreducible. It must not be possible wholly to explain the supernatural or impossible away, by seeing it simply as a disguised projection of something within our "nature." Beast and moral fables are not really fantasies. Of the latter Britain boasts many examples in the form of the century and more of child-improving fairy-tales written from about 1750 onwards, among the first of which are the stories in Sarah Fielding's *The Governess; or, the Little Female Academy* (1749): one describes the escape of its hero from the clutches of a giant by means of a magic fillet he discovers on a statue, and is followed by this exhortation from Mrs. Teachum simply to translate supernatural beings and events into moral data as one reads:

> "Giants, Magic, Fairies, and all sorts of supernatural Assistances in a story, are introduced only to amuse and divert: For a Giant is called so only to express a Man of great Power; and the magic Fillet round the Statue was intended only to show you, that by Patience you will overcome all Difficulties. Therefore by no means let the notion of Giants or Magic dwell upon your minds." (2nd ed. [1749], p. 41)

Nor, again, where the supernatural is seen as a symbolic extension of the purely human mind is the work in which it appears a fantasy. This is the case in the *Alice* books, where the happenings are presented as Alice's dreams: as Tolkien says, "since the fairy-story deals with 'marvels,' it cannot tolerate any frame or machinery suggesting that the whole story in which they occur is a figment or illusion," and, "The very root (not only the use) of their [the *Alice* books'] 'marvels' is satiric, a mockery of unreason; and the 'dream' element is not a mere machinery of introduction and ending, but inherent in the action and transitions" (*Tree and Leaf*, pp. 19, 64). In "Gothic" novels—Walpole's *The Castle of Otranto,* Matthew Lewis' *The Monk*, or Charles Maturin's *Melmoth the Wanderer*, for instance—the presence of the supernatural is of a piece with dislocated plots, frenzied passions, the use of chiaroscuro and underground passages and vaults containing guilty secrets and unbridled lusts: it expresses the revolt of a purely human subconscious against reason, figured in organized religion and social civility. Those Gothic novels in which the supernatural is revealed to be some merely natural phenomenon or a trick of the light—as in the works of Mrs. Radcliffe—are really no different in kind from those which offer no such explanation, for in both the purpose is simply to stimulate the reader's unconscious terrors. A work such as Henry James's *The Turn of the Screw* would, however, be impossible to categorize here: are the ghosts of Quint and Miss Jessel real, or are they figments of the governess' warped imagination?

It is true that in fantasy the supernatural may in part belong to our reality by being a disguised physical, moral or mental phenomenon, but it is never more than partly these things. Kingsley's Mrs. Bedonebyasyoudid and her actions in *The Water-Babies*, for instance, are an allegory of the law of action and reaction in nature; Tolkien's Middle-earth is in one aspect a projection of our world as it would be if we would only see it aright; George MacDonald's North Wind, Mara, and the grandmother in the "Curdie" books are mother surrogates or even versions of the Jungian *anima.* At the same time, however, Mrs. Bedonebyasyoudid is seen as the sub-vicar of God without whom there would be no laws; Middle-earth is a world created and considered for its own sake; and MacDonald's supernatural agents are portrayed as expressions of God's immediate purpose within creation.

Evoking wonder. By *wonder* is meant anything from crude astonishment at the marvellous, to a sense of "meaning-in-the-mysterious" or even of the numinous. Wonder is, of course, generated by fantasy purely from the presence of the supernatural or impossible and from the element of mystery and lack of explanation that goes with it. The science-fiction writer throws a rope of the conceivable (how remotely so does not matter) from our world to his: the fantasy writer does not—or, where like Kingsley he tries to, it falls short. Thus the unexplained mirror apparatus through which MacDonald's Mr. Vane reaches fairyland in *Lilith* excites more wonder than the optical pseudo-science employed by Wells in *The Invisible Man* to account for his hero's powers of self-effacement.

But in fantasy wonder is not only the sort of by-product described above, but a central feature—or as Tolkien puts it, "the realisation, independent of the conceiving mind, of imagined wonder" (*Tree and Leaf*, p. 19). The worlds of science fiction have as much potential as fantasy for the strangeness, which is one precondition of wonder: think of the superbly imagined landscape of Brian Aldiss' *Hothouse,* where a giant banyan tree covers half a static globe beneath a dying sun, and a whole new variety of predatory fauna and flora war with the remnants of mankind for survival; or the drowned or crystal worlds of J. G. Ballard; or the equally surreal landscapes of Ray Bradbury. Yet our contemplation of that strangeness is rarely allowed full scope; the setting is absorbed by an insistent narrative of war, the struggle for survival, or discovery and consequences, the dominant leitmotivs of the genre. The jungle in Aldiss' book, however exotic, is the antagonist of man and exists only to be circumvented, not looked at; the triffids, krakens, chrysalids, lichens, and Midwich cuckoos of John Wyndham (pseudonym for John Beynon Harris) are little more than initiators of quiet epics of the human will to survive; the Lithians of James Blish's *A Case of Conscience* are purely the data of a developing theological dispute: little is present for its own sake. It would, of course, be wrong to declare that this situation is true of all science fiction or even exclusively true of any one story—one thinks of Asimov's *Fantastic Voyage* or of some moments in the work of Ballard or Bradbury—and equally false to say that everything is otherwise in fantasy. Nevertheless there is a definite tendency for fantasy to be more contemplative in aim and character, concerned at least as much with states of being as with processes of becoming. In *Perelandra,* for example, C. S. Lewis is as concerned to portray the planet and the Lady's innocence as the Un-man's temptation of her and its struggle with Ransom. In his Gormenghast Trilogy, Peake is in fact rather more interested in the character of Castle Gormenghast than in the plots against the castle. Frequently in a fantasy one finds description slowing or halting the narrative: so much is this so with Peake that one could at times say rather that the narrative interrupts the description.

This strong element of contemplation in fantasy can be related to other factors. Fantasy often draws spiritual nourishment from the past (even when set in the present day, as with Lewis' or Williams' fiction), particularly from a medieval and/or Christian world order—for example, the work of George MacDonald, William Morris, Lord Dunsany, E. R. Eddison, Charles Williams, C. S. Lewis, J. R. R. Tolkien, Mervyn Peake—where science fiction is usually concerned with the future and the way we may develop. Again, in fantasy the direction of the narrative is often circular or static, where in science fiction it is generally evolutionary or dynamic. Tolkien's *The Hobbit* is subtitled *There and Back*

Again, and the same title might apply to The Lord of the Rings, in which the quest begins and ends in the Shire. The dynamic of time is present, but in the form of what is lost of the old rather than of what is gained of the new. In some fantasies there is a supernatural irruption followed by a return to normality: a phoenix, a genie or the principles behind creation appear, cause havoc, whether grim or amusing, and finally remove or are removed. This is the basic pattern in the work of, for example, F. Anstey, E. Nesbit and Charles Williams; "Whereyouwantogoto" (or don't—the title is from one of E. Nesbit's stories) ends as "Whereyoustartedfrom." Of fantasy, in general, the title *The Worm Ouroboros* ("The Endless Worm") by E. R. Eddison is perhaps a fair description, though the nature of the story itself is an extreme version: at the end, when they have killed off all the villains and restored peace and plenty, the heroes grow bored, and with supernatural help have their enemies resuscitated so that they can start all over again.

With which the mortal characters in the story or the readers become on at least partly familiar terms. The supernatural or impossible in fantasy is not simply strange and wonderful, nor is it considered in terms only of distance: the reader becomes partially familiar with or at home in the marvellous worlds presented, and the mortal characters establish relationships with beings or objects from the "beyond." In fantasy children meet and talk with a phoenix, or men with angels, or the reader becomes closely acquainted with a world like Gormenghast or Arcturus. Often a relationship or contract between the supernatural and natural orders is central. This is, of course, *de rigueur* in Christian fantasy, and in those stories where in return for co-operation the supernatural imposes conditions, as in the traditional fairy tale and those fantasies of which it is a forebear—for instance Ruskin's *The King of the Golden River,* Thackeray's *The Rose and the Ring,* Kingsley's *The Water-Babies* or the stories of F. Anstey and E. Nesbit.

It is this, more than anything else, that distinguishes fantasy from the ghost and horror story. In the latter the supernatural is left entirely alien, for the point is the shock, the "*frisson* of the supernatural,"[13] that is experienced both by the characters and the reader. That *frisson* is invariably one of numinous rage. Some of the most effective stories use familiar or domestic situations to make that rage at once more terrifyingly near and more dreadfully "other." One thinks of the apt incongruity of the name "familiar" given to the fiend in the form of a monkey that is revealed to the minister in J. Sheridan le Fanu's "Green Tea," when his addiction to green tea finally opens his "inner" and "spiritual" eye: the furious creature, visible only to him, plagues his every activity until he is tormented into violent suicide. The master of the method is M. R. James: a good example is his "The Diary of Mr. Poynter." This describes a bibliophile, one James Denton, who buys four early-eighteenth-century quarto volumes relating to the area in which he has his country house. His aunt, who lives in the same house, finds a beautiful piece of curtain material of strange design pasted in one of the books and arranges for it to be copied to provide curtains, although the man employed for this task feels that the nature of the design is somehow evil. When the job is done and the curtains are up in the bedrooms of the house, we resort to Denton, sitting late one evening in his room, alternately reading and dozing in an armchair until he

> bethought himself that his brown spaniel, which ordinarily slept in his room, had not come upstairs with him. Then he thought he was mistaken: for happening to move his hand which hung down over the arm of the chair within a few inches of the floor, he felt on the back of it just the slightest touch of a surface of hair, and stretching it out in that direction he stroked and patted a rounded something. But the feel of it, and still more the fact that instead of a responsive movement, absolute stillness greeted his touch, made him look over the arm. What he had been touching rose to meet him. It was in the attitude of one that had crept along the floor on its belly, and it was, so far as could be recollected, a human figure. But of the face which was now rising to within a few inches of his own no feature was discernible, only hair. Shapeless as it was, there was about it so horrible an air of menace that as he bounded from his chair and rushed from the room he heard himself moaning with fear: and doubtless he did right to fly.[14]

The syntax drifts, like Denton's hand, into contact. The hand hangs within a few inches of the floor, the object rises to within a few inches of his face; the poise of civility and terror is caught neatly in the "absolute stillness *greeted*" and "What he had been touching *rose to meet* him"; the final dry comment, as if there were any question in the matter, mocks irrelevant reason, and its cool tone heightens the terror of the scene. Denton's stroking of the thing, mistaken for his dog, brings the horror so close to domesticity as to drive it to the limit of sheer alien otherness. The whole object is the production in the reader of as powerful a jolt of shock as is possible.

Sometimes terrifying supernatural beings are present in fantasy, but they are generally matched by at least equally potent supernatural powers for good that work on man's side. In MacDonald's *Phantastes* the deceptive Alder Maiden with her back in the form of a coffin and the devouring Ash Tree with the hollow heart are countered by the friendly Beech Tree and the Knight in Rusty Armour; in W. H. Hodgson's *The Night Land*, the surreal horrors from the outer darkness that surround the Last Redoubt of mankind are frequently foiled by a magic light emanating from some power for good. Nearer, though unintentionally so, to the horror story is Tolkien's The Lord of the Rings where the power and dread of Sauron are much more vividly felt than the forces of right.

The character of 'fantasy' now outlined is, to repeat, that of *A fiction evoking wonder and containing a substantial and irreducible element of supernatural or impossible worlds, beings or objects with which the mortal characters in the story or the readers become on at least partly familiar terms.* This definition takes in works told or written since the beginnings of human history—for example, myths, fairy tales, the voyage section of the *Odyssey*, Ovid's *Metamorphoses*, the Bible, *Beowulf*, saints' legends, Dante's *Divine Comedy*, medieval romance, the Grail story, Ariosto's *Orlando Furioso*, Spenser's *Faerie Queene* Book I, Milton's *Paradise Lost*, the *Märchen* of the German Romantics as well as modern fantasy as we know it. Not that these works are homogeneous: modern fantasy tends to be far more self-conscious, ratiocinative, cultural, and descriptive than, say, the traditional fairy tale of the sort found in Grimm; and twentieth-century fantasy differs from Victorian in being even more lavish in its descriptions, with values rather more discovered than imposed, with cultural values stressed more than social or moral ones, and often with fewer rules and prohibitions and less naked use of the supernatural. But this is only to say that like most other genres fantasy is a plastic one, taking individual character from each phase of its history.

AFTERWORD

Looking back at this definition, I find myself less inclined to be so guarded in my use of the term "fantasy." It seems to me that there is in practice a certain amount of agreement as to what is and is not a fantasy, and that since the definition started with a broad range of the best-known of works so described and then tried to find common distinctive features among them, the literary kind it isolated may be said to have a reasonable claim to the title of fantasy.

Definitions can be too inclusive to be definite or too definite to include very much. As regards fantasy, no doubt E. F. Bleiler and possibly Eric S. Rabkin in his *The Fantastic in Literature* (Princeton, N.J.: Princeton University Press, 1976) can be taken as examples of the former. However, it should be said that Rabkin's object is rather more to describe an element that is for him to be found throughout literature than to isolate a genre (p. 118n.). With Rabkin and Bleiler, one can only ask for the kind of specificity that has been refused. More productive disagreement occurs with the narrower definitions. An example is Tzvetan Todorov's *The Fantastic: A Structural Approach to a Literary Genre,* trans. Richard Howard (Cleveland: Case Western Reserve University Press, 1973 [1970]), which defines the fantastic as "that hesitation experienced by a person who knows only the laws of nature, [when] confronting an apparently supernatural event" (p. 25):

> The fantastic . . . lasts only as long as a certain hesitation: a hesitation common to reader and character, who must decide whether or not what they perceive derives from "reality" as it exists in the common opinion. At the story's end, the reader makes a decision even if the character does not; he opts for one solution or the other, and thereby emerges from the fantastic. If he decides that the laws of reality remain intact and permit an explanation of the phenomena described, we say that the work belongs to another genre: the uncanny. If, on the contrary, he decides that new laws of nature must be entertained to account for the phenomena, we enter the genre of the marvellous.
>
> The fantastic therefore leads a life full of dangers, and may evaporate at any moment. (p. 41)

So defined, "fantasy" exists for Todorov only in the late eighteenth and nineteenth centuries and is limited to such authors as the Gothic novelists, E. T. A. Hoffman, Poe, Gautier, and Nerval (though he could have extended the list to include, say, the *Alice* books). Now, few people, given the existence of Tolkien, C. S. Lewis or Mervyn Peake, would so restrict the province of fantasy; and most, if one may risk the assumption, would place "fantasy" where Todorov puts his genre of "the marvellous," that is, where we are dealing with the unambiguously supernatural almost from the outset. Clearly, then, while Todorov's definition may be useful in isolating a class of literature, it has very little value in describing fantasy as we know it.

Another recent book on the fantastic, W. R. Irwin's *The Game of the Impossible: A Rhetoric of Fantasy* (Urbana: University of Illinois Press, 1976) is limited by focussing on only one class of fantasies. Like Todorov, Irwin is a structuralist, concerned with what he sees as the basic strategy of fantasy. Thus, "a narrative is a fantasy if it presents the persuasive establishment and development of an impossibility, an arbitrary construct of the mind with all under the control of logic and rhetoric" (p. 9). For Irwin, we never lose sight of the fact that we are playing a game: if we do, we are reading a "romance," not a fantasy:

> romance is not an intellectual game, and . . . it fosters a credence different from that which fantasy requires. In a romance the reader is induced to lose his sense of fact; in a fantasy he is persuaded to play the new system of "facts," which he has wilfully and speculatively accepted, against the established facts, which he only pretends to reject. (p. 67)

Irwin disconnects fantasy from truth, credence and even moral effect, seeing it as an essentially therapeutic activity of make-believe: "fantasy is a result of intellectual play. The capacity for play is an amiable human characteristic. . . . But human play is a diversion, and after the game is over, the 'serious business of living' must be resumed" (p. 197). Doubtless such a definition might do some justice to the work of, say, Edith Nesbit. But fantasy as it is generally known comprises a large group of directly or indirectly Christian works, such as those by Kingsley, MacDonald, Williams, Lewis or Tolkien, many of which seek to produce in the reader a measure of belief in God, and present worlds that are intended to partake no less in ultimate reality than our own.[15] And most writers of fantasy do not ask merely for make-believe in their worlds, except at the outset: they hope that the power with which they bring to life a Gormenghast, an Arcturus or a Middle-earth will make us feel at once that it does and does not exist.[16] The astonishing thing is that with a definition of fantasy that so excludes them, Irwin talks at length about MacDonald, Williams, Lewis and Tolkien—whom he even terms writers of "theological romance"—as though they still belonged within the genre (ch. 10). And as with Todorov, it is not only his definition of fantasy which is narrow, but the time-scale—roughly 1880–1957—he allows for its existence.

It is only fair at this point to discuss some criticism of my own definition. It has been pointed out by one reviewer that my notion of "supernatural or impossible" need not be that of other people, and that what looks impossible here and now need not always be so:

> to me the gateway in [Charles Williams'] *Many Dimensions* is no more impossible than the interstellar gateways of science fiction, and while I see no reason to believe in the existence of the Oyéresu, I also see none to believe in their impossibility: except for making a stone so large He can't lift it, nothing is impossible to an infinite God. The supernatural is subsumed by the impossible only in the mind of the unbeliever, and therefore must not be so subsumed in definitions that depend on the responses of believers as well as unbelievers. . . .
>
> . . . We do not and cannot know what is possible for mankind in the future or for psychozoa in other parts of the natural-order universe.[17]

To this I should say first that I had no intention of subsuming the supernatural in the impossible in the sense of saying that it could not happen. My point was that no extension of nature can arrive at supernature, just as no extension of possibility can arrive at impossibility: the two are equivalent only in the sense of being, as I said, "of another order of reality from that in which we exist and form our notions of possibility." It seems to me that this phrase must also be my answer to the final sentence of the passage: from an Olympian point of view perhaps all could be seen as supernatural or natural, and anything as possible; but in practice we live in one temporal and spatial locality and found our notions on that. And most people, including Christians, would accept that there is a clear difference between our apprehensions of nature and supernature:[18] with nature, it is a matter of knowing (or not knowing), but with supernature, it is a matter of belief—and the latter mode is significantly the one to which the above reviewer resorts in this connection. But I think that a central answer here must be that fantasists can often themselves be seen portraying the very distinction I have made. Frequently the protagonist of a fantasy is forced to accept that his experiences have no rational explanation, and to respond with increasing awe, dread, joy or wonder—in short with emotions conditioned by the unknowable and mysterious—to events. Where the distinction is made by the work itself it ceases altogether to be open to question.

It has also been suggested that there is less difference than I maintain between fantasy and science fiction.[19] The reinforced definition of "supernatural or impossible" in the last paragraph may go some way toward answering this. There are also several criteria by which the two genres may be still further distinguished. Science fiction commonly portrays technological societies, whether in praise, blame or indifference. These societies need not always be industrial, but they involve the notion of intelligent beings changing their physical environment or else adapting to changes in it for their own benefit. The genre is rightly named *science* fiction in that it involves knowledge, or finding out how things work, on the part of the protagonist, who is often quite coolly rational and impersonal in his approach: indeed it is its functional tone, its concern with practicality, that profoundly marks off the bulk of science fiction from fantasy. Fantasy is almost invariably pastoral in setting and often antitechnological: MacDonald opposes the scientific intellect in *Phantastes*, Tolkien the industries of Sauron and Saraman, Peake the machine-based society Titus finds on leaving Gormenghast. In fantasy we have the realization of wonder at created things rather than the desire to know in order to master: even in the novels of Charles Williams, where the workings of the supernatural have to be found out in order that it may not do harm to mankind, the ultimate purpose is the depiction of what Williams sees as the glory of the "co-inherent" web of reality.[20]

The hero of fantasy usually has an emotional and spiritual life that we do not often find in science fiction, and his heroism is frequently of the sort that involves helping others. Fantasy tends to be moral in character, depicting the different natures of good and evil, and centrally concerned with viewing conduct in ethical terms. Science fiction is not so interested: certainly there can be "good" and "evil" personages in the genre, but the nature of their goodness or evil is not of great concern. In science fiction the criterion is often one of adaptation, of adjustment to new situations for survival; in fantasy it is one of conduct, of how well or badly the characters behave by timehonoured standards. In fantasy the hero is often brought under some protection or restraint, whether it originate in god, fairy or mortal, while in science fiction he must usually rely on his own wits and carve out a path for himself. It is of a piece with this that fantasy often looks back to and draws on the great literature of the past, where the work of science fiction tends to conceal its indebtedness and, where it is obliged, tends to be so only to works from within its own modern genre. The difference may be put as originality versus novelty: the fantasist tries to recreate, the science-fiction writer to make the wholly new. Science fiction will often try to reverse our presuppositions or upset our notions of order: it will, for example, invite us into the "mind" of a roadside tree convinced that it moves towards all the objects that pass it rather than that they move towards it, or present us with situations in which humans are used as farm animals, machines come to rule men, women run the world alone, or the past turns out to be the future.[21] The genre is fundamentally exploratory in character.

All the above statements can only be on the whole true, for the aim here has been to define fantasy in its purest form. There will always be exceptions and crossings of the border with science fiction at certain points, since the two genres, radically different though they are, do lie alongside one another to the extent that they are part of a larger class of "alternative world" fiction. But if this imposes reserve on the maker of definitions, it should also ask moderation of his reader. There are cases in which not every one of the above distinctions applies and yet the work remains basically science fiction or fantasy. Ursula Le Guin's *The Left Hand of Darkness* and *The Dispossessed* portray heroes of emotional and spiritual life who act on behalf of others,[22] but in most other respects, the works remain science fiction. Traditional fairy tales, such as those of the brothers Grimm, in contrast to modern fantasy, portray the disruption of the *status quo* in the form of lowly protagonists who become kings or queens, and they are not much concerned with contemplation or celebration; yet they otherwise come under the head of fantasy as we have defined it.

One further characteristic of fantasy may be added to the original definition. In its modern form, at least, fantasy shows a central interest in celebrating identities of created things. Other modern writers in other genres—Gerard Manley Hopkins, Virginia Woolf or Alain Robbe-Grillet, for example—show a similar interest in the individual, but the trait is peculiarly pervasive in fantasy. And the concern of fantasy is not simply with the minutely faithful record for the sake of fidelity to fact, but with that sense of individuality that, as Tolkien has said, comes from making things strange and luminous with independent life in a fantastic setting.[23] At the core of the genre is a delight in being, whether it be Kingsley's sense of the miraculous in all physical nature, MacDonald's view of the wonder of reality as seen by the unconscious mind, C. S. Lewis' transmutation of the solar system into something rich and strange, Tolkien's love of "tree and grass; house and fire; bread and wine"[24] as portrayed in The Lord of the Rings, the theme of the restoration of the true being of oneself or one's world in Ursula Le Guin's Earthsea Trilogy, or T. H. White's special love of the Middle Ages as he depicts them in *The Once and Future King*.[25] Even a fantasy so ascetic and sense-denying in aim as David Lindsay's *A Voyage to Arcturus* ends, through the very riot of its images, in appearing to delight in the very things it spurns (rather as Spenser's Guyon in Acrasia's Bower).[26]

The great evil in fantasy is that which seeks to possess—evil not only because such a desire is selfish but because it reduces being. In *The Water-Babies* Tom's greed brings him near to degenerating to an eft in a pond, and the lazy Doasyoulikes devolve from men to apes. The Shadow in MacDonald's *Phantastes* turns all the wonders that are seen to the commonplace and the everyday, and Anodos has to learn how to relinquish his desire for the white lady. The enemy in David Lindsay's *Voyage to Arcturus* is Crystalman, who seeks to enslave all being in sensual chains. Charles Williams' novels are all concerned with the struggle against magic, which tries to subdue all things to the self. The central theme of Lewis' *Perelandra* is giving the self willingly into Maleldil's hand rather than taking things independently (symbolized in the forbidden Fixed Land). The Ring in Tolkien's Lord of the Rings makes the people who wear it desire to subdue others to their will while it subdues them to its own: Sauron's object is to enslave Middle-earth, but Frodo's quest is to dispossess himself of the Ring and restore their individual freedoms to the variety of races in Middle-earth. In Ursula Le Guin's Earthsea Trilogy, it is the desire of self to aggrandize itself at the expense of others that causes evil—whether in the form of the evil shadow (of himself) that Ged releases in his pride to show himself a powerful magician in *A Wizard of Earthsea,* or in the subjugation of Arha to service to the Old Ones in the dark and eventually-destroyed labyrinth in *The Tombs of Atuan,* or in the desire of the magician Cob to live forever, even by destroying all other being, in *The Farthest Shore.* And at a general level one would even go so far as to say that the very "supernatural or impossible" character of fantasy is a way of freeing it from possession as an extension of our reality. In Tolkien's words,

> Creative fantasy . . . may open your hoard and let all the locked things fly away like cage-birds. The gems all turn to flowers or flames, and you will be warned that all you had (or knew) was dangerous and potent, not really effectively chained, free and wild; no more yours than they were you.[27]

NOTES

1. E. F. Bleiler, *A Checklist of Modern Fantastic Literature* (Chicago: Shasta, 1948), p. 3.

2. Bovet, *Pandaemonium, or The Devil's Cloyster* . . . (London: for J. Walthoe, 1684), pp. 172–76, 207–10.

3. Bishop Leadbeater, *The Hidden Side of Things,* 3rd ed. (Madras: Theosophical Publishing, 1923), pp. 100–101.

4. Arthur Conan Doyle, *The Coming of the Fairies* (London: Hodder and Stoughton, 1922), p. 71 et passim.

5. C. S. Lewis, *The Pilgrim's Regress,* 3rd ed. (London: Geoffrey Bles, 1943), p. 9.

6. J. R. R. Tolkien, *The Fellowship of the Ring,* 2nd ed. (London: Allen and Unwin, 1966), pp. 23–25. Tolkien maintained that the mortal beholder of stories dramatized by the elves would come to forget that the tales were fictions: "If you are present at a Faërian drama you yourself are, or think that you are, bodily inside its Secondary World" (*Tree and Leaf* [London: Allen and Unwin, 1964], pp. 47–48). See also my *Modern Fantasy: Five Studies* (Cambridge: Cambridge University Press, 1975), pp. 162, 286 n. 22.

7. See *Modern Fantasy: Five Studies,* pp. 111, 280 n. 41.

8. *Charles Kingsley: His Letters and Memories of His Life,* ed. F. E. Kingsley (London: Kegan Paul, 1876), II, 137.

9. See *Modern Fantasy: Five Studies,* pp. 34, 267 n. 54.

10. Theodore Cogswell, "The Wall Around the World," in *Yet More Penguin Science Fiction,* ed. Brian Aldiss (Harmondsworth: Penguin, 1964), p. 40.

11. H. Beam Piper, "He Walked Around the Horses," in *Best SF Three,* ed. Edmund Crispin (London: Faber and Faber, 1962), p. 67.

12. Robert Sheckley, "The Store of the Worlds," in *More Penguin Science Fiction,* ed. Brian Aldiss (Harmondsworth: Penguin, 1963); Frederik Pohl, "Let the Ants Try" and "Target One," *Alternating Currents* (Harmondsworth: Penguin, 1966); Arthur Porges, "The Rescuer," in *Yet More Penguin Science Fiction,* ed. Brian Aldiss; and Ray Bradbury, "A Sound of Thunder," in *Science Fiction Through the Ages,* ed. I. O. Evans (London: Panther, 1966).

13. For this phrase, see Davendra P. Varma, *The Gothic Flame* (London: Arthur Barker, 1957), p. 211.

14. M. R. James, *A Thin Ghost and Others* (London: Edward Arnold, 1919), pp. 67–68.

15. See Tolkien, *Tree and Leaf,* p. 63.

16. See also the review of W. R. Irwin's book by Jane Mobley in *Extrapolation,* 18 (May 1977), 146–47.

17. R. D. M[ullen] in *Science-Fiction Studies,* 3 (1976), 206, 207.

18. This point, however, will not hold for young children; for them, few things are impossible and much of life is magical.

19. Letter to me from Brian Aldiss, 19 November 1975.

20. See my "The Liturgical Novels of Charles Williams," *Mosaic,* 12 (Winter 1979), 161–81.

21. References here are, respectively, to Ursula K. Le Guin's "Direction of the Road," *The Wind's Twelve Quarters* (New York: Harper & Row, 1975); Piers Anthony, "In the Barn," in *Again, Dangerous Visions,* ed. Harlan Ellison (Garden City, N.Y.: Doubleday, 1972); Karel Capek, *R.U.R.* (1920; rpt. Garden City, N.Y.: Doubleday, 1923); Isaac Asimov, *I, Robot* (New York: Gnome, 1950) and many other works by him; John Wyndham, "Consider Her Ways," *Consider Her Ways & Others* (London: Michael Joseph, 1961); and Brian Aldiss, *An Age* (London: Faber and Faber, 1967).

22. See also Ursula K. Le Guin's statement of her interest in this in her "Science Fiction and Mrs [sic] Brown," in *Science Fiction at Large . . .*, ed. Peter Nicholls (London: Victor Gollancz, 1976). It is significant to note that Le Guin is also a writer of fantasy.

23. Tolkien, *Tree and Leaf,* p. 53.

24. Ibid.

25. On the last, see my "Flight to Aleppo: T. H. White's *The Once and Future King*," *Mosaic*, 10 (Winter 1977), 65–83.

26. For a similar point, see John Herdman, "The Previously Unpublished Novels of David Lindsay," *Scottish Literary Journal*, 3 (Winter 1976), 16.

27. Tolkien, *Tree and Leaf*, p. 53.

From Fancy to Fantasy: Coleridge and Beyond

W. R. Irwin

FANCY AND FANTASY. We easily assume that we know what both are and that the exercise of the former yields the latter. Thus if we define the faculty, we have a reliable access to the product, whether this takes a literary form or some other. But before we rest assured with this simple cause-to-effect reasoning, let us pause and consider. Do we know what the fancy is? Is it always the same? Does the fancy alone produce fantasy? Regrettably, we discover, no one of these questions can be answered simply. It will be the business of this essay to explore various answers and to reach, not definitive understanding, but a further stage toward clarification.

What is the fancy? If we turn to those whom we expect to provide illumination—historians of criticism, literary theorists, writers making notes on their craft—we find a bewildering richness of answers. Fancy is defined as wit, invention, free play of the mind, the "mimic" of reason that frolics while reason sleeps. It is the source of imagination, immature imagination, another term for imagination, a lower order (younger sister) of imagination, a servant, a competitor, an enemy of imagination, and an agent of fraud and triviality of taste. The fancy is embodied in a thousand metaphors, distilled in a thousand epithets.

Fancy (*phantasia*) and imagination (*imaginatio*) were long synonymous. In the history of their usage, now one and now the other has been regarded as the more important or the superior faculty. You will have noticed in the phrases of the preceding paragraph that the fancy has often been deprecated, disapproved; so has the imagination, as when the astronomer in *Rasselas,* after perceiving his error, gives thanks for deliverance from the "dangerous prevalence of the imagination." But with the distinction between fancy and imagination that Coleridge propounded and elaborated, but did not devise, the aesthetic, intellectual, and even moral ill repute of the fancy has become almost dogmatic, despite the rehabilitating efforts of some recent critics.

The reader of this essay does not need a full rehearsal of Coleridge's definition and devaluation of Wordsworth's modifying contributions. Suffice it to quote again Coleridge's last, familiar words on the subject from the unfinished *Biographia Literaria*:

> Fancy, on the contrary, has no other counters to play with but fixities and definites. . . . The Fancy is indeed no other than a mode of memory emancipated from time and space; while it is blended with, and modified by, that empirical phenomenon of the will, which we express by the word Choice. But equally with ordinary memory the Fancy must receive all its materials ready made from the law of association.[1]

The pejorative words and phrases leap at us: "counters," "play," "fixities," "definites," "empirical phenomenon of the will," "choice," "ready made," 'law of association." With the fancy we have mechanism and artifice, as well as the baneful legacy from the dead and trivial rationalism of the eighteenth century, especially from David Hartley. So the legend runs.

The fault deriving from an over-simple understanding of this passage is shared by Coleridge and his readers: Coleridge, because the passage, being spectacular, encourages a reductive reading; his readers, because few of them have troubled themselves with the many other passages in which Coleridge refined and modified his distinction by giving the fancy a more worthy essence and function.[2]

Various people have deprecated Coleridge's pronouncement. Ruskin advised readers to ignore Coleridge's distinction as "insignificant."[3] Lascelles Abercrombie called it "one of Coleridge's chimeras."[4] T. S. Eliot warned against it as being "specious" and "too simple."[5] Sir Herbert Read dismissed imagination and fancy, as defined by Coleridge, labeling them "the twin humbugs of romantic criticism."[6] These are potent voices, but they cannot drown the echoing roar of Coleridge's edict, especially as his authority has been asserted by I. A. Richards.[7]

I have no desire to join a quarrel over the validity of this perpetuated distinction between fancy and imagination, either in its cognitive or evaluative aspects. So complex are the two faculties, in themselves and in their relationships, that one can forgive Coleridge for not effectively bringing them to a final clarification. And the pejorative understanding of the fancy is fortified by the fact that it appears in the final chapter of the unfinished *Biographia Literaria,* widely regarded as Coleridge's major work of literary theory. Elsewhere he did grant that the fancy can operate organically as well as mechanically, that it is more than monistic, that the difference between the two can be one of degree and operation as well as of kind, that there can be an equal co-functioning of the two. These possibilities have been noted also by Wordsworth, Leigh Hunt, Ruskin, even by I. A. Richards. But several critics in the twentieth century, playing off the seeming finality of the quoted passage, have asserted the constitutive powers of the fancy. In their different ways T. S. Eliot, T. E. Hulme, and Sir Herbert Read have revalidated the claim of intellect to a central part in the creative process, and with this have contributed to rehabilitating the fancy by clarifying it.

T. S. Eliot's comments on the fancy are few but rich in suggestion. In one of his Norton Lectures of 1932, entitled "The Age of Dryden," he notes especially that in the preface to *Annus Mirabilis* Dryden proposes that the fancy functions with "invention" and "elocution" to form the totality "imagination." By "moulding the thought," the fancy is an activity of both imagination and intellect. But also being "partly verbal," it contributes to the elocution. So there is no part in shaping a poem from which the fancy is absent. It is both assimilative and dynamic.

In the lecture entitled "Wordsworth and Coleridge," Eliot objects that to restrict fancy to "a mode of memory" and to make as a result no connection between memory (which we may remember as the mother of the Muses) and imagination is to ignore both experience and what we know of the poetic process. Also to imply that intellect and imagination are quite separate, perhaps confiicting, powers is at best simplistic, at worst fallacious. For him, as for Dryden, the fancy participates in both and exerts its force throughout creativity. Though Eliot was by no means a total anti-Coleridgean, he makes clear that in his view Coleridge's discussions of fancy and imagination were basically as much preferential as judicious.

Some caution is advisable in considering the statements of T. E. Hulme, that brilliant, hasty, contentious corrector of vulgar errors. For him, romanticism was a malaise, to be remedied by the renewed health of classicism. In the recovery that he forecast, the most potent medication will be the fancy, superior to the imagination. It cleanses and orders poetry, feelings, thought. The fancy concentrates on the beauty of "small, dry things," which it perceives as they are. The fancy not only promotes accurate observation, but—more important for poetry—by creating new images and figures, it perceives essences as the beclouded and self-indulgent visions of imagination never can. This is the proposed message of Hulme's essay "Romanticism and Classicism."[8]

As he goes on, however, there are hints that if Hulme were to make his favored faculty the source of poetry rather than versification, he must ascribe its essential power to something other than accurate observation and clear images. Observation is mainly an instrument of intellect, and Hulme seems to be advocating a theory of poetry in which intellect is dominant. But he states that "the characteristic of intellect is that it can only represent complexities of the mechanical kind" (p. 139). He has just been saying that "the vital and organic" is what a poet must perceive and express. Rather than work out the difficulty, he calls up invention. This must be used to deal with what Bergson called "intensive," that is, vital complexities, in contrast with "extensive" complexities, which, being only mechanical, have multiplicity but no unity. It seems that, to reach essences, the poet must use invention. Is this the same as fancy? Probably, but he does not say so. He does state that "a powerfully imaginative mind seizes and combines at the same time all the important ideas of its poem or picture, and while it works with one of them, it is at the same instant working with and modifying all in their relations to it and never losing sight of their bearings on each other . . ." (pp. 139–40). If fancy and invention are the same or closely alike, it seems that the fancy has become almost identical with imagination.[9] Earlier in the essay, fancy was the superior faculty.

In an attempt to explain what Hulme meant, but did not state, Michael Roberts suggests this:

> In Hulme's use, "imagination" is an act of apprehending things in their essence and grasping all of their implications

and interrelations; and "fancy" is the instrument through which the imagination expresses itself.[10]

Hence, presumably, his insistence on separate sharp images and precise language. In his essay "Bergson's Theory of Art," Hulme makes his most emphatic remarks on the forming thought itself by accurate and fresh language. This Hulme had made the peculiar power of the fancy, though in his discourse he does not mention the fancy. We may infer that for Hulme the fancy is central in the unified poetic process. As Murray Krieger summarizes his concept, "Hulme does not allow for the possibility of a pre-existing fresh idea for which we then seek fresh embodiment. The idea becomes fresh as it is worked by us across the grain of language habits."[11]

Considerations of the fancy recur in the critical writings of Sir Herbert Read. Not only does he give it more attention than do Eliot and Hulme, he also more clearly distinguishes between fancy as a faculty and fantasy as a product: a necessary distinction, though scarcely the final word on the relationship. "A fantasy is more than a conceit, implying a sustained invention in the realm of fancy."[12]

Read's treatment is different also in that he makes the fancy and fantasy part of a scheme of rhetoric which conforms to principles of Jungian psychology. In chapter 9 of *English Prose Style*, entitled "Fantasy (Fancy)," he sets out the following paradigm:[13]

	Extraversion	*Introversion*
Thinking	exposition	narrative
Feeling	fancy	imagination (invention)
Sensation	impressionism	expressionism
Intuition	eloquence	unity

Coleridge's definition of the fancy provokes Read to no dissent, but he denies Coleridge's devaluation. Read ends the cited chapter with a hope that the future will bring "a less romantic age," in which the fancy will be rescued from an "aspersion . . . entirely sentimental in origin," and in which writers "will turn to fantasy as to a virgin soil" (p. 135). From Coleridge, Read understands that the fancy is an objective faculty, that is, one which deals with the concrete rather than the vague, or with phenomena rather than numena. Because it is emancipated memory, it has nothing to do with exposition and narrative, the two modes which result from thinking. "It deliberately avoids the logic and consistency of these types of rhetoric and creates a new and arbitrary order of events" (p. 126). Thus he allows, though he does not stress, a close alliance of the fancy and wit. It seems that in its initiating concept and maneuver such wit is free, but once the fancy begins developing its invention, it becomes arbitrary, controlled by the logic which its chosen illusion requires. It follows that a resulting fantasy is totally obedient to its parent; conforming to discursive logic, fantasy is deliberate and rational. Given Read's insistence on rationality, I confess myself at a loss to know why he considers the fancy and fantasy to be emanations from feeling rather than from thinking. And Read himself acknowledges that Jung would not have accepted his confinement of fantasy to "extraverted feeling," for Jung thought "phantasy activity" or reverie a possibility in any of the four functions of the psyche.

When Read passes from theorizing to exemplifying, he chooses, as the form that best embodies "objectivity and apparent arbitrariness," the fairy tale, which has its verse correspondence in the ballad. This comes, despite his previous exclusion of narrative, as we commonly understand it, from works of the fancy. He cites approvingly an account of green children as given in Thomas Keightley's *The Fairy Mythology* and Southey's "The Three Bears." And here one perceives an interest that led him to write his own unsurpassed fantasy entitled *The Green Child*, an unusual activity for a theoretician of the fancy and fantasy. For Read, the supreme exemplar of pure fantasy produced from the fancy is *The Thousand and One Nights*, which has no English equivalent. Indeed, most of the fantasies written in English, from English traditions, he dismisses as emanations from a fancy corrupted or sophisticated.

Though neither Eliot, Hulme, nor Read was an uncompromising opponent of Coleridge's views, each of them contributed some important understandings to a liberated and respectful idea of the fancy. All three connect the fancy and wit, and all value wit more highly than did Coleridge by implication in his definition. All grant the fancy a persistent verbal component, saying in effect that its perceptions cannot be separated from expressions and thus that the fancy operates constitutively throughout development and not simply as a faculty that, having served the imagination at the outset, then is excluded as a writer proceeds to attain high seriousness. Nor is it simply the provider of diversions, giving "a release from the serious business of living, a playful enjoyment of that to the reality of which we are indifferent."[14] The fancy and fantasy are consistent with the play principle to which, as formulated by Johann Huizinga in *Homo Ludens*, we owe much of our high culture. In short, Eliot, Hulme, and Read encourage taking the fancy seriously for itself and for its literary potential.

We should be grateful to Eliot, Hulme, and Read for refusing to take Coleridge's one pronouncement as the final word on the fancy.[15] Coleridge himself modified his statement in other, less well-known remarks, and some of these modifications appear, or are hinted at, in the later critics' considerations. But in the end the ambiguities and shifts of meaning remain, and there is no way of assigning certain ones to correctness and others to error, for what is right in one context is wrong in another. Let us then regretfully abandon the effort to make meaning correspond to some abstract essence and try to describe (not define) it by use in works of fantasy. The results will still be unfixed, but at least there will be an objective component in the operation.

The reader will have observed that the theoreticians whom I have cited approach the fancy through its actions and results. Sometimes they attempt to get no closer to the essence. Such effect-to-cause reasoning, or surmising, seems inescapable in this kind of consideration. The same is true of most—perhaps all—qualities whose names indicate abstractions, qualities which have manifestations but such being and attributes as the human understanding cannot perceive directly.

Most observers give to fancy a facile energy, an inherent activeness that is quick to mobilize and quick to bring its results. It does not contemplate; it seizes. This might be called an immediate responsiveness, in which sensibility and wit move together as one. Coleridge might say that this responsiveness is limited to an apprehension of phenomena only and that the energy of fancy cannot exert itself beyond manipulation of "fixities and definites." I doubt this, for such a contention ignores the fictive potentialities of the fancy, which operate perhaps from the moment of response, perhaps as a separate continuance of the excitement the response produces. That the fictive potentiality is present can, I believe, be demonstrated by examining a passage, the well-known Queen

Mab speech in *Romeo and Juliet,* which has been repeatedly cited (by Wordsworth among others) as an exhibit of the fancy at work (or at play). Romeo is apprehensive about attending the Capulets' masque; it appears that he has had a warning dream. But Mercutio forestalls his telling it by a brilliant, though non-functional,[16] descant on Queen Mab as a maker of dreams:

O, then I see Queen Mab hath been with you.
She is the fairies' midwife, and she comes
In shape no bigger than an agate stone
On the forefinger of an alderman,
Drawn with a team of little atomies
Athwart men's noses as they lie asleep;
Her wagon spokes made of long spinners' legs,
The cover, of the wings of grasshoppers;
Her traces, of the smallest spider's web;
Her collars, of the moonshine's wat'ry beams;
Her whip, of cricket's bone; the lash, of film;
Her wagoner, a small grey-coated gnat,
Not half so big as a round little worm
Prick'd from the lazy finger of a maid;
Her chariot is an empty hazelnut,
Made by the joiner squirrel or old grub,
Time out o' mind the fairies' coachmakers.
And in this state she gallops night by night
Through lovers' brains, and then they dream of love;
O'er courtiers' knees, that dream on curtsies straight;
O'er lawyers' fingers, who straight dream on fees;
O'er ladies' lips, who straight on kisses dream,
Which oft the angry Mab with blisters plagues,
Because their breaths with sweetmeats tainted are.
Sometime she gallops o'er a courtier's nose,
And then dreams he of smelling out a suit;
And sometime comes she with a tithe-pig's tail
Tickling a parson's nose as 'a lies asleep,
Then dreams he of another benefice.
Sometimes she driveth o'er a soldier's neck,
And then dreams he of cutting foreign throats,
Of breaches, ambuscadoes, Spanish blades,
Of healths five fathom deep; and then anon
Drums in his ear, at which he starts and wakes,
And being thus frighted, swears a prayer or two

And sleeps again. This is that very Mab
That plats the manes of horses in the night
And bakes the elflocks in foul sluttish hairs,
Which once untangled much misfortune bodes.
This is the hag, when maids lie on their backs,
That presses them and learns them first to bear,
Making them women of good carriage.
This is She——— (I, iv, 53–95)

Mercutio's response is prompted by the talk of dreams, with which he immediately associates the folklore that grants Queen Mab a particular power over pregnant women; he himself arbitrarily adds the assumption that sleepers are pregnant with dreams. There is no perceptible pause between this assumption and his development. But for seventeen lines he says nothing of dreams or midwifery, for he is concerned to elaborate an image of Queen Mab and her accoutrements. The latter are more fully described than the former, as if to visualize her chariot, its maker, the wagon-spokes, cover, traces, and the rest, all in consistent miniature, were to visualize by inference the figure herself. The total picture might be called a phantasm, a summoned-up, fabricated, cohesive appearance. To think of this as made from nothing is quite wrong. The picture is actually assembled from easily envisioned things, some familiar in themselves and some in which a familiar object, arbitrarily reduced in size, is assimilated to a less familiar, already small and delicate. Many images of the passage seem almost designed to illustrate Edmund Burke's ideas of the beautiful, which is generally consistent with the fancy. The engraftment produces an image of what no one has ever seen, which is nonetheless completely vivid and plausible. This rapid process, completed in richly detailed language, occurs repeatedly in these first seventeen lines and carries over, somewhat modified, into the account of Queen Mab's travels by night, an account which converts the representation from static to dynamic.

Being logical in his ebullience, Mercutio turns to Queen Mab as a midwife. As she drives her chariot, she delivers the vain wish-fulfilling dreams with which the sleepers are pregnant. So successful has been the cumulative illusion that the chariot's first route, "through lovers' brains," seems entirely plausible. This first image is tactically advantageous, since it implies in the later points of contact ("O'er courtiers' knees,"

"O'er lawyers' fingers," etc.) an effectual, though not specified, pressing on the brain to release the dream. The reader is not allowed to forget what midwives actually do. After a brief digression, Mercutio returns to the sexual associations of Queen Mab. Now, however, she is transformed into a hag, the incubus, which, though it is the dread "nightmare demon," Mercutio pretends is still as benevolent as a midwife, for she "learns them first to bear, making them women of good carriage." It is hard to guess what entertaining bawdry and inversion of ordinary thought might have followed but for Romeo's impatient interruption: "Thou talk'st of nothing." Mercutio disingenuously agrees, without sharing Romeo's lugubrious literalness and without abandoning his original fancy:

> True, I talk of dreams
> Which are the children of an idle brain,
> Begot of nothing but vain fantasy.

In Mercutio's speech, energy of conception and expression are steadily evident. His original invention, the finding, is instantaneous; his development follows without pause through a series of witty, seemingly free, but actually controlled associations. Though the speech is long and interruptive, there is no tedium in it, because the reader is hurried from one image to the next and from one movement to the next. This rapidity can have no other result than to make the language rapid.

Mercutio's is a young man's speech. One of the amusing effects is that here Mercutio seems younger than the hesitant and still bemused Romeo, who can exercise his wit, such as it is and what there is of it, only in self-pity. It has been many times suggested that the fancy is a youthful faculty. As I previously noted, one of Wordsworth's propositions was that fancy is the immature state of the imagination, and even Coleridge granted that fancy "is the power/That first unsensualizes the dark mind,/ Giving it new delights. . . ."[17] To make youthfulness an attribute of the fancy is acceptable if youthfulness is freed from a necessary link with chronology.

What is so unusual about Mercutio's notion? Its abrupt departure from the context of thought. Romeo does not wish to attend the Capulets' masque; he is still caught in the self-indulgences of an unreal love. He pretends—perhaps he believes—that going is folly, and not only because the Capulets are enemies. He has had a dream, and the implication is that the dream warned him not to go for fear of disaster. He rejects the notion that the dream was a lie. Thus is advanced as the norm of discourse a standard superstition of dream lore, that dreams portend evils to come. To this, Mercutio introduces a sudden and violent counter. Somewhat like Pertelote's scoffing at Chauntecleer's flatulence, Mercutio's aetiology stresses a detailed physical causation of dreams that robs them of any sinister meaning. Dreams come from the sports of a mischievous fairy; they are transitory and insignificant. Mercutio's rhetorical purpose is presumably not to make Romeo believe in Queen Mab but to shake him from an equally unfounded conviction. By a mundane standard of verification, Mercutio's demonstration mocks the validity of his causation as much as it asserts it; though, once the fanciful standard replaces the mundane, the temporary plausibility of Mercutio's account is overwhelming.

Thus, I believe, it always is with the fancy. Some norm, convention, evident fact, conclusion validated by experience or consent or the like is overtly or implicitly challenged and, by a strong play against it, temporarily routed and replaced. This creates novelty in its extreme form, and while the novelty persists with a detailed and coherent development, its factitiousness disappears from sight. When the performance is over or the excursion finished, the norm reasserts itself, though often not so firmly established as it was before.

The foregoing generalizations suggest the way in which freedom and arbitrariness operate in productions of the fancy. To the routine-minded, such freedom seems complete, lawless, outrageous. Actually, it is contingent because it is derived by speculative subversiveness. If we did not know that the human body is composed of flesh, bones, tissue, nerves, organs, and the rest, there would be no occasion to posit a living man of glass, as in Cervantes' *The Licentiate of Glass*. If we were not sure that angels are phenomenally non-existent, no one would be disturbed by a report that the archangel Michael appeared in someone's kitchen to bring a message of warning, as he does in T. H. White's *The Elephant and the Kangaroo*. This second example indicates, of course, that the arbitrariness of the fancy operates against an established arbitrariness. Thus, again, the fancy is characteristically responsive in a subversive way; it is not originating, but an interlude of revolution or misrule.

Within this interlude, however, an activity occurs in which

there is little freedom. Details, images, ideas arrange themselves as by a kind of internal necessity into a closed system of plausible relations. This too may be seen in Mercutio's speech. He appears to be inventing spontaneously as he goes along. Actually, his whole development, with the exception of the three lines about manes and elflocks, is a carefully though simply ordered discourse on the statement "She is the fairies' midwife."[18] There can be two motives, often complementary, for seeking to fabricate the perfect internal logic of a projection from the fancy: a performer's delight in consistency as he lays out his show of a rational process, and the need to demonstrate that the new formulation, competing against the customary acceptance accorded to the standard, is within itself as firm intellectually. In the execution of these motives, there is ordinarily an element of gamesmanship. Were there not, it might be hard to distinguish the purveyor of fancy from a madman.

The sanity of the fancy's productions is also maintained by persistent reminders of connections, sometimes of contrast and sometimes of skewed comparison, between the construct and the ordinary development of the norm from which it departs. This is but another way of saying that, without something to react against, the subversiveness of the fancy would be meaningless. Mercutio's whole speech is a demonstration against a general superstitious notion of dreams that Romeo accepts. Queen Mab's chariot and its accoutrements can be visualized by the distortion of the mind's miniaturizing an ordinary carriage and its accoutrements. This same relationship of the fictive and the known through systematic alteration of size invests the overall effect and the details of Books I and II of *Gulliver's Travels,* as Samuel Johnson perceived. Lilliput and Brobdingnag, and all that is in them, are so different from contemporaneous England as to be amusing and so like as to be embarrassing. The same may be said of the exotic little world, a tight little island, created in *The Rape of the Lock.* One can have little understanding of *Hudibras* except against two backgrounds: the adventures and *morale* of *Don Quixote,* which Butler affectionately perverts, and current Presbyterianism, which he degrades. The examples might be multiplied, but the point remains the same: the fancy must play, sometimes with more complexity than I have suggested, against a context, whether this be stated or assumed. And it is part of the reader's obligation and delight to keep continuously in mind the context and the subversive production which it prompts.

Here one reaches a real and unresolvable paradox: a successful play of the fancy is coherent and self-contained, yet it has no significant existence except against a referent.

In the interplay of convention and new construct lies one aspect of that meeting of contraries that is attributed to the fancy. Admittedly, this is different from what the operation is usually thought to be—the making of unexpected, indeed bizarre, analogies. The conceits of metaphysical poetry are no doubt emanations of the fancy, but it is not just one collection of elements of a conceit that startles by rejecting the other, but first the collocation of what seems radically disparate and second the perception that this joining has an intellectual validity, even though it may be factitious and temporary. These generalizations remain true, I believe, even when one part of a conceit is *outré* and the other familiar. In such case the first may sharply alter the usual understanding of the other, but it does not deny or replace it.

Briefly, a conceit is a strange but recognizable analogy, or elaborated metaphor, and this definition only repeats a commonplace understanding. In oxymoron, association between opposites occurs as a surprise, but each element reciprocally modifies the other and the completed figure represents an entity, a synthesis that, though forced and unstable, may be apprehended. Also, images that simply acknowledge the coexistence of opposites, held in brief suspension together, are combinations of which neither element is a refutation or replacement of the other. Examples of this may be found generously in the poetry of Keats, who in my view had as clear a practical understanding of the fancy as did Coleridge or Wordsworth, though he does not theorize about it. Keats's untitled fragment "Welcome joy, and welcome sorrow" is composed of little else than such joinings to illustrate the assertion "I do love you both together."

Accordingly, the operation of fancy with which I am most concerned is not straightforwardly analogical, as in some way are the other three that I sketched in the foregoing paragraph. Indeed, that work of the fancy that seeks to displace a convention is overall the opposite; the general logical connection between old and new is contrast. Within this pattern, however, will occur what I have called "skewed comparisons," large and small. This complication requires some explaining. They are not straightforward comparisons because a degree of likeness is introduced in order to suggest a more prominent unlikeness and thus further to develop and strengthen the competing, subversive construct. This is really an inversion of a characteristic maneuver of analogies that are more than simple, whereby an evident common feature of the two elements is made the means to discover or force the recognition of other similarities that are not evident, sometimes to an extent that strains the reader's capacity for acceptance. The more ingenious and plausible are these extended similarities, the more successful is the analogy as a display of wit, unless in the development it becomes tedious. But in the inverse operation, the result is the discovery through superficial similarities of fundamental differences. This process may be seen repeatedly at work in the details and the larger movements of *Gulliver's Travels.* Consider the description, in Chapter 1 of Book IV, of Gulliver's first sight of the Yahoos:

> At last I beheld several Animals in a Field, and one or two of the same Kind sitting in Trees. Their Shape was very singular, and deformed, which a little discomposed me, so that I lay down behind a Thicket to observe them better. Some of them coming forward near the Place where I lay, gave me an Opportunity of distinctly marking their Form. Their Heads and Breasts were covered with a thick Hair, some frizzled and others lank; they had Beards like Goats, and a Long Ridge of Hair down their Backs, and the fore Parts of their Legs and Feet; but the rest of their Bodies were bare, so that I might see their Skins, which were of a brown Buff Colour. They had no Tails, nor any Hair at all on their Buttocks, except about the Anus; which, I presume Nature had placed there to defend them as they sat on the Ground; for this Posture they used, as well as lying down, and often stood on their hind Feet. They climbed high Trees, as nimbly as a Squirrel, for they had strong extended Claws before and behind, terminating on sharp Points, hooked. They would often spring, and bound, and leap with prodigious Agility. The Females were not so large as the Males; they had long lank Hair on their Heads, and only a Sort of Down on the rest of their Bodies, except about the Anus, and Pudenda. Their Dugs hung between their fore Feet, and often reached almost to the Ground as they walked. The Hair of both Sexes was of several Colours, brown, red, black and yellow. Upon

> the whole, I never beheld in all my Travels so disagreeable an Animal, or one against which I naturally conceived so strong an Antipathy.

The tone of this passage is that of the whole work—sober, careful reporting; even the antipathy which pervades the passage is carefully wrought from diction which is officially neutral but actually charged with revulsion, especially the quasi-technical language. Twice Gulliver refers to them as animals, and his comparisons, for various purposes, are with goats and squirrels. His first qualitative observation is "Their shape was very singular, and deformed, which a little discomposed me. . . ." Their shape was "deformed" from what? Why was Gulliver "discomposed"? Because he has a glimmer of what is evident to the reader who, because of distance, has no personal pride to maintain, that these creatures are an ugly parody of the human being. In this passage Gulliver uses only the imagery of sight, though the images have a secondary effect of smell. It is no surprise, then, that a few lines later images of sound and smell, both hideous, swarm over the description.

Throughout this passage—and others—Swift is developing an analogy between Gulliver and the creatures that parody him. He observes no more than does anyone who visits the larger simians on display in a zoo. Later the analogy, less evidently physical, between Gulliver and the Houyhnhnms will be developed to complete the frame. Gulliver is both Yahoo and Houyhnhnm, and neither, a being "plac'd on this isthmus of a middle state." Try though he may, as he did in Lilliput and Brobdignag, Gulliver cannot become a citizen, for he is both like and unlike either dominant group of this polarized society, like and unlike the Yahoos physically, like and unlike the Houyhnhnms spiritually. The comparisons and contrasts are there for all to see, even Gulliver, but they are skewed. Instead of analogy being used to bring disparate components together, it is used as much to keep them apart. The method of analogy has the effect both of making and displacing analogy. Formally this passage is a parody in which one element, the deviant construct, is elaborated, and the other, the standard, may be taken for granted. The Yahoos need description; Gulliver does not, for he is like us. Some version of this method of skewed comparisons, in which like and unlike remain unresolved, recurs in fantasy, whether by Swift or others.

What concerns me in this working of the fancy is a competition, an overt or implied argument, which is not conspicuous in those other results of fancy in which contraries or disparates are brought together. Hence the one operation imposes rhetorical requirements which the others do not necessitate. The original subversive concept and its development must be so coherent and plausible as to form an apparently independent system, strong enough temporarily to usurp the dominance of the convention that it counters. One means to this end, likely the most promising, is narrative, which has the tactical advantage of taking demonstration out of the conceptual range and making it concrete, sequential, and illustrative. Other operations of the fancy—conceit, oxymoron, images of opposition in confrontation—scarcely need narrative; they will succeed, or not, as of their immediate presentation. And it is hard to see how any of these might generate a story. But this version of parody, which I am belaboring, has an intrinsic potential for narrative, and one realization of this potential is prose fiction fantasy.

If the reader has accepted my description of what may be called the rhetoric of fancy, he has also perceived that this cannot be mobilized except by a person free from the domination of established conclusions even when he essentially accepts them, willing to turn his capabilities of thought to any novel proposition. To Caesar such men are dangerous, to Erasmus precious. The play of his mind may have any aim from serious to frivolous, but his development, if he chooses to develop beyond the initial invention, will be a calculated counter-demonstration. If his chosen form is narrative, he may produce a work as grim as Orwell's *1984,* as exotic as Read's *The Green Child*, as entertaining as Beerbohm's *Zuleika Dobson*, or as impudent as Douglas' *South Wind*. All these possibilities and more are within the range of narrative that originates with that fancy which is controlled by wit.

It is fortunate for my purpose that, in such twentieth-century theoretical discussion as can be found, the transition has already been sufficiently made from concentration on the faculty (fancy) to concentration on the product (fantasy). And since about 1880 the product has more and more been prose fiction. In the nineteenth century, as I have shown, critics sketched their notion of the fancy and sometimes cited examples. Their exposition of the chosen passages, however, was usually perfunctory. Exceptional instances are Wordsworth's incomplete comments on "Winter" by Charles Cotton and some of Leigh Hunt's analyses.

Presumably the reader, already persuaded that the fancy is a simple capability that works mechanically, could make his own inferences from the passages without help. I do not remember an instance among these critics of illustrating the operation of the fancy by citing a work of prose fiction fantasy. This was certainly not for lack of adequate examples which would have been well known to them. Several narratives of Lucian, *The Golden Ass* of Apuleius, various Utopias, *Gulliver's Travels,* some of the satirical tales of Voltaire, perhaps Beckford's *Vathek*—to name only the most prominent possibilities—would have yielded aids to understanding. The answer likely is that, as I have said, the romantic critics were interested in the fancy only as a way of defining (and exalting) the imagination, and this honorific quality they were predisposed to find in the works of major poets.

No modern critic has demurred from shifting attention to prose fiction fantasy in considering the works of the fancy. Indeed, it seems to be one of Sir Herbert Read's unstated assumptions that only narrative fiction illustrates the faculty. Perhaps the propriety of the shift has become self-evident. Perhaps recent commentators have recognized that, from late in the nineteenth century on, prose fiction has extended its empire, so that readers are accustomed to its now including areas once thought the domain of poetry alone.[19] In any event, there is nothing that restricts the fancy to expressing itself only in poetry. If it be that aspect of imagination controlled and energized by wit of a free, playful, speculative kind, the persuasive forming of sustained impossible fictions would seem to be its most congenial activity. The frequency with which *Hudibras* and *The Rape of the Lock* are cited as works of the fancy supports the consanguinity of the faculty and a kind of narrative that projects an exotic order as if it were real.

Yet there is an important distinction to be observed here. To say that fancy is a capability of bringing opposites together is not to suggest that its joinings are all of the same kind. Keats was fond of combining known disparates in a series of pleasing, though unstable, unions. The metaphysical poets, not content with a series of collocations, created systems of ingenious and unlikely extended metaphors, and thus offended Dr. Johnson. But the fancy can work as well by making a narrative from the consequences of a single controlling and generative contrast between the known of the accepted world and a posited impossibility. The former already exists and needs no development; the latter is developed in a story. This is what one perceives in *Hudibras*, *The Rape of the Lock*, *The Hunting of the Snark*, and in prose fiction fantasy. The common element in these is not just the material—the "fixities and definites"—which authors manipulate, but in the displacement of nominal acceptation resulting from the exercise of free and inventive speculation, which is always available but rarely put into play. This produces delight and a responsive participation in readers of sufficient mental agility, as they see the new construct emerge and place it *vis-à-vis* the routine. In the most successful fantasies, this new construct takes on a speculative validity of its own, which a reader may accept without being perverse or surrendering himself to insanity. For this reason, the world as perceived by Miss M in Walter de la Mare's *Memoirs of a Midget*, for example, rather than fading once the reader is finished and leaves the book for a bed accommodated to his own size, remains memorable and in a manner "true."

Sir Herbert Read posits two forms of art. "One is the elaboration of the given reality, of the classified data of experience. It is a grace added to life: a plaything. The other is an extension of the given reality, an extension of experience, an exercise of consciousness."[20] These may be thought of as roughly equivalent to emanations from the fancy and the imagination. We are still under the domination of Coleridge. But a comprehensive mind and taste, like Coleridge's, will find value in both, as they are separately and as they interact. Actually, we need playthings as well as monuments.

NOTES

1. Samuel Coleridge, *Biographia Literaria*, ed. T. Shawcross (London: Oxford University Press, 1907), I, 202.
2. See Owen Barfield, *What Coleridge Thought* (Middletown, Conn.: Wesleyan University Press, 1971), pp. 81, 85, 91, 111, et passim.
3. John Ruskin, *Modern Painters*, in *The Works of John Ruskin*, ed. E. T. Cook and Alexander Wedderburn (London: Allen; New York: Longmans, Green, 1903), IV, 219.
4. Lascelles Abercrombie, *The Idea of Great Poetry* (London: Secker, 1925), p. 53.

5. T. S. Eliot, *The Use of Poetry and the Use of Criticism*... (London: Faber, [1950]), pp. 56–57.

6. Herbert Read, *Wordsworth: The Clark Lectures 1929–1930* (London and Toronto: Cape, 1930), p. 161.

7. Those who seek a general understanding of the imagination and fancy will profit from reading the two excellent articles so entitled in the *Princeton Encyclopedia of Poetry and Poetics,* enlarged edition, ed. Alex Preminger, et al. (Princeton: Princeton University Press, 1974). See also R. L. Brett, *Fancy and Imagination* ([London]: Methuen, [1969]).

8. T. E. Hulme, *Speculations: Essays on Humanism and the Philosophy of Art,* ed Herbert Read (New York: Harcourt, Brace; London: Kegan Paul, Trench, Trübner, [1936], pp. 113–40. See also Herbert Read's essay entitled "The Isolation of the Image: T. E. Hulme," in *The True Voice of Feeling*... (London: Faber, 1953), pp. 101–15.

9. It is worth noting that Sir Herbert Read in the paradigm cited below makes imagination and invention synonymous.

10. Michael Roberts, *T. E. Hulme* (London: Faber, [1938]), p. 68.

11. Murray Krieger, "The Ambiguous Anti-romanticism of T. E. Hulme," *English Literary History,* 20 (December 1953), 314. Krieger's article is throughout a careful explication and assessment of Hulme's aesthetic ideas, which Krieger makes more cogent than did Hulme himself.

12. Herbert Read, *English Prose Style* (1952; rpt. Boston: Beacon, [1955]), p. 125. This work was first published in 1928, and in a revised form re-issued in 1952.

13. Ibid., p. 85.

14. D. G. James, *Scepticism and Poetry* (London: Allen and Unwin, [1937]), p. 49.

15. Yet, if one is not to spend one's life in confusion, a reductive definition is necessary. Owen Barfield has done more than any other to show that in Coleridge's view fancy and imagination are protean. Even so, Barfield stresses finally the very contrast that Coleridge himself reached in his most famous passage: "And so fancy (as Coleridge uses the word) is that which is responsible for, that which produces, the kind of imagery, or combinations of images, that come to mind ready-made and almost unbidden simply out of the impressions of the senses which the memory has stored and retained. Thus, he speaks of 'the law of the passive Fancy and the mechanical Memory.' Fancy is predominantly a passive thing and its products (by contrast with those of the imagination) are 'fixed and dead.' "

"Whereas the imagination is essentially vital. The images begotten by imagination are alive and creative, and have a sort of germinating power of their own. When true imagination is at work, the same power is operating in man as operated, in the Beginning, in the creation of the world; only now it flows from an individual mind, and in association with what Coleridge calls 'the conscious will.' Fancy and imagination are both needed for composing poetry (and, in a sense, imagination must work by 'irradiating' fancy); but the truly great poet is the poet of the imagination rather than the poet of mere fancy." ("Where is Fancy Bred?" in *The Rediscovery of Meaning and other Essays,* Middletown, Conn.: Wesleyan University Press, 1972, pp. 88–89).

16. "The Queen Mab speech . . . is as much and as little to be dramatically justified as a song in an opera is" (Harley Granville-Barker, *Prefaces to Shakespeare,* Second Series [London: Sidgwick and Jackson, Ltd., 1930], p. 7).

17. Coleridge, "The Destiny of Nations," 11. 80–82. Coleridge allowed this passage to stand unchanged when the poem was included in *Sibylline Leaves* (1817) and in the editions of 1828, 1829, and 1834.

18. My colleague Miriam Gilbert suggests that as this speech proceeds it becomes less controlled, as if Mercutio were overwhelmed with his own wit and cannot stop except by being interrupted.

19. See Dean B. Doner, "The Burdening of Narrative," Ph.D. diss., University of Iowa, 1953, pp. vii–xviii.

20. Read, *The True Voice of Feeling . . . ,* p. 154.

The Secondary Worlds of High Fantasy

Kenneth J. Zahorski
and Robert H. Boyer

Perilous realm, legendary land, mythic country, Faërie, home of the gods: these are a few of the generic names for the landscape or "secondary world" (Tolkien's term) of high fantasy. This secondary world, fully as glamorous as its various epithets suggest, is the subject of this essay. However, since there is such an integral connection between "secondary world" and "high fantasy," this latter term should be examined before going any further into the former.

High fantasy is, in fact, distinguished from low fantasy largely on the basis of setting. Low fantasy (*low* is a descriptive, not evaluative, term here) is set in a conventional here and now, in our "primary world," to again use a Tolkien term. Low fantasy is like high fantasy in that it contains nonrational phenomena, that is, creatures or events that cannot be explained scientifically or rationally according to our norms of what is real. But unlike its opposite number, low fantasy offers no explanations for its nonrational happenings; in fact it cannot, precisely because it is set in the ordinary, primary world. In the secondary worlds of high fantasy, on the other hand, there are explanations that are plausible in those other-world settings, explanations that point to magical (faery tales) or supernatural (myth-based) causality. Having defined high fantasy in general, we can now begin to understand it better by exploring, as systematically as is feasible without distorting matters, a variety of its secondary worlds.

It is J. R. R. Tolkien, appropriately enough, who has provided us with some of the most perceptive and illuminating observations on the nature and function of setting in faery stories and other types of fantasy literature. His seminal essay, "On Fairy-Stories," should be placed first on any required reading list for students of the genre. Indeed, this essay serves as our primary lexicon of terms used in contemporary fantasy criticism. Page quickly through it and the terms pop out: "sub-creator," "Primary World," "Secondary World," "arresting strangeness," "Perilous Realm," "Recovery," "Escape," "Consolation," "Eucatastrophe." Most contemporary critical treatises on fantasy reflect, in one way or another, Tolkien's germinative ruminations. Perhaps most influential, however, have been his comments about setting. Let us examine some of these.

To begin with, Tolkien makes it quite clear that there is a close correlation between successful fantasy and successful sub-creation. The sub-creator must invent secondary worlds that are credible: worlds that possess their own "inner consistency of reality." Although it isn't necessary for an invented world to be governed by laws and causality identical, or even similar, to those of our primary world, there must be some internal logic at work in the sub-creator's invention. Tolkien is clear on this point:

> What really happens is that the story-maker proves a successful "sub-creator." He makes a Secondary World which your mind can enter. Inside it, what he relates is "true": it accords with the laws of that world. You therefore believe it, while you are, as it were, inside. The moment disbelief arises, the spell is broken; the magic, or rather art, has failed. You are then out in the Primary World again, looking at the little abortive Secondary World from outside.[1]

The secondary world of high fantasy, then, should possess a consistent order that is explainable in terms of the supernatural (i.e., deities), or in terms of the less definable, but still recognizable, magical powers of Faërie (e.g., wizards and enchantresses).

Although of vital importance, verisimilitude is not enough. A secondary world must also create in the reader a feeling of "arresting strangeness," a feeling of awe and wonder. Thus, an invented world must be wondrous, or at least extremely interesting, as well as credible. The sub-creator must attempt to depict a world with truly marvelous aspects. The new worldscape should also be different from our own. So different, as a matter of fact, that we are allowed to escape for a while from the mundane existence so often experienced in the primary world. Furthermore, we should be given the opportunity to recover a new and fresh perspective on the primary world (Tolkien's concept of "Recovery"). And, finally, if everything works exactly right, we should be able to experience the greatest joy of all, the joy of Consolation (i.e., the joy of the happy ending).

The creation of such a secondary world is not, as might be expected, an easy task. Tolkien vividly describes the difficulty of the challenge:

> To make a Secondary World inside which the green sun will be credible, commanding Secondary Belief, will probably require labour and thought, and will certainly demand a special skill, a kind of elvish craft. Few attempt such difficult tasks. But when they are attempted and in any degree accomplished then we have a rare achievement of Art: indeed narrative art, story-making in its primary and most potent mode.[2]

It is clear from Tolkien's statement that to have any hope of successfully practicing the "elvish craft" of world-making an artist must be gifted, industrious, and adventurous. But even the possession of these rare qualities does not automatically guarantee success. It is a truly mysterious process, this invention of other worlds, and even the master-fantasist, Tolkien, has difficulty trying to explain it. When he attempts to define the process, he admits that the word which most readily comes to mind is "magical," but he resists the temptation to use this term, explaining that "Magic should be reserved for the operations of the Magician."[3] He finally settles upon "Enchantment" as the term which best describes the "elvish craft" of the fantasist:

> Enchantment produces a Secondary World into which both designer and spectator can enter, to the satisfaction of their senses while they are inside; but in its purity it is artistic in desire and purpose.[4]

Operating under this artistic Enchantment, writers of high fantasy have dealt with the secondary world as related to the primary world in three different ways. Some have created remote secondary worlds; others have created juxtaposed primary and secondary worlds with magical portals serving as gateways between them; and still others have created worlds-within-worlds. Each of these treatments deserves examination.

Many fantasists choose to ignore the primary world completely, introducing readers to their remote secondary worlds from the outset. Thus, Ursula K. Le Guin's Earthsea, a maritime secondary world of countless islands and vast oceans, has no connection with our world; there is no portal through which one may pass from one world to the other. The primary world simply does not exist—physically or geographically. Spiritually, of course, the two worlds are related, since Le Guin lives in the primary world and writes, as do all authors, from her human imagination and experience. As Tolkien explains:

> Fantasy is made out of the Primary World, but a good craftsman loves his material, and has a knowledge and feeling for clay, stone and wood which only the art of making can give. By the forging of Gram cold iron was revealed; by the making of Pegasus horses were ennobled; in the Trees of the Sun and Moon root and stock, flowers and fruit are manifested in glory.[5]

Authors of high fantasy have created a large variety of remote secondary worlds. Most of these worlds, however, can be placed into four broad categories. Our categories do not neatly pigeonhole all works of high fantasy, but they can help the reader come to grips with the many types of invented worlds.

The first category consists of works set in secondary worlds vaguely defined in terms of their relationship to our world and to our time. While these worlds do bear some resemblance to our primary world, their geographical and chronological settings are too nebulous to permit solid identification. This is not to say that the specific features of the worlds are vague and general. Indeed, the worlds have their own unique personalities; it is simply difficult to place them in the history of the primary world, if that is where they belong. Like faery tales, they are usually set "a long time ago in a far away kingdom," or "once upon a time, in the heart of the country." Into this category we can place such works as Patricia McKillip's land of Eld, Peter Beagle's land of the last unicorn, Piers Anthony's magical land of Xanth, and Ursula K. Le Guin's Earthsea.

The invented worlds of the second category are those clearly set in the primary world of the very distant past. Their milieu is frequently mythic or legendary in nature. The myth fantasy novels of Thomas Burnett Swann offer the best collective example. His *Day of the Minotaur* (1966), for instance, is purportedly "an authentic record of several months in the late Minoan period soon after the year 1500 B.C., when the forests of Crete were luxuriant with oak and cedars and ruled by a race who called themselves the Beasts."[6] Also featuring the fantastic inhabitants of the Country of the Beasts is his *Cry Silver Bells* (1977). *Lady of the Bees* (1976), an imaginative retelling of the Romulus and Remus legend, is set on the banks of the Tiber at the very dawn of Roman civilization, and *Queens Walk in the Dusk* (1977), which tells the story of Dido (Queen of Carthage), Aeneas and Ascanius, is also set in the hazy mythic past. A little closer in time, but still back in the druidic mists, are many of the works inspired by the *Mabinogion*. Prime examples are the Prydain books of Lloyd Alexander; Evangeline Walton's *The Prince of Annwn* (1974), *The Children of Llyr* (1971), *The Song of Rhiannon* (1972), and *The Island of the Mighty* (1970); and Kenneth Vennor Morris' *The Fates of the Princes of Dyfed* (1913) and *Book of the Three Dragons* (1930). Tolkien's Middle Earth is on the cusp of this classification. A strong argument can be made for its inclusion here, but an equally strong one can be made for its inclusion in the first category.

The works in the third category bear some similarity to those in the second in that they too are set in our world, but instead of being set in the past, they are set at a time in the very distant future. Jack Vance's *The Dying Earth* (1950) and *The Eyes of the Overworld* (1966) nicely exemplify this category. At the beginning of *The Dying Earth,* we are told: "Once [Earth] was a tall world of cloudy mountains and bright rivers, and the sun was a white blazing ball. Ages of rain and wind have beaten and rounded the granite, and the sun is feeble and red. The continents have sunk and risen. A million cities have lifted towers, have fallen to dust. In place of the old peoples a few thousand strange souls live. There is evil on Earth, evil distilled by time. . . ."[7] It is this setting—a dying earth inhabited by incredible beings, where magic has replaced science—that forms the eerie backdrop of the thirteen stories that comprise the two Vance volumes. A more recent work of high fantasy that displays this type of backdrop is Terry Brooks's *The Sword of Shannara* (1977). The setting is earth some hundreds of years after the "Great Wars," clearly nuclear holocausts. One of the consequences of the atomic devastation is the appearance of races other than man: dwarves, trolls, gnomes. Elves, on the other hand, have always existed but have never had much commerce with humanity. It is important to note that in many respects the works fitting this classification resemble science fiction. The similarities to dying-earth and post-holocaust science fiction novels such as H. G. Wells's *The Time Machine* (1895) and Walter M. Miller, Jr.'s *A Canticle for Leibowitz* (1960) are readily apparent.

The fourth, and final, category contains works featuring pseudomedieval settings. Most of these works are based upon the Arthurian legend. This is true of T. H. White's *The Once and Future King* (1958); Mary Stewart's *The Crystal Cave* (1970), *The Hollow Hills* (1973), and *The Last Enchantment* (1980); and Vera Chapman's *The King's Damosel* (1976), *The Green Knight* (1975), and *King Arthur's Daughter* (1976). Although not set in Arthur's England, James Branch Cabell's Manuel novels are also medieval in flavor and setting (the imaginary French province of Poictesme). Another continental, pseudomedieval world is the Nordic one of Poul Anderson's two pure fantasies, *The Broken Sword* (1954) and *The Merman's Children* (1979). Also deserving mention are such William Morris classics as *The Story of the Glittering Plain* (1891), *The Wood Beyond the World* (1894), *The Well at the World's End* (1896), and *The Water of the Wondrous Isles* (1897). While it is true that many of the works of this fourth category are set in countries and realms that we know and in times not far removed from our own, they still feature convincing secondary worlds. This is true because the customs, the beliefs, and the languages of these worlds are still different enough from ours to seem wondrous and strange. Then, too, as Tolkien points out in "On Fairy-Stories," historical figures like Arthur have been put into the great "Cauldron of Story," and there they have been "boiled for a long time, together with many other older figures and devices, of mythology and Faerie,"[8] until they come out something quite different from what they were when first dropped into the pot. Arthur, for example, has "emerged as a King of Faerie."[9] The fantasists who have written works belonging to this final category have learned how effectively to ladle out soup from the Cauldron of Story, and have also learned how to spice it satisfactorily with their own magical and supernatural condiments.

The secondary worlds cited as examples in the preceding discussion, especially those in the final category, reveal an interesting pattern. While these worlds do display variety, most are nonetheless Occidental in setting, flavor, and tradition. It is clear that most modern English and American fantasists have turned to Western myths for their inspiration. Even with the diversity, then, there has been an Occidental emphasis so strong as to display a kind of chauvinism, or at least mythic myopia.

Some writers, it is true, have turned to Middle-Eastern myth rather than Northern or Southern European myth. Lord Dunsany is certainly the primary example here. His Pagāna is a well-defined Middle-Eastern imaginary world. Among more recent authors, one of the finest sub-creators of a Middle-Eastern worldscape is Joyce Ballou Gregorian in *The Broken Citadel* (1975). A lengthy novel with archetypal and mythic foundations reminiscent of McKillip's *The Forgotten Beasts of Eld* (1974) or even more closely of Le Guin's *The Tombs of Atuan* (1971), *Citadel* provides the reader with a complete Pantheon, basically Middle Eastern in flavor, but with echoes of most other major mythologies. Gregorian entertains us with a series of beautifully described exotic landscapes and with the implied comparison between this Arabian Nights otherworld and our own world where a sense of the supernatural has been smothered by mundane pursuits. Some of Kenneth Morris' short stories, such as "The Rose and the Cup" (1916), also feature exotic Middle-Eastern settings.

Although the Far East seems like a natural for the sub-creator because of its exotic nature, not many fantasists have taken advantage of its vast potential. One of those who has is Richard Lupoff, whose *Sword of the Demon* (1978) is distinctly Oriental in character—more specifically, Japanese. The reader is introduced to a colorful world of samurai, geishas, *naga-suyari* spears, *kabuto* battle helmets, graceful wooden ships "with tall masts and slatted bamboo sails square-rigged to capture a following breeze,"[10] pastel lanterns, and hot saki. It is a landscape featuring exotic places like the mysterious Sea of Mists, and the "chill-water-dripping" Forest of Ice. Versatile Kenneth Morris has also exploited the Oriental milieu in stories like "Red-Peach-Blossom-Inlet" (1916) and "The Eyeless Dragons" (1915), as has Ernest Bramah in his Kai Lung tales.

In short, fantasists have not yet fully exploited primary world settings, traditions, and cultures that can serve as inspirations for their invented worlds. Rider Haggard made excellent use of the Dark Continent, as did John Buchan, but few have taken it up since the turn of the century. On this side of the Atlantic, the mysterious and intriguing Incan and Aztec myths beckon, but few have answered the summons. A notable exception is Felix Martí-Ibáñez, who, in stories like "The Sleeping Bell" (1963), "Niña Sol" (1963), and "Seekers of Dreams" (1963), has vividly displayed the great potential of this exotic milieu.

The second major technique used by fantasists is to set their secondary worlds in some sort of more direct relationship to the primary world, enabling them to further define their secondary worlds by comparison with this one. Lord Dunsany takes full advantage of this juxtaposition in his fantasy classic, *The King of Elfland's Daughter* (1924). This novel is unusually rich in evocative descriptions, but some of the most memorable are those involving the "frontier of twilight," that magical border separating Elfland from "the fields we know." Witness, for example, Alveric's first crossing into the land of Faërie:

> And then, as he pushed through a hedge into a field untended, there suddenly close before him in the field was, as his father had told, the frontier of twilight. It stretched across the fields in front of him, blue and dense like water; and things seen through it seemed misshapen and shining. He looked back once over the fields we know; the cuckoo went on calling unconcernedly; a small bird sang about its own affairs; and, nothing seeming to answer or heed his farewells, Alveric strode on boldly into those long masses of twilight.[11]

As Alveric takes a few strides through this gossamer curtain the sounds of his own world grow dim, the images of familiar earthly things fade, and, finally, the "wonders and splendours of Elfland" appear before him:

> The pale-blue mountains stood august in their glory, shimmering and rippling in a golden light that seemed as though it rhythmically poured from the peaks and flooded all those slopes with breezes of gold. And below them, far off as yet, he saw going up all silver into the air the spires of the palace only told of in song. He was on a plain on which the flowers were queer and the shape of the trees monstrous. He started at once toward the silver spires.[12]

The physical features of the primary world seem rather pale and plain next to the glamorous landscape of the secondary world of Elfland, and Dunsany makes effective use of the contrast. But he does not stop here. He also emphasizes the radically different pace at which time progresses in the secondary world, where a few moments may be equal to years in this world. As might be expected, it is this time differential that first attracts the attention of those who cross the magical boundary. It is especially noticeable, of course, to those who leave the essentially timeless and changeless Elfland for a sojourn in the swiftly changing primary world. One who does so is the capricious troll, Lurulu, and his sage and witty comments on the advantages and disadvantages of change represent one of the highlights of the work. Ultimately, we are not only entertained by this novel, we are also given a fresh perspective on our lives and our world.

As is the case with Dunsany, one of the most fascinating aspects of the relationship of secondary to primary worlds is the nature and variety of portals, and portal-like agents, by which characters pass to and fro. There are so many types of portals and agents, as a matter of fact, that we have devised a system of classification to help in examining them. Our system, broad and flexible, contains the following categories: (1) conventional portals; (2) magical and supernatural conveyors; (3) Platonic shadow worlds; and (4) scientific or pseudoscientific portals. Let us examine each of these categories.

Few fantasy writers have created conventional portals as ingenious, convincing, and remarkable as those found in C. S. Lewis' Narnian Chronicles. In the first volume, *The Lion, the Witch and the Wardrobe* (1950), for example, Lucy Pevensie is exploring the ancient rooms of Professor Digory Kirke's sprawling country house when she walks into a large wardrobe and there encounters the snow-covered landscape of Narnia, instead of the back wall of the closet. Her surprise changes to delight when she is invited to tea by the first Narnian inhabitant she meets, a genial Faun called Mr. Tumnus. With this memorable passage into Narnia begins a whole series of remarkable adventures for Lucy, her brothers Peter and Edmund, and her sister Susan. The portal of Book 3, *The Voyage of the "Dawn Treader"* (1952), is probably the most inventive of Lewis' passageways. Edmund and Lucy Pevensie and their disagreeable cousin, Eustace Clarence Scrubb, are looking at a picture of a ship hanging on the wall of Lucy's bedroom when it suddenly comes to life. They rush toward the picture, momentarily stand on its frame, and then find themselves actually swimming beside the ship. After being hoisted aboard, they discover that they have been saved by their old friend Prince Caspian, who is on a quest to find seven Telmarine lords who have mysteriously disappeared. Once again the children have inadvertently found their way to Narnia, and in truly memorable fashion.

It would be a mistake to think that all conventional portals lead into attractive secondary worlds, however. On the contrary, some lead into demonic domains that few dare, or care, to enter. One of the most intriguing examples is found in James Blish's *The Day After Judgment* (1971). In this worthy sequel to Blish's critically acclaimed *Black Easter* (1968), the action begins on the "sullen full morning of the day after Armageddon";[13] the earth is horribly pockmarked with H-bomb craters, fires race across cities and the surrounding countryside, and the anguished cries of survivors pierce the poisoned air. The stench of death covers the planet. The earth has become not only a figurative hell, but in one respect a literal one as well—for the city of Dis, "the fortress surrounding Nether Hell," actually exists in Death Valley, California. All four of the central characters of the novel finally find their way to the demonic city of Dis, enter through its hellish gates, and there have an audience with that "archetypal dropout, the Lie that knows no End, the primeval Parent-sponsored Rebel, the Eternal Enemy, the Great Nothing itself SATAN MEKRATRIG."[14] As terrifying as this portal is the awful Pit that seems to lead to a hellish underworld in William Hope Hodgson's *The House on the Borderland* (1908). Through his vivid portrayal of this portal and the grotesque swine-creatures who use it, Hodgson informs his novel with an almost unbearable feeling of suspense and evil foreboding. The feeling of dread intensifies as the novel progresses and reaches a peak when the protagonist discovers that the ancient trap door in his "great cellar" seems also to serve as a portal to the subterranean world of the swine-creatures. Although he places stones on the door to prevent the creatures from gaining entry into his home, his efforts apparently fail, since the last anguished entry of his diary records that "someth——" crawls out of the "great, oak trap" in the basement, pads up the steps, and confronts the diarist, causing him to break off his writing in midsentence.

In many works of fantasy, magical and supernatural conveyors of different types function virtually as portals. The Chronicles of Narnia display two fine examples of such conveyors. In the second book, *Prince Caspian* (1951), we discover that the portals into Narnia are not always as tangible as a magic wardrobe or a picture hanging on a wall. *Caspian* begins with the four Pevensies sitting in an "empty, sleepy, country station" despondently awaiting their school-bound train. Suddenly they find themselves irresistibly drawn back into Narnia. They later learn that it was Prince Caspian's signal on Susan's magic horn that had pulled them back. In Book 6, *The Magician's Nephew* (1955), there are several magical agents at work. First, young Digory Kirke and Polly Plummer are transmitted from the primary world of London to "The Wood between the Worlds" through the power of magical rings. Then, they discover that this "in-between" place is dotted with magical pools, each of which provides transport to still another world. Lewis' preoccupation with magical agents as portals or conveyors probably derives from one of his favorite E. Nesbit books, *The Story of the Amulet* (1906). The amulet is an ancient Egyptian artifact on which is inscribed the name of power. When one of the four children invokes this name and states a destination, the amulet becomes a magical arch through which the children enter other realms and times.

One of the most fascinating magical agents in all high fantasy appears in A. Merritt's *The Ship of Ishtar* (1926). Couched in the author's inimitable brand of ornate poetic prose, this novel relates the fantastic exploits of John Kenton, an American scholar and adventurer who enters a secondary world through the magic of an ancient stone block that "Forsyth, the old archaeologist, had sent him from the sand shrouds of ages-dead Babylon." The vehicle for Kenton's journeys into this strange world is a miniature ship with toylike figures that he discovers when he breaks open the Babylonian relic.

In some fantasies, the magical agent/portal is important enough to become the focus of the entire work. This is true, for instance, in Jane Langton's *The Diamond in the Window* (1962), an all-ages fantasy set in Concord, Massachusetts, some time in the first half of the twentieth century. One day Edward and Eleanor Hall, the two children who are the central characters of the novel, discover an attic room furnished for two children about their own age, with a large stained-glass, keyhole-shaped window with an enormous diamond set in the middle. Edward and Eleanor discover a series of riddles in a poem scratched into one of the facets of the keyhole-shaped window. The poem includes clues to nine treasures. The children move into the attic room, which, when light comes through the key-window at the proper angle, acts as a portal to various secondary worlds. The children enter these worlds as though in dreams, but they really aren't dreams because one can get trapped in them, especially if one cannot solve the riddles; for each dream presents the children with one of the nine riddles from the poem.

While the majority of conveyors are magical in nature, some of the most memorable are supernatural. One of the best examples of this type of portal can be found in C. S. Lewis' *Perelandra* (1943), where the protagonist, Elwin Ransom, is literally spirited away by angel-like creatures called Eldils to another planet, Perelandra (Venus), in a "white and semi-transparent" oblong box "big enough to put a man into";[15] in short, a celestial coffin.

In all of the examples of portal worlds discussed so far, the perspective has been chiefly a human one, viewing the other world as "secondary" to the human or "primary" one. And the traffic has been from the human to the other world and back again. Several writers of fantasy from George MacDonald (mid-nineteenth century) to the present have chosen a different perspective, viewing our world as a mere shadowy reflection of the authentic world. They adopt Plato's conception of our world as simply an imitation of the real world where pre-exist all the ideal forms from which the creatures of our world are copied. In this type of fantasy, our world is the secondary, the other world the primary one. And the traffic is from the other world to this one and back again—ideally. Three authors that present our world as a Platonic shadow world are Lord Dunsany, E. R. Eddison, and Roger Zelazny.

In Dunsany's *The Gods of Pegāna* (1905), Māna-Yood-Sushāi creates lesser gods and worlds of men in his dreams as Skarl plays the drums. If Skarl stops, the creator awakens and the creatures return to nothingness. Eddison's King Mezentius, in *A Fish Dinner in Memison* (1941), manages to give his creation an existence apart from his thoughts which initially give it life. Our world—it is earth that Mezentius creates—remains as fragile as Māna-Yood-Sushāi's, however, and just as vulnerable. Most recently (1970–1978), Zelazny's royal family of Amber—approximately fourteen members in all—have the power to construct "shadow earths" for their own purposes. Our earth is but one creation of many, though the favorite one of Prince Corwin, who uses "the primal pattern of order" in Amber to shape mentally our shadow earth. A direct line of influence may, in fact, connect these authors, but what is important is that all three use a shadow world as both a link (portal) between worlds and as a thematic device. Eddison will serve to illustrate these points.

It took Eddison three books to discover how best to relate our world to the other world, both practically and thematically. In *The Worm Ouroboros* (1922) he failed completely in this regard. But Eddison wanted such a connection and in his next book, *Mistress of Mistresses* (1935), the first of his Zimiamvian Trilogy, he comes nearer to the mark. Eddison wisely opts for myth fantasy and suggests (and examines) supernatural causality. Zimiamvia in *Mistress* is, for the hero, Lessingham, a Valhalla, a place for those "that were great upon earth and did great deeds when they were living."[16] The explanation of how Lessingham, and the reader, get to the other world is a satisfactory one, but Eddison is clearly not content simply to get there. He wants to connect Zimiamvia with our world in more substantive ways. Thus he allows Lessingham, who has forgotten his previous existence, to occasionally and vaguely remember his other life. His doing so unfortunately confuses the reader, who knows nothing of Lessingham's earthly life.

Eddison remedies this situation and finally achieves what he wants, a meaningful interrelationship between primary and secondary worlds, in *A Fish Dinner in Memison.* He alternates scenes from our world, England during the period from the turn of the century until a few years after World War I, with scenes from the other world, the Three Kingdoms of Zimiamvia, where, however, only a single month passes. Throughout most of the novel, Lessingham and his wife Lady Mary, the earthly hero and heroine, lead the lives of an English aristocratic couple, attempting to act honorably in a largely ignoble world. Meanwhile, in Zimiamvia the lords and ladies are experiencing an awakening to their divine natures of which they had been unaware. These two alternating plots converge in the dazzling climactic chapter fifteen, "The Fish Dinner: Symposium." King Mezentius' Duchess asks the question: "If we were Gods, able to make worlds and unmake 'em as we list, what world would we have?"[17] All are content with the status quo, until Fiorinda (Aphrodite) dictates the details of a different world (Earth) and the King (Zeus) actually bodies it forth from his thoughts. More striking still, King Mezentius and his mistress, Duchess Amalia (another Aphrodite figure) enter this world where they live, forgetting their previous existence, as Lessingham and his wife Lady Mary. When they return after fifty years—a mere blink of the eyes in Zimiamvia—

the banquet ends, but not before Fiorinda, as an afterthought, destroys Earth with a pinprick. Eddison has, on his third attempt, discovered the successful formula for interweaving his two worlds. The plot connection works with striking effect, and the thematic implications, in relation to men and the gods and time and place, are manifold and breathtakingly original in their presentation.

But Eddison is not done; he refines his Platonic linking of earth and Zimiamvia a step further in his last book, *The Mezentian Gate*. This book overlaps the time settings of the first two Zimiamvian works. In the "Praeludium," Lessingham dies. The rest of the book follows the career of King Mezentius in Zimiamvia and concludes with his death. Clearly Mezentius is Lessingham, who is going to come alive in the Valhalla-like Zimiamvia, where Mezentius has just died. Neat, but more significantly, the implication is that, as Lessingham forgets that he is the divine Mezentius in another existence, Mezentius has forgotten that he is a divinity in still another world from which he created—and entered—Zimiamvia. The final effect is to raise significant philosophical questions about the nature of divinity and its relationship to man.

One last type of portal that is profitable to discuss is the scientific or pseudoscientific portal found in science fantasy. In many instances, including those that will be given here, the only scientific elements in science fantasy are the explanations for the bare existence of the secondary world and of the means of getting there from here. Once we arrive in the secondary world, scientific devices or explanations give way to the magical or the supernatural. A species of scientific portal found in some prominent works written in the first half of this century is the space voyage to a real or imagined distant planet whereon exists a magical or supernatural secondary world. The assumption in such works is that such distant places could contain almost anything; the challenge, however, is how one manages to get there. As mentioned previously, Eddison's *Worm Ouroboros* contains a mythopoeic world much like Tolkien's Middle Earth, for which it in fact served as a model; yet it is set on the planet Mercury. And the earthling, Lessingham, travels thither in a most curious chariot with the guidance of a talking bird. In David Lindsay's classic work, *A Voyage to Arcturus* (1920), the hero, Maskull, journeys in a capsule-shaped rocket to reach one of the most unusual but vividly described secondary worlds ever created, the planet Tormance, which revolves around the twin suns of Arcturus. The best known work of this sort is C. S. Lewis' *Out of the Silent Planet* (1938), a work influenced by H. G. Wells and in no small part by Lindsay's *Voyage*. Lewis' spaceship is a much more plausible vehicle than either Eddison's chariot or Lindsay's capsule, and it is probably more plausible than Well's pseudoscientific travel machines. Like his fantasy predecessors, however, Lewis is concerned not so much with how one gets to the distant planet as with what happens after one arrives. Lewis' hero, Ransom, gradually discovers that Malacandra (Mars) is a planet that can be understood in terms of gods and angels and devils rather than in terms of science.

The science in all of these earlier works is meager in comparison to its incidence in some of the more contemporary science fantasies that use scientific portals. Poul Anderson, in his delightful *A Midsummer Tempest* (1974), employs the device of parallel universes, which provides an explanation for the existence of the secondary world of Faërie in which the book is principally set. The idea of the parallel universe is that more than one universe exists simultaneously and in the same place, but occupies different dimensions. In *A Midsummer Tempest* the premise is that a parallel world exists in which Shakespeare's plays are not fiction but history. The faery court of Oberon and Titania, and the magic book and staff of Prospero, are realities. Such a spatial dimension positing a world parallel to our own is itself a kind of portal through which one can upon occasion pass; yet Anderson specifies a particular location—portal—where such a passage takes place. Prince Rupert, the hero of the book and an inhabitant of the Shakespearean world, stumbles into the Old Phoenix Tavern, where he finds a young woman from the United States who has read Shakespeare as a dramatist. The young woman is able to tell Rupert some facts about Prospero's book and staff that help him in his quest. The Old Phoenix, it seems, is a neutral point of contact where numerous parallel universes intersect. One finds a different one simply by choosing a different door to exit through.

Clifford Simak also employs the parallel universe device to good effect in his *Enchanted Pilgrimage* (1975). Alexander Jones uses some undefined machine to pass on his motorcycle between our dimension and the Wasteland, a faeryland inhabited by goblins, trolls, and unicorns, as well as by monks and medieval university students. The year is 1976.

Two other recent science fantasy writers, Andre Norton and C. J. Cherryh, use the device of alternate worlds. Alternate worlds are not simply parallel dimensions of a single universe, but are separate worlds entirely, though some connection links them to our own. This connecting link or portal is thus much more important than the dimension-connection portals in Anderson's and Simak's works. Both Norton and Cherryh give considerable attention to place or time-warp portals for transportation. In *Witch World* (1963), the first volume of her celebrated Witch World Series, Norton uses the *Siege Perilous* of Arthurian vintage to transfer her hero from our world to the Witch World, where Witches use magic to defend themselves against their suspicious and warlike neighbors. C. J. Cherryh, in *Gate of Ivrel* (1976), uses the "Gates Between Worlds" as portals "into elsewhen as well as elsewhere," a secondary world in which one encounters the fascinating witch-woman, Morgaine.

In all of the instances of scientific portals, the most important effect is to help persuade the reader of the reality of the secondary world. In one sense the device is a way of coaxing the skeptic to read fantasy; as C. S. Lewis put it, scientific elements offer a "sop" to the intellect.[18] Similarly, however, this blending of rational and nonrational has the intriguing effect of merging the two types of phenomena and challenging the reader to some healthy questioning about "what is real?" In C. S. Lewis' case, science helps to persuade us of the truth of myth, both Christian and pre-Christian. Science and magic and myth in these works are integrated in an effective and thematically functional manner. Science fantasy is a relatively new direction in high fantasy, an attractive one that should continue to expand and enhance the genre in the future.

The third major category of secondary worlds includes writers who use the world-within-a-world technique. There are no portals; the secondary world is simply a particular location within the primary world. It is usually marked off by physical boundaries within which events transpire that do not occur elsewhere, that is, within which a different set of laws pertain. These inner worlds, it should be noted, can take many forms and can assume many different sizes and shapes. They can be as small and esoteric, for example, as the "neat pentagram" that Jehan Lenoir draws on the floor of his Parisian garret in Ursula K. Le Guin's "April in Paris" (1962), or the "Grand Circle" that Theron Ware, Doctor of Theology and Black Sorcerer, uses to practice his hellish arts in Blish's *Black Easter*. An inner world a little larger, but not by much, is the church that serves as the backdrop for the Archdeacon's final High Mass in Charles Williams' *War in Heaven* (1930). More typical, perhaps, but still highly unusual because of its exotic Oriental setting, is the supernatural other-world that Wang Tao-Chen accidentally discovers in Kenneth Morris' superb myth-fantasy story, "Red-Peach-Blossom-Inlet." Although very small in area, the idyllic inlet is a well-defined secondary world, rich in sight, smell, and taste delights, all of which are vividly conveyed by Morris' sensuous imagery:

> Forthwith and thenceforward the place was all new to him, and a thousand times more wonderful. What had seemed to him cottages were lovely pagodas of jade and porcelain, the sunlight reflected from their glaze of transparent azure or orange or vermilion, of luminous yellow or purple or green. Through the shining skies of noon or evening you might often see lordly dragons floating: golden and gleaming dragons; or that shed a violet luminance from their wings; or whose hue was the essence from which blue heaven drew its blueness; or white dragons whose passing was like the shooting of a star.[19]

The point to be made here is that it is the quality of the world-within-a-world, and not the quantity, that determines its credibility and effectiveness. Through a few deft strokes on their literary canvasses, gifted artists can create inner worlds that are truly believable and memorable.

One of the finest examples of an elaborately defined world-within-a-world is found in Peter Beagle's *A Fine and Private Place* (1960), where the walls of the Yorkchester Cemetery mark it off as a secondary world surrounded by New York City. Inside these walls, if you are like Jonathan Rebeck, you can commune with ghosts, or, if you are a ghost, you can think yourself anywhere—except beyond the gates of the cemetery where your body lies. In the case of Beagle's novel, the ghosts of Michael Morgan and Laura Durand circumvent this law by having their bodies exhumed and transferred to another place.

There are several reasons why Beagle's cemetery-world works so well. To begin with, the boundaries of the cemetery are very clearly defined; it is never difficult to determine where this land of the dead ends and the land of the living begins. The boundaries of the Yorkchester Cemetery are especially clear, of course, because massive stone walls surround it. Secondly, Beagle's description of the cemetery is extraordinarily concrete, detailed, and vivid. This was relatively easy for Beagle to do, since he grew up near the cemetery described in the novel. As he explains in his playful but highly informative introduction to *The Fantasy Worlds of Peter Beagle*: "The cemetery is a very real place (I grew up playing there, going for walks, or sitting at the kitchen window with my brother, peacefully watching funeral processions winding over the green-and-white slopes). . . ."[20] Finally, a cemetery has an ambience that makes it a natural choice for a secondary-world setting. Beagle does exploit this ambience—but only up to a point. Do not expect to find the sense of dread that permeates most Gothic high fantasy. This is not an H. P. Lovecraft graveyard with its moldering skeletons, frightening shadows, and howling dogs. Beagle's cemetery-world, on the contrary, is a rather bizarre, eccentric, and often downright comic, world featuring drunken caretakers, a poetic red squirrel (who can talk, of course), and a baloney-stealing raven that serves as a delightful parody of all of its doom-croaking predecessors.

The world-within-a-world classification contains a broad and heterogeneous collection of tales. It cannot, therefore, be readily subdivided. Three subgroups, nonetheless, deserve to be examined: the enchanted wood, the magical or supernatural garden, and the primary world in which still lingers a remnant of Faërie, dormant but easily roused.

Contemporary high fantasy offers many interesting, but archetypally recognizable, variants of the enchanted wood motif. There is, for instance, the strange wood at the edge of the village of Treegap that serves as the central setting of Natalie Babbitt's beautifully written novelette, *Tuck Everlasting* (1975). In this all-ages fantasy, the narrative focuses upon the relationship between ten-year-old Winnie Foster and the Tuck family, four mortals who have unwittingly acquired everlasting life by drinking the water of a magical spring located in the forest. Their life seems idyllic indeed, until we discover, through revealing conversations that Winnie has with the Tucks, that there are serious drawbacks to a life without death or change. The forest, although only a "slim few acres of trees," is convincing enough as a secondary world to make the supernatural events that transpire therein seem credible. It is a forest so "strange," after all, that even roads refuse to pierce its borders, preferring instead to veer sharply in wide arcs around its circumference.

Another fine example of the enchanted forest setting is given in Abraham Merritt's "The Woman of the Wood" (1926), one of his most popular tales of Gothic high fantasy. In this violent but poignant story about the primeval conflict between humankind and nature, the battlefield. oddly enough, is a lush and tranquil coppice nestled along the shore of an equally tranquil lake:

> Between the lodge and the shore, marching down to the verge of the lake was a singularly beautiful little coppice of silver birches and firs. This coppice stretched for perhaps a quarter of a mile; it was not more than a hundred feet or two in depth, and not alone the beauty of its trees but also their curious grouping vividly aroused McKay's interest. At each end were a dozen or more of the glistening, needled firs, not clustered but spread out as though in open marching order; at widely spaced intervals along its other two sides paced single firs. The birches, slender and delicate, grew within the guard of these sturdier trees, yet not so thickly as to crowd one another.[21]

The significance of this "curious grouping" of trees within the coppice is vividly revealed later in the story when a bizarre and ultimately deadly battle rages between the nature spirits of the wood and the ill-fated Polleau family.

Many other enchanted woods deserve our exploration—for example, the magical forest of Robin McKinley's *Beauty* (1978) and the Forest Sauvage of T. H. White's classic, *The Sword in the Stone* (1939)—but space allows for only one other example. And what better to end with than the truly wondrous, but perilous, enchanted forest of Lord Dunsany's *The King of Elfland's Daughter*. Since it is situated in the realm of Elfland, we expect this wood to possess the powerful glamour of the land of Faërie. We are not disappointed. To make us fully aware of the wood's arcane qualities, Dunsany sends his hero, Alveric, through the middle of it in his journey to claim as his bride the Elfin princess, Lirazel. He barely escapes with his life. It is only his potent sword of "thunderbolt iron," magically forged by the witch Ziroonderel, that ultimately saves him from the savage attack of the pines and ivy tendrils of the enchanted wood.

> So he returned his father's sword to the scabbard by his side and drew out the other over his shoulder and, going straight up to the tree that had moved, swept at the ivy as it sprang at him: and the ivy fell all at once to the ground, not lifeless but a heap of common ivy. And then he gave one blow to the trunk of the tree, and a chip flew out not larger than a common sword would have made, but the whole tree shuddered; and with that shudder disappeared at once a certain ominous look that the pine had had, and it stood there an ordinary unenchanted tree. Then he stepped on through the wood with his sword drawn.[22]

Dunsany's treatment of the enchanted wood is a fine example of his intuitive understanding of the ambivalence of the realm of Faërie. The forests of Faërie can be places of repose and retreat, but if one isn't wary or doesn't act in the proper fashion, the forests can be frightening realms.

Perhaps even more ambiguous than the enchanted wood, in regard to humans at least, is the enchanted garden. And this has to do very likely with the fact that, while both have ancient archetypal associations, the garden is the older, at least in literature. The enchanted wood is more frequently featured in the French fairy tales and German Märchen that were recorded, and sometimes embellished, in the seventeenth and eighteenth centuries by writers and folklorists such as Charles Perrault and Jacob and Wilhelm Grimm. The garden, on the other hand, appears primarily in myth fantasy, in some of the earliest written myths and legends. It appears in the Bible as the Garden of Eden. It appears likewise in a wide variety of classical sources.[23] The major tradition, however, remains the biblical one, transmitted to us through the pens of some of the greatest writers of the Middle Ages, including Dante and Chaucer. Chaucer was clearly influenced by one of the most extensive uses of the garden in medieval literature, *The Romance of the Rose*, from which the following description comes:

> I entered then upon that garden fair.
> When once I was inside, my joyful heart
> Was filled with happiness and sweet content.
> You may right well believe I thought the place
> Was truly a terrestrial paradise,

For so delightful was the scenery
That it looked heavenly; it seemed to me
A better place than Eden for delight,
So much the orchard did my senses please.[24]

The garden, as it eventually does in the *Rose,* becomes a complex symbol, ideally suited to medieval allegory. It could be a place of innocence, symbolic of rebirth, spiritual fecundity, virginity, or the Virgin. Alternatively, it could be a place of the fall from innocence, of frivolity and spiritual or physical seduction like the medieval gardens of courtly love. Or the garden could be a place both of innocence and of seduction simultaneously, on different allegorical levels.

Subsequent writers have retained both elements, innocence and fall, from the medieval tradition of the garden, most often blending the two in the same story. One of the most famous writers to use the tradition is Nathaniel Hawthorne. Hawthorne, who uses the wood in "Young Goodman Brown" (1835) as an unambiguous symbol of evil, uses the garden in an ambiguous way, as a symbol of innocence tainted by selfishness, in "Rappaccini's Daughter" (1844). Through his malignant intelligence, Rappaccini introduces evil to pervert the innocence of his daughter, who becomes the forbidden and deadly fruit of the garden.

Other more contemporary fantasists are divided in their use of the garden. Some, like Kenneth Morris, Selma Lagerlöf, and C. S. Lewis, recognize the element of evil or potential evil in the garden, but they see innocence as the vanquisher of evil, at least for the moment. In Morris' "The Rose and the Cup," the Persian rose garden becomes sacred ground on which the famed Cup of Jamshid, a parallel to the Holy Grail, appears to quell the fury of the invader and avert a massacre. Two gardens form the focal points in Lagerlöf's "The Legend of the Christmas Rose" (1904). The first is the monastery garden, symbolic of order restored after the fall; the second is the garden of the Göing Forest, a verdant garden that appears at midnight every Christmas Eve, a garden of childlike innocence, even though, ironically, the only humans to witness it are a family of outlaws. When a monk introduces evil into the Christmas garden through his suspicion and lack of faith, the garden disappears forever—all except the Rose which remains and is transferred to the monastery, where it blooms as a symbol of lost innocence. The entire planet of Perelandra (Venus) in the novel of that title by C. S. Lewis is a garden of

Eden, since it is an unfallen world. The Tempter enters the scene but is vanquished, albeit only after a fearful struggle. While Perelandra is an unfallen world, an Eden, earth is very much a world of lost innocence, a Wasteland, in Lewis' *That Hideous Strength* (1945). The garden at St. Anne's is, however, an antique oasis of pre-fall conditions. Jane, a young woman, has the following vision when she passes through the gate of the garden wall:

> A flame coloured robe, in which her hands were hidden, covered this person from the feet to where it rose behind her neck in a kind of high ruff-like collar, but in front it was so low or open that it exposed her large breasts. Her skin was darkish and Southern and glowing, almost the colour of honey. Some such dress Jane had seen worn by a Minoan priestess on a vase from old Cnossus. The head, poised motionless on the muscular pillar of her neck, stared straight at Jane. It was a red-cheeked, wet-lipped face, with black eyes.[25]

The fertility goddess is appropriate here, not only because of the garden, but because Jane has been denying her femininity and has been in danger of losing her innocence. The goddess recalls her to both a physical and a spiritual fertility.

Writers who use the garden for its associations with the fall from innocence include Barry Pain, John Buchan, and Sanders Anne Laubenthal. In his story "The Moon-Slave" (1916), Pain tells a tale of erotic but sinister seduction. Princess Viola, a headstrong girl, finds herself increasingly drawn to "an old forsaken maze" in an almost forgotten and overgrown portion of the palace gardens. There, during the full moon, she dances in a trancelike state, until one night she comes out of her trance long enough to realize that she is dancing with a cloven-hoofed god. Buchan's story, "The Grove of Ashtaroth" (1912), is a poignant tale of a young Englishman named Lawson who is torn by his conflict between the bewitching but heathen rites of Ashtaroth and his Christian upbringing. The conflict centers about a small grove or garden on his estate in a remote part of South Africa. The grove is a timeless place, and in its center is a shrine to the goddess Ashtaroth. Lawson's conflict and ambivalent feelings about the grove affect even his close friend, who, after he has destroyed the shrine, thinks of his deed as a desecration. "And then my heartache returned, and I knew that I had driven something lovely and adorable from its last refuge on earth."[26] Rather less ambiguous in its presentation of lost innocence—or the temptation thereto—is the description of the garden in Laubenthal's *Excalibur*. Laubenthal is clearly familiar with the detail of medieval gardens, as the following description shows:

> The place was large as a cathedral, walled with roses and roofed with rain as with silver and glass. It was half-dark—darker, he thought, than the stormy wood outside. There were trees of a kind he had never seen before, with smooth trunks like black marble and strange, curving branches clothed with red leaves. And the leaves, it seemed to him, were not red with autumn; it was their native color, instead of green. The trees stood in a perfect circle and seemed too symmetrical in shape, as if they grew obedient to some force of mind. Lamps hung from their boughs to light the dusk of the garden, gold and silver lamps fantastically wrought and encrusted with gems. There was no grass or ground to be seen; underfoot was a carpet of short-growing crimson flowers, shaped like starflowers and springy like moss, with no green leaf showing. They gave out a strong, sweet scent, a little like gardenias but more subtle and powerful. In the center of the garden rose a pyramid of circular steps of some shining black stone, perfectly smooth and without carving, except that from the lowest step a fountain of water poured thinly out of an opening carved like a leopard's mouth, and lost itself under the short flowers. On the low, flat height of the pyramid stood a black stone chair like a throne, also shining and smooth as glass; and on it sat an image like a woman.[27]

The description is attractive, but suspect ("too symmetrical"), and the enthroned woman turns out to be the false seductress Lilith.

The Yorkchester Cemetery of Beagle's *A Fine and Private Place*, the enchanted wood of the faery tale, and the gardens of innocence and fall of myth-based tales are worlds-within-a-world in the sense of a definite enclosure within which laws operate that are different from those on the outside. There is another sense in which a secondary world can be considered a world-within-a-world. Some works present a contemporary primary-world setting, quite normal and rationally or scientifically explainable but within which the powers of Faërie or the gods are dormant, though just on the threshold of awakening. These powers can be roused at the appropriate time, frequently with the aid of some sort of magical talisman. Of all the secondary worlds of high fantasy, this one is closest to the primary world and offers the challenge of merging the magical and supernatural with the natural. Numerous authors have found this challenge an attractive and productive one, including Nancy Bond, William Mayne, Alan Garner, Susan Cooper, and Charles Williams, as a sampling of their works will illustrate.

Two major devices link these authors into the sleeping-world group: first, their use of a primary-world setting that has legendary or mystical associations and, second, their use of a magical or mystical talisman. Nancy Bond in *A String in the Harp* (1976) and Alan Garner in *The Owl Service* (1967) both use the area around Aberystwyth, Wales, for its associations with Taliessen and other characters and events found in the *Mabinogion.* William Mayne, in *Earthfasts* (1967), uses rural North of England settings whose very names evoke the glamour of the past: Garebrough, Haw Bank, High Kelk, Eskeleth, and Arkingathdale. Susan Cooper sets *The Grey King* (1975) in Wales, fittingly because she employs in it the Pendragon. Charles Williams uses a village with ancient Roman roots, Caer Parvulorum (camp of the children), as the setting for his modern grail novel, *War in Heaven* (1930).

The talismans that these five authors use function differently than do the magical agents that convey people back and forth in the portal worlds books. The talismans don't convey people out of the primary world; rather, they are catalysts for arousing the unsuspected magical or supernatural powers out of the past and blending them with natural ones of our contemporary world. In *A String in the Harp,* the talisman is the harp of Taliessen, which is discovered by a young boy. It periodically vibrates and enables its owner and others to observe scenes from Taliessen's life occurring on the very ground where they first happened fourteen centuries earlier. The dinner setting decorated with the figures of owls that three young people discover in *The Owl Service* becomes the means by which the three begin to reenact the tragic legend of Blodeuwedd, the woman made out of flowers by the magician Gwydion in the *Mabinogion.* A particularly appropriate talisman is the lighted candle in *Earthfasts*; when it is removed from its underground setting, Arthur and his men awaken, but they are bewildered because the time is not yet ripe for their return. The motif of the talisman literally awakening a sleeper from the ancient past appears again in *The Grey King*. The hero seeks and finds the golden harp that must be used to rouse the six Sleepers, Arthur's men, who are then united with the Pendragon. In *War in Heaven* the talisman is also Arthurian, the grail. It becomes the repository of power used by both sides in a good-evil struggle: after the struggle, Prester John collects the grail and it is seen no longer in England.

In all of the above works, and in several other works by these same authors, the pattern is clear. They are set in the contemporary primary world but in a place with legendary or mythic associations, and they employ a talisman as a means of tapping the powers resting just beneath the surface of these locations. The immediate, practical effects of this pattern are to dissolve the barriers of time, thereby joining past and present, and fantasy reality. The aesthetic and thematic possibilities of the sleeping-world fantasies, which the above authors effectively realize, are numerous. In *War in Heaven,* for example, the reader shares the sense of awe expressed by the Archdeacon and his associates for the sacred and ancient grail. Even more affecting is the Archdeacon's agonizing acceptance, through the power of the grail, of the burden of another (Williams calls this "transference").

In the foregoing material, we have explored a variety of landscapes of the secondary worlds of high fantasy. This variety is one of the particular riches of fantasy literature. Readers can get as far away from our own world as the remote islands of Earthsea, or they can go to as close a place as Wales. Or readers can choose a work in which they move back and forth between our world and a faery world like Narnia, or a mythic world like Zimiamvia. In each case, however, the reader will be travelling in the realms of high fantasy, wondering at their "arresting strangeness," and returning to the real universe both renewed and with a fresher perspective.

NOTES

1. J. R. R. Tolkien, "On Fairy-Stories," in *The Tolkien Reader* (New York: Ballantine, 1974), p. 37.
2. Ibid., pp. 48–49.

3. Ibid., p. 52.
4. Ibid., pp. 52–53.
5. Ibid., p. 59.
6. Thomas Burnett Swann, "Preface," *Day of the Minotaur* (New York: Ace, 1978), p. vi.
7. Jack Vance, *The Dying Earth* (New York: Pocket Books, 1977), p. 42.
8. Tolkien, pp. 28–29.
9. Ibid., p. 29.
10. Richard Lupoff, *Sword of the Demon* (New York: Avon, 1978), p. 187.
11. Lord Dunsany, *The King of Elfland's Daughter* (New York: Ballantine, 1977), p. 13.
12. Ibid., p. 14.
13. James Blish, *The Day After Judgment* (New York: Doubleday, 1971), p. 18.
14. Ibid., p. 153.
15. C. S. Lewis, *Perelandra* (New York: Macmillan, 1972), p. 17.
16. E. R. Eddison, *Mistress of Mistresses* (New York: Ballantine, 1978), p. 23.
17. E. R. Eddison, *A Fish Dinner in Memison* (New York: Pan/Ballantine, 1972), p. 247.
18. C. S. Lewis, "On Science Fiction," in *Of Other Worlds: Essays and Stories,* ed. Walter Hooper (New York: Harcourt, Brace and World, 1967), p. 68.
19. Kenneth Morris, "Red-Peach-Blossom-Inlet," in *The Fantastic Imagination II,* ed. Robert H. Boyer and Kenneth J. Zahorski (New York: Avon, 1978), p. 99.
20. Peter S. Beagle, "Introduction," *The Fantasy Worlds of Peter Beagle* (New York: Ballantine, 1979), p. x.
21. A. Merritt, "The Woman in the Wood," in *Dark Imaginings,* ed. Robert H. Boyer and Kenneth J. Zahorski (New York: Dell, 1978), p. 47.
22. Dunsany, p. 19.
23. See Howard Rollins Patch, *The Other World, According to Descriptions in Medieval Literature* (1950; rpt. New York: Octagon, 1970).
24. Guillaume de Lorris and Jean de Meun, "The Dreamer Enters the Garden of Mirth," *The Romance of the Rose,* trans. Harry W. Robbins (New York: E. P. Dutton, 1962), p. 14, 11, 76–84.
25. C. S. Lewis, *That Hideous Strength* (New York: Macmillan, 1977), p. 304.
26. John Buchan, "The Grove of Ashtaroth," in *The Fantastic Imagination,* ed. Robert H. Boyer and Kenneth J. Zahorski (New York: Avon, 1977), p. 127.
27. Sanders Anne Laubenthal, *Excalibur* (New York: Ballantine, 1973), p. 123.

Ethical Fantasy for Children

Francis J. Molson

I

My favorite books back in grade school were Francis Finn's. My classmates and I thoroughly enjoyed his stories about boys with names like Percy Wynn and Tom Playfair because they were about Catholic boys—as all of us were—and about winners—as all of us imagined we were or dreamed we would become. We wholeheartedly identified with Finn's heroes, for they had exciting adventures, always whipped the public school boys in sports competitions, and were the hub of all that went on around them. While reading Finn's stories, we felt—rather, we knew!—that there wasn't anything we couldn't do, and that whatever we did the world not only would be the better for it but would gratefully acknowledge its debt.

Examining Finn's books recently, I was surprised to discover just how propaganistic Finn was as in story after story he sought to ram home the thesis that pious practices were essential to growing up Catholic and that Catholics were as good Americans as Protestants were. As best I can now recall, my classmates and I missed much of Finn's thesis. We paid little heed to the strictures on piety because, hearing them on all sides, we just tuned them out. We never suspected that Percy and Tom were Irish or German Catholic and, hence, the objects of prejudice; to boys whose last names, e.g., Kaminsky and Soroka, were clearly foreign, the surnames of Finn's heroes sounded genuinely American and much like Jack Armstrong, our collective hero. Why, then, did we enjoy Finn's books?

The answer, I believe, is relatively simple. Stripped of their sectarian narrative veneer and preaching, Finn's books are actually series fiction: i.e., his versions of school story, sports story, or adventure story expressed in series pattern. Consequently, what we had responded to were those story elements and presumptions concerning childhood that all series fictions—whether old examples like Tom Swift or the Bobbsey Twins, or more recent ones like the Hardy Boys or Nancy Drew—incorporate when they accept eight- to eleven-year-olds as they are and try to satisfy their fantasies of accomplishment, purpose, and recognition.[1] Finn's fiction, then, worked for his readers as long as it was true to the conventions of series fiction; on the other hand, when Finn's books aspired to a supposedly realistic, exhortative recounting of growing up Catholic in America, they often sputtered and missed. Put another way, Finn's fiction succeeded wherever it gratified certain key fantasies of youngsters and failed when it sought explicitly to prescribe moral behavior and religious practice.

Selma Lanes has perceptively discussed the ways series fiction is designed to meet the needs of children:

> Decidedly regressions so far as literary or human content are concerned, they play subtly upon the restlessness and idealism of older children, perhaps even staving off adolescent depressions with their pure fantasies of the power of youth and the glory of the life of action. Lo the poor ten- and eleven-year-olds, for whom time hangs suspended between childhood and man's estate, for whom little that is meaningful seems ever to happen in the here and now. They have outgrown the best of childhood's privileges, yet have attained almost none of the prerogatives of adulthood. Their parents and assorted elders still control large areas of their lives. To their frequent lament that nothing ever happens, the authors of such popular series have their heroes and heroines move all over the globe in cars, planes, steam-yachts, air gliders and submarines to solve a seemingly endless chain of mysteries and best assorted villains of all ages.[2]

Lanes is not as clear as she might be in distinguishing the dual function of fantasy in series fiction. For not only is a particular series book the product of an author who is aware that he or she actually has created fantasy, although when published it masquerades as realism,[3] but that book also is the means whereby youngsters can fantasize, choosing deliberately to put aside the reality of their routine-filled, uneventful lives and escape to another "real" world of excitement, achievement, and recognition.

Paradoxically, as Lanes points out, series fiction, even though gratifying fantasy needs, at the same time provides practical advice to boys and girls concerning coping effectively in the actual world:

> Each action-packed adventure . . . rests on the bedrock of conventional practicality and sensible rules of day-to-day behavior which surely would rate general grownup approval. Though the Hardy boys and Nancy Drew encounter assorted wicked villains who behave bizarrely, they themselves always act with commendable decorum, paragons of well-brought-up young citizenry. . . . Beneath the façade of exotic adventure, these stories are practical handbooks for getting along successfully in the workaday world.[4]

Lanes goes on to call attention to the fact that series fiction graphically demonstrates for young readers the usefulness of applied intelligence.

> Just as everything in children's first picture books suggests an ordered, comprehensible universe, so, too, these mystery adventures always yield ultimately to the heroes' or heroines' applied intelligence. The constantly repeated message that the forthcoming mysteries of adult life are manageable, using one's own good sense, is part of these books' perennial appeal.[5]

Series fiction, then, is both fantastic and didactic.

Two important observations can be made concerning Lanes' remarks on series fiction. The first is that adults tolerate series books, in spite of their simplistic plotting, two-dimensional characterization, stylistic infelicities, and naked appeal to children's fantasizing, because grown-ups realize that series books are didactic, offering real, albeit limited, practical advice on how to succeed in life. The second observation is that the didacticism of series fiction reflects an understanding of evil that children can comprehend and do accept. In the fictive world of series fiction, generally speaking, evil exists outside the child protagonist and within one or, at most, several individuals; evil does not inhere in human institutions or in the universe. Often evil is not called by that name or even recognized as such; moreover, and most importantly, it is always subject ultimately to human intelligence and resourcefulness. Accordingly, when intelligence, especially as exercised by a clever young boy or girl, is directed towards a troubling or unfair situation, "evil" is readily overcome, revealed as stupid or ill-mannered, and perceived as temporary.

Since the series book is intended for the pre-pubescent child, virtually all children as they mature outgrow it and themselves dismiss series books as "for kids." Let us be very clear. What many older children and young adolescents reject when they dismiss Nancy Drew, for example, is a specific narrative pattern and cast of characters, the complex of feelings and needs the specific pattern and cast were designed to appeal to and gratify, and a simplistic, absolutist understanding of life. What these young persons are not necessarily rejecting is a predisposition to seek out and read books that, while addressing an increasingly sophisticated and morally ambiguous view of life, appeal to and satisfy the feelings and needs of the various stages of adolescence. Nor do these young persons necessarily reject didacticism unless it is corrupted into moralizing or proselytizing.

By and large older children and young adolescents acknowledge that life does seem increasingly complex and its difficulties relatively immune to the mere application of intelligence. They are willing to admit that something called evil does exist not only in individuals but in human institutions as well. Many are prepared to concede that they too can do wrong and, hence, may become part of an evil bedeviling humanity at large. Yet, at the same time, these young people also want—rather need—assurances that still they have intrinsic worth and that, their wrong-doing forgiven and their guilt assuaged, they are capable of actions which can contribute significantly to the redressing of serious wrongs and the enhancing of good. In short, older children and young adolescents need assurance that they matter and can be relied on to choose and act responsibly and competently. Consequently, they are likely, given the opportunity, to prefer fiction which, while respecting their steadily maturing intellect and sense of ethics, supplies all these assurances.

I propose—and most of what follows in an elaboration of the proposal—that what can be called ethical fantasy is both a source of many of the assurances older children and young adolescents seek and one that should prove especially attractive to them. In addition, I suggest that, because it is an attractive source of these assurances, ethical fantasy can be considered the series book grown up, so to speak, and become sophisticated or, at the least, one of its legitimate successors. To forestall any possible misunderstanding, I am not claiming that the mechanical plotting, stereotypes, and awkward style of series fiction are also characteristic of ethical fantasy. All I claim is that, like series fiction, ethical fantasy deliberately appeals to and seeks to gratify key fantasies of its audience and, while doing so, is unabashedly didactic. Finally, I suggest that with the development of ethical fantasy we may be witnessing the emergence of a new literary formula.

II

What is ethical fantasy? It is contemporary fantasy for older children and young adolescents that is explicitly concerned with the existence of good and evil and the morality of human behavior. Neither technical nor argumentative, ethical fantasy takes for granted that good and evil exist and that there are substantive, discernible differences between them. At the same time it concedes that the differences are not always easily discernible. Actually, the plots of ethical fantasy often focus on the difficulty and, sometimes, even the necessity of discerning right from wrong and then of acting accordingly. Also, ethical fantasy presumes that the choices and decisions of young people, whether they are fully aware or not, involve taking sides between good and evil and sometimes may have results different from what the individual intends or foresees. Further, ethical fantasy presumes that choosing between right and wrong and accepting the consequences of that choice are marks of maturity. In ethical fantasy, then, making moral decisions is an important plot element. Obviously, ethical fantasy is didactic, its creators intending that young readers will find either corroboration for their previous acceptance of the validity of the basic presumptions of the genre or, at the least, justification for maintaining an open mind towards the possible validity of these presumptions.

Not a particularly neat and tidy genre, ethical fantasy

sprawls, cutting across traditional sub-categories of children's fantasy. Sometimes, for example, ethical fantasy can be the heroic fantasy or romance that depicts a world Northrop Frye describes as "of heroes and gods and titans . . . a world of powers and passions and moments of ecstasy far greater than anything we meet outside the imagination."[6] Sometimes ethical fantasy can be high fantasy as characterized by Robert H. Boyer and Kenneth J. Zahorski: featuring other-world setting and causality; imposing characters who "with unearthly powers, inspire wonder or fear, or often both: dragon kings, elves, dryads, demon princesses"; concern with "archetypal figures, motifs, and themes such as the temptress, death and renewal, and the spiritual quest, with its demands for courage and selflessness"; and style that is "a fittingly elevated one, characteristically working through imagery and metaphor to evoke its imaginary worlds."[7] Ethical fantasy can be also the high fantasy that Eleanor Cameron, the widely recognized author and critic of children's books, portrays as fantasy that reveals

> a striking attitude regarding the human condition and our relationships with one another. For within these tales lies the essence of their creators, the philosophy of their lives subtly woven through the pages of a story that children love and remember and which may, quite unbeknown to the children themselves, become a lasting influence.[8]

Other times, ethical fantasy can be what Boyer and Zahorski call low fantasy that, containing mimetic elements, is "much closer to reality as we know it."[9] Finally, ethical fantasy may be time fantasy, space fantasy, or psychological fantasy. The point of all this is that "ethical fantasy" qua term is not meant to signal the preeminence of either the high heroic or low mimetic in the plot, or the presence of a secondary world and otherworld principles of causality, or a high degree of seriousness in tone. Rather, the term "ethical fantasy" designates children's fantasy with distinctive subject matter and specific intent.

Ethical fantasy, it is true, may not be a familiar term. However, its usefulness should become evident once its several advantages are noted. First, the term avoids the occasional confusion or invidious comparisons involving intrinsic worth, seriousness of tone, or scope of intention that may occur when a person employs traditional terms like high, low, or heroic when attempting to delineate or discuss the kind of fantasy this essay is concerned with. Second, the term "ethical fantasy" accurately indicates the content and purpose of a work so designated whether or not it features traditional heroic, mythic, or mimetic elements. Third, by indicating that the content and purpose of a particular fantasy involve ethics, the term "ethical fantasy" acknowledges openly that the latter is didactic, and does so without embarrassment or defensiveness, well aware that didacticism is not the same as moralizing or proselytizing. Incidentally, its openly avowed didacticism situates ethical fantasy firmly within the longest-lived and still intellectually respectable tradition of children's literature, namely, the use of imaginative writing to influence the thoughts and actions of children. Ethical fantasy as a term, then, is "up front" and refreshingly direct.

Because ethical fantasy is didactic does not mean that its assumptions about good and evil and the importance of ethical decision-making in the lives of young people need appear as inert propositions, stale maxims, and hackneyed morals inserted into the plot at supposedly appropriate places. On the contrary, these assumptions become grist for the mill of the imagination and emerge transformed into narrative patterns and plot elements, aspects of characterization, and even symbols. Thus, the most important of these assumptions, the existence of good and evil and their interrelationship, is imaginatively rendered in a variety of patterns. Most times good and evil are rivals or combatants locked in a seemingly perennial struggle for dominance. Sometimes the clash between good and evil becomes entangled in the stirring of some elemental, amoral power whose manifestations are dangerous or even fatal. And in at least one instance good and evil are complementary forces whose equilibrium is disturbed only at great risk to individuals and the world.

Andre Norton, for instance, in *Steel Magic* has Huron speak about a war between good and evil:

> "The enemy . . . are those powers of darkness who war against all that is good and fair and right. Wizards of the Black, witches, warlocks, werewolves, ghouls, ogres—the enemy has as many names and faces as Avalon itself—many bodies and disguises, some fair, but mainly foul. They are shadows of the darkness, who have long sought to overwhelm Avalon and then win to victory in other worlds,

> yours among them. Think of what you fear and hate the most, and that will be part of the enemy and the Dark Powers."[10]

Although she uses the terms Light and Dark, Susan Cooper is just as direct and explicit as Norton when, in *Silver on the Tree,* Will explains to Stephen, his oldest brother:

> "But beyond the world is the universe, bound by the law of the High Magic, as every universe must be. And beneath the High Magic are two . . . poles . . . that we call the Dark and the Light. No other power orders them. They merely exist. The Dark seeks by its dark nature to influence men so that in the end, through them, it may control the earth. The Light has the task of stopping that from happening. From time to time the Dark has come rising and has been driven back, but now very soon it will rise for the last and most perilous time. It has been gathering strength for that rising, and it is almost ready. And therefore, for the last time, until the end of Time, we must drive it back so that the world of men may be free."[11]

Other authors may be less detailed but just as clear as Norton and Cooper. Mr. Bass, in Eleanor Cameron's *Time and Mr. Bass,* refers to a "blind, one-track-minded evil" that seeks to disrupt the Mycetians.[12] Jane Louise Curry has Maelin, one of the major characters of *Beneath the Hill,* attribute the "ugliness and destruction of the Bane" to something profound and extensive:

> "It is our hearts which tell us most surely that what dwells below is some power which hates us, which hates things that live and flourish freely. . . . Do you not feel that here in this chamber something more than man's greed troubles this mountain?"[13]

In *The Giant Under the Snow* by John Gordon, Elizabeth is terse as she explains the source of the problem troubling the countryside: "A very long time ago, . . . in this part of the country from the backlands to the coast there was a struggle between great powers that was never properly ended."[14] Cadellin, the wizard of Alan Garner's *The Weirdstone of Brisingamen*, recites the origin of evil in this fashion:

> "Long years ago . . . beyond the memory or books of men, Nastrond, the Great Spirit of Darkness, rode forth in war upon the plain. But there came against him a mighty king, and Nastrond fell. He cast off his earth-shape and fled into the Abyss of Ragnarok, and all men rejoiced, thinking that evil had vanished from the world for ever: yet the King knew in his heart that this could never be. . . . And it was prophesied that, when the day should come, Nastrond must be victorious, for there would be none pure enough to withstand him since, by that time, he would have put a little of himself into the heart of all men."[15]

Cadellin, this time in Garner's *The Moon of Gomrath,* speaks of elemental powers, the Old Magic, that, becoming entangled in the contest between good and evil, may be dangerous: "These may not be evil, but they are wild forces, which could destroy one not well acquainted with such things." And later he says, ". . . the Old Magic is wrong for these times. It does not fit the present scale of good and ill."[16]

Instead of placing good and evil in a constant struggle, Ursula Le Guin envisages them as the Light and the Dark which are in balance but affected by any and all acts.

> ". . . Do you see, Arren, how an act is not, as young men think, like a rock that one picks up and throws, and it hits or misses, and that's the end of it. When that rock is lifted, the earth is lighter; the hand that bears it heavier. When it is thrown, the circuits of the stars respond, and where it strikes or falls the universe is changed. On every act the balance of the whole depends."[17]

Regardless of how they become involved in the struggle or relationship between good and evil, the youthful protagonists of ethical fantasy eventually do side with the good. Yet knowing in every instance who or what is good is not always clear or easy to determine, and this difficulty is a dominant plot element in ethical fantasy. Jesse and Rich, for instance, the heroes of Jay Williams' *The Hero from Otherwhere,* are dismayed by the task of recognizing evil.

> "And I've been thinking . . . I wonder if that phantom we saw was put there by Skrymir? Or if it could have been Skrymir himself?

> "We're going to have an awful time recognizing the enemy. . . . How can we tell who he is? He might be anybody."[18]

Having succumbed to a bribe of Turkish Delight, Edmund in C. S. Lewis' *The Lion, the Witch and the Wardrobe* mistakenly believes at first that the evil White Witch is good. In *The Weirdstone of Brisingamen,* Fenodyre warns Colin and Susan that the evil morth brood "mingle with others unnoticed, and can be detected only by certain marks, and that not always."[19] Colin, in *The Moon of Gomrath,* is chagrined to discover that Pele's being a dwarf does not guarantee his allegiance to the cause of goodness: "Why's he doing all this? . . . We didn't think twice about trusting him, with his being a dwarf."[20] In Cooper's *Over Sea, Under Stone,* although Barney's instinct warns him that Mrs. Palk is untrustworthy, his older brother Simon does not recognize the woman's complicity in evil and is skeptical about his younger brother's distrust:

> Barney's hair was ruffled, and his eyes shadowed with sleep. It was very easy to believe that what he was describing had been no more than a dream.[21]

A more significant plot element or pattern in ethical fantasy than surmounting obstacles in discerning good from evil is facing up to the necessity of choosing between the two, once they have been recognized, and then screwing up the courage to act accordingly. For instance, when Merlin in *Steel Magic* explains to Greg, Eric, and Sara that they have the option of aiding him in opposing "the evil tide" or not, the children volunteer to help but only hesitantly.

> "Then I choose to do as you wish," Greg answered. "It's for Dad, in a way." He looked questioningly at Sara and Eric.
>
> "All right." Eric's agreement was reluctant. He looked as scared and unhappy as Sara felt inside.
>
> She held to the basket which was the only real thing now in this mixed-up dream. And her voice was very small and thin as she said, "Me, I'll help too," though she did not want to at all.[22]

In *The Marrow of the World* by Ruth Nichols, Ygerna informs Linda, her half-sister, that because she is part witch she must choose between the immortality and great power of witchcraft, or the inevitable death mere humans face. "Stay here and live. . . . Stay with me and be powerful. Your other choice is to die and be extinguished, as though you had never been."[23] Choosing proves anything but easy for Linda and she needs support. "You are burdened," the wizard Leo tries to comfort the girl, "and with a choice not wholly of your seeking. Rest here, and be at peace for a while."[24] Arthur in *Beneath the Hill* is acutely aware of the importance of choosing:

> The non-Periel, the fogs, Mr. Dekany's tale—and, above all, the perilous power of the Bane to bend other wills to its own—all these had made fearfully clear that if he closed his eyes and ears to that darkness, its movement into the sunshine from the depths where wisdom had sealed it would be the freer.[25]

Jesse and Rich also clearly understand in *The Hero from Otherwhere* the importance of deciding for the good and of doing something positive. Rich remarks:

> ". . . and when he said that about saving our world and this one I felt that if I didn't speak up, I'd never be able to look myself in the face again."

As Jesse agrees that indeed they had a free choice, he says:

> "But I felt I was making the choice he'd have made if he had been in my place. It made me feel good."
>
> "Yeah. That's right."[26]

In *A Swiftly Tilting Planet*, Madeleine L'Engle, as if presuming the reader's familiarity with this important pattern, employs an interesting variation. Young Charles already accepts the necessity of choosing only what is pleasing to the good, but exactly what good deed to do is the problem. Taking advantage of the boy's eager willingness, the false unicorn tempts Charles to act—even precipitately, if necessary—so that his good deed will affect positively the future of the world:

> ". . . you have the ability to see the difference between right and wrong, and to make the correct decisions. You

were selected because you are an extraordinary young man and your gifts and your brains qualify you. You are the only one who can control the Might-Have-Been. . . . Come, Charles Wallace. You have been chosen. You are in control of what is going to happen. You are needed. We must go."[27]

Although tempted and suffering from the pain of his uncertainty, still Charles demurs: "I don't know what I'm supposed to use, but it's not my intellect or strength."[28] In this way L'Engle depicts the young boy's permanent change from arrogance to humility—in other words, his maturation.

Another significant pattern or plot element found in much ethical fantasy involves the chagrin or surprise experienced by the protagonists when they learn that their actions have consequences quite different from what they intended or imagined. In Lewis' *The Magician's Nephew,* for example, Polly and Digory just want to look at and barely touch a golden bell and hammer that they are forbidden to tap. But the youths' mere looking and touching lead, as often occurs, to their tapping the bell, which action precipitates not only the collapse of the building the children are in but also evil Jadis' awakening, the introduction of evil into Narnia, and eventually that world's end. Wanting more status, Taran of Lloyd Alexander's *The Book of Three* is elevated to Assistant Pig-Keeper. Shortly after, Wen, the magic pig, runs away in fear and Taran holds himself responsible. Impulsively rushing out to track down the pig, the boy unknowingly initiates a sequence of events that culminate in his becoming the High King of Prydain. Envious of Jasper's rank, Ged in Le Guin's *The Wizard of Earthsea* demonstrates his superior magic by a summoning from the dead. As he does so, he also releases an evil shadow that sorely plagues him. Further, when Ged decides to stop running away from the shadow and, instead, confront it, he unwittingly takes the one essential step towards learning his true identity. In L'Engle's *A Wrinkle in Time,* Charles, brimming with the confidence of young genius, challenges the evil "It," expecting an easy triumph, but, instead, he loses and becomes imprisoned. His sister Meg, believing that she possesses no distinctive gift or talent, is astounded that her simple and seemingly impotent declaration of love releases both Charles and her father and beats back Evil. One final example should suffice. In Susan Cooper's *Greenwitch,* Jane impulsively wishes the stuffed effigy of the Greenwitch happiness, and the girl's single act of disinterested benevolence prompts the Witch to give Jane and the forces of Light the lead case containing the manuscript they need to unravel the secret of the grail. It should be clear, then, that this pattern in ethical fantasy underscores that human actions and choices matter, whether they are large or small, deliberate or not, and sometimes they have even worldwide consequences.

III

The several narrative patterns and plot elements just distinguished are reason enough, it may be argued, to entice readers to ethical fantasy. For indeed the plots of the books already mentioned do make for interesting, exciting, and often intense, suspenseful reading. The best indication of the relatively high level of skilled storytelling found in ethical fantasy is that *A Wrinkle in Time, The High King, The Grey King, Silver on the Tree, The Marrow of the World* and *The Farthest Shore* are Newbery Medal, National Book Award, or Best Book of the Year in English winners—awards given to the best children's book of the year. Moreover, three authors who have written some ethical fantasy have been highly praised by reviewers and critics—Alan Garner, Andre Norton, and Jane Louise Curry. And one ethical fantasy sequence, the Narnian Chronicles, has already become a classic of children's literature. Nevertheless, besides telling engrossing stories, ethical fantasy possesses three other features that should aid considerably in attracting young readers and, one would hope, furnish gratification for some of their key fantasies and dreams. These features, furthermore, comprise the basis for suggesting that ethical fantasy is a legitimate successor of the series book, if not the latter grown up.

The first of these features is the prominent, sometimes essential, role of youth in the plots of ethical fantasy. Consider, for one example, the centrality of children in *The Lion, the Witch and the Wardrobe*. The young Pevensies—Peter, Susan, Edmund, and Lucy—enter Narnia, and their exploits, complementing Aslan's, enable the land to free itself from winter and the White Witch's reign of terror. As a result, the children are crowned kings and queens whose reign is recalled in subsequent Narnian history as a golden age. What young reader would not wish a similar destiny—achievement, recognition, status—all earned and not just given by an accommodating or patronizing adult! As if this were not enough, in *Prince Caspian* the children return to restore Caspian to his throne and the Narnians to their senses. And the other Narnian Chronicles also speak of the essential role of young persons in that world's history, both secular and religious.

There are other examples of the paramount role youth enjoy in ethical fantasy. Essential characters in the defeat of the Dark in Cooper's "The Dark Is Rising" sequence, Susan, Barney, and Jane decipher codes, read maps, and find lost items the Masters of the Light need. When Martha, Sue, and William in Penelope Lively's *The Whispering Knights* inquire if they can assist elderly Miss Hipplewaite in her struggle against the "bad side of things," she assures them that being young does not ipso facto rule out their participation: "It doesn't matter what you look like or who you are. It's courage and conviction that count."[29] After final victory, the elderly woman praises the children for their help: "You have done magnificently . . . the task is complete."[30] At the end of *The Giant Under the Snow,* Elizabeth returns just to reward Jonk, Bill and Arf for their contributions to the triumph of good. When they demur, she insists: "But you must have it. Pattern, remember? Things must be fitted into place, and a reward is one of them."[31] In *The Sleepers,* Hugh and Jennifer have the satisfaction of Myrddin's pointing out to Arthur that the king does not have any more "faithful guardians to the Treasures than these . . . children."[32] For without their aid, Myrddin, Arthur, and all his knights would have been defenseless against the machinations of evil. Near the beginning of *Steel Magic,* Merlin stresses the great importance of the children's entering the fray:

> "Then you can understand why we are excited at your coming. We lose three talismans, and then you arrive. What else can we believe but that your fate is tied to our loss?"[33]

After Avalon has been saved, Merlin graciously acknowledges the land's debt to Greg, Sara and Eric:

> "Also know this—Avalon gives thanks and Avalon cherishes her own. For you are now a part of her, which in time to come may be more to you than you can now guess."[34]

At the climax of *Time and Mr. Bass,* David is of major assistance to Mr. Bass in his struggle with and defeat of the black shape that has threatened the Mycetians, a struggle and defeat, incidentally, that only David foresees. Although it is Ged in *The Farthest Shore* who restores death to its rightful place and power, the mage would have been unable to depart from the dark land except for the courageous aid of young Prince Arren. Le Guin's description of Arren's realization of the great import of his accomplishment aptly bears out the contention that ethical fantasy serves to validate youth's key fantasy of competence and achievement: "And he smiled then, a smile both somber and joyous, knowing, for the first time in his life, alone, unpraised, and at the end of the world, victory."[35]

The prominence accorded youth in ethical fantasy indicates convincingly that its creators deliberately seek to capitalize on the still strong inclination of older children and young adolescents to identify with the protagonist of whatever they read. Obviously, by capitalizing so extensively on this desire to identify, ethical fantasy hopes to enhance its appeal and didactic effectiveness. However, ethical fantasists are not, generally speaking, crass manipulators of their readers or subscribers to the naive belief that through some mechanism of intense empathy readers can themselves experience whatever the characters in a story feel and do. On the contrary, the kind of identification ethical fantasy provides is a rich and subtle one, similar to what D. Harding invokes in his discussion of what happens when people read:

> Although . . . desires . . . will not be satisfied in drama or fiction . . . , there may still be a highly important gain in having joined with the novelist or dramatist in the psychological act of giving them statement. . . . What, after all, is the alternative to defining and expressing our attained and perhaps unattainable desires? It is to acquiesce in the deprivation and submit to the belief that with our personality or in our circumstances we ought not even to desire such things; and to forfeit the right to the desire is even worse than to be denied the satisfaction.
>
> . . . wish-fulfillment in novels and plays can . . . be described as wish-formulation or the definition of desires. . . . It is the social act of affirming with the author a set of values.

> . . . fictions contribute to defining the reader's values.
>
> Empathic insight allows the spectator to view ways of life beyond his own range. . . . he can achieve an imaginary development of human potentialities that have remained rudimentary in himself . . . . The spectator enters imaginatively . . . into some of the multifarious possibilities that he has not himself been able to achieve.[36]

Especially pertinent is Harding's reiteration of the familiar, but still important, observation that empathic identification allows for imaginative trying on or trying out of roles and options currently beyond a reader's range or circumstances. Also pertinent is Harding's suggestion that wish formulation (that is, value formulation) is a more precise description than wish fulfillment of what actually occurs in the reading process. Perhaps most pertinent and provocative is the contention that worse than fiction's feeding unrealizable dreams would be its conniving with circumstances to suggest that readers ought not have dreams, desires, and fantasies but must forsake any rights to them.

Harding's observations concerning the process of "empathic insight" can help us appreciate how enticing and helpful ethical fantasy can be as it provides readers with opportunity for identification. That is to say, it invites and encourages young readers to look at their fantasies and dreams of achievement and recognition and to recognize them for what they are—signs of both willingness and competence to try out new, possibly exciting options once they become available. Further, ethical fantasy validates a young reader's sense of self-esteem as genuine or, at the least, still potentially realizable. Finally, in any case, it assures individual readers that, since others harbor similar fantasies and dreams, they need not be ashamed or feel defensive about theirs.

The second feature of ethical fantasy that may attract young readers derives from its nature as fantasy. As is widely recognized, fantasy employs a technique of displacement that—transferring basic human situations and emotions into exotic, bizarre, or novel settings—often restores to these situations or emotions the original sheen and importance overfamiliarity or cynicism has eroded. Through an analogous form of displacement—i.e., translating certain assumptions concerning good and evil and their several relationships into various story patterns—ethical fantasy can restore to the pressing concern with good and evil and to ethical decision-making some of their luster and their challenge, which have gradually been dimmed by peer pressure, rote, conventional presentation, and uncomfortable *ad hominem* proselytizing. Because it does not fret over the laws of probability to the same degree as realism, ethical fantasy convincingly places its young protagonists at the center of significant action. Thus, far more readily and plausibly than realism, ethical fantasy can give young people the center stage they yearn for but seldom enjoy in the real world.

Adults who like to use children's books that reflect the ideas and values of Judaism and Christianity can find ethical fantasy a handy supplement. Clearly, the latter's concern for the existence of good and evil and the importance of ethical choosing is compatible with a belief in God, the presence of evil in both individuals and universe, free will, and the necessity of admitting responsibility for the consequences of one's actions. But ethical fantasy may be a more effective substitute than supplement to children's books reflecting the Judaic-Christian ethos. That is to say, because it avoids conventional theological formulations and eliminates allusions to particular religions and sects, ethical fantasy need not worry about readers' ignoring it on account of overfamiliarity, or misunderstanding it on account of lack of knowledge or recognition, or rejecting it on account of an association with religious institutions. Ethical fantasy can "talk about" good and evil without unduly irritating those among its readers who may be offended by explicit "God-talk." Even Lewis and L'Engle, the two authors of ethical fantasy who come the closest to insisting on a belief in God, do so only obliquely or so quietly and infrequently that many readers may not even notice. Put another way, ethical fantasy presupposes and encourages a fundamental certitude or faith in transcendence without linking that certitude or faith in God to a particular religion.

Ethical fantasy can be said to enjoy the best of two worlds. On one hand, it shares with children's books reflecting the Judaic-Christian ethos a belief in the existence of good and evil and the importance of moral choice. On the other hand, ethical fantasy does not run as great a risk of being rejected or ignored as does explicitly religious, didactic literature because the former employs virtually no technical, theological formulations and does not make traditionally formulaic demands (e.g., "Thou shalt not . . ."). This "best of both worlds" advantage is the third feature of ethical fantasy that may be potentially very attractive to older children and young adolescents.

This advantageous situation of ethical fantasy may be similar to that which Bruno Bettelheim suggests fairy tales have over old-fashioned Bible stories for children:

> As long as parents fully believed that Biblical stories solved the riddle of our existence and its purpose, it was easy to make a child feel secure. The Bible was felt to contain the answers to all pressing questions: the Bible told man all he needed to know to understand the world, how it came into being, and how to behave in it. In the Western world the Bible also provided prototypes for man's imagination. But rich as the Bible is in stories, not even during the most religious of times were these stories sufficient for meeting all the psychic needs of man.
>
> Part of the reason for this is that while the Old and New Testaments and the histories of the saints provided answers to the crucial questions of how to live the good life, they did not offer solutions for the problems posed by the dark sides of our personalities. The Biblical stories suggest essentially only one solution for the asocial aspects of the unconscious: repression of these (unacceptable) strivings. But children, not having their ids in conscious control, need stories which permit at least fantasy satisfaction of these "bad tendencies, and specific models for their sublimation.[37]

Still another way of appreciating ethical fantasy's "best of both worlds" advantage derives from the paradox that, in spite of eschewing explicit allusion to the Bible and organized religion, ethical fantasy may be more "biblical" than traditional, explicitly religious stories that ostensibly are Bible-grounded. Here I am indebted to John Shea's insights into the nature of biblical story, in particular story as a medium for transmitting fundamental religious truths. In Shea's view, biblical story speaks of the existence of "darkness" in life, e.g., frailty, tragedy, death, as part of "Mystery" without using explicit "God-talk."[38] So, too, does ethical fantasy speak of evil, wrong, and dark as essential, virtually inexplicable components of all life. Biblical story attempts to create "root metaphors" which provide "unity and meaning" to the lives of its audience.[39] So, too, ethical fantasy attempts to shape "root" story patterns that help give point to the lives of its readers by embodying and validating various key fantasies and dreams.

Just as biblical story does, ethical fantasy retells "basic stories" and, in refashioning them, hopes to "unthicken" situations and emotions in order that they may function once more as mediators between readers and "Mystery."[40] Unlike traditional story that often assumes pat answers to everything, biblical story features growth, change, searching, and questioning: so, too, does ethical fantasy. According to Shea, biblical story shows that myth undergirds human society.[41] Indirectly, ethical fantasy functions similarly when through its mythlike story patterns it not only sustains its audience's sense of self-worth but also demonstrates graphically that it is responsible for its actions which may very well affect all society. Like the function of myth in biblical story, the story patterns of ethical fantasy urge readers to stand up and be counted, to choose, and to act. And like biblical story, ethical fantasy urges through "broad directionality" that suggests direction without providing detailed guides to the complexities of each concrete situation.[42] Finally, ethical fantasy, like biblical story, is weighty, gives dignity to its characters and, indirectly, to its audience, and cultivates an awareness of "Mystery."

IV

Whether the development of ethical fantasy owes more to chance or to the nicely calculated response to a potentially large market by publishers, authors, librarians, reviewers, and even specialists in children's literature is unclear. Given the nature of the book business—where success breeds imitation and constant testing and retesting of the market—and a long-lived tradition of didacticism in children's books, the second explanation seems more likely. Regardless of its causes, however, ethical fantasy has emerged as a distinctive type of children's fantasy, in other words, a literary pattern. What is also unclear is whether this pattern is what John Cawelti has called literary formula—"a structure of narrative conventions employed in a great number of individual works."[43] The reason for the uncertainty is simple. Since reader acceptance over an extended period of time is the single most important criterion for determining whether a literary pattern has become literary formula, there is no way ethical fantasy, a very recent development, can qualify unconditionally as formula. Unfortunately, as a consequence, the final, perhaps clinching, piece of evidence (that ethical fantasy, like series fiction, is also formula fiction) to support the suggestion that ethical fantasy is the series book grown up does not yet exist!

Despite the fact that it cannot claim unequivocally to be literary formula, ethical fantasy does possess many of the characteristics of literary formula: discernible pattern; moral fantasy; an emphasis on action, suspense, and excitement; gratification of the need for escape and identification; an imaginary world; and ego enhancement.[44] In view of all that has already been presented concerning ethical fantasy, it would be redundant to show that it possesses each and every one of the characteristics Cawelti distinguishes. There is one exception. What he means by moral fantasy needs defining so any confusion between it and ethical fantasy can be prevented. Moral fantasies, according to Cawelti, are fictive worlds, made up from a variety of story patterns, in which

> the audience can encounter a maximum of excitement without being confronted with an overpowering sense of the insecurity and danger that accompany such forms of excitement in reality. Much of the artistry of formula literature involves the creator's ability to plunge us into a believable kind of excitement while, at the same time, confirming our confidence that in the formidable world things always work out as we want them to.[45]

Moral fantasy, then, is not the same as ethical fantasy or material or secondary world.

Two points remain. Cawelti remarks that most formula fiction in practice can be located somewhere between the two poles of pure formula and complex fiction, i.e., serious adult fiction, usually in a realistic mode.[46] If ethical fantasy should develop into formula, it would most likely be located at a point, perhaps midway, between the two poles—a point where we might expect to find types of formula fiction for children. Cawelti also remarks that the essential cultural function of formula is to reflect accurately the values and tastes of various groups of people.[47] Ethical fantasy's becoming formula, then, would imply that many, if not most, of the young people for whom it is intended have found it indeed attractive and gratifying. A further implication would be that adults convinced of the potentially high didactic impact of ethical fantasy might derive some satisfaction in observing that its didacticism is, at least, not so obtrusive as to repel many readers. On the other hand, if ethical fantasy fails to become formula but still remains a pattern, at least two conclusions are possible. One is that sufficient numbers of older children and young adolescents do not or cannot find in ethical fantasy the various assurances and gratifications they need. The other is that ethical fantasy ultimately is located much closer to the pole of complex fiction than is usually expected of formula fiction. Such an eventuality is possible when we recall the relatively high level of storytelling already manifest in ethical fantasies. Obviously, only time and the reading habits and needs of young people will determine whether ethical fantasy remains pattern (or even survives) or becomes formula.

NOTES

1. A. S. Neill, the famed educator, comments about children's need for stories that gratify their needs: "Children love to be told of their own prowess; they have little realistic evaluation of their own skills. If you make Bert, aged nine, fly the latest jet, looping the loop and at the same time hitting six eggs in the air with his gun, he will accept the statement without reservation. But he may suspect that you underrated his prowess in the matter of the *number* of eggs. A story should satisfy a child's wish to perform miracles . . . the fairy tale up to date" (*The Last Man Alive* [New York: Hart, 1969], pp. 6–7).

2. Selma Lanes, *Down the Rabbit Hole* (New York: Atheneum, 1972), p. 133.

3. Leslie McFarlane, writing as Franklin W. Dixon, the originator of the Hardy Boys series for the Stratemeyer syndicate, makes it very clear in his autobiography that he was well aware that he was writing fantasy. *Ghost of the Hardy Boys* (New York: Metheun, 1976).

4. Lanes, p. 134.

5. Ibid., pp. 134–35.

6. Northrop Frye, *The Educated Imagination* (Bloomington, Ind.: Indiana University Press, 1964), p. 100.

7. Robert H. Boyer and Kenneth J. Zahorski, eds., *The Fantastic Imagination II: An Anthology of High Fantasy* (New York: Avon, 1978), pp. 2–3.

8. Eleanor Cameron, "High Fantasy: *A Wizard of Earthsea*," *Horn Book*, April 1971, p. 130.

9. Robert H. Boyer and Kenneth J. Zahorski, eds., *The Fantastic Imagination II: An Anthology of High Fantasy* (New York: Avon, 1978), p. 2.

10. Andre Norton, *Steel Magic* (Cleveland: World, 1965), pp. 41–42.

11. Susan Cooper, *Silver on the Tree* (New York: Atheneum, 1977), p. 14.

12. Eleanor Cameron, *Time and Mr. Bass* (Boston: Little, Brown, 1967), p. 163.

13. Jane Louise Curry, *Beneath the Hill* (New York: Harcourt, Brace, 1967), pp. 140–41.

14. John Gordon, *The Giant Under the Snow* (New York: Harper & Row, 1968), p. 78.

15. Alan Garner, *The Weirdstone of Brisingamen* (New York: Ace, 1978), pp. 34–35.

16. Alan Garner, *The Moon of Gomrath* (London: Collins, 1972), pp. 28, 87.

17. Ursula K. Le Guin, *The Farthest Shore* (New York: Bantam, 1975), p. 66.

18. Jay Williams, *The Hero from Otherwhere* (New York: Dell, 1973), p. 82.

19. Garner, *The Weirdstone of Brisingamen,* p. 170.

20. Garner, *The Moon of Gomrath,* p. 137.

21. Susan Cooper, *Over Sea, Under Stone* (Harmondsworth: Penguin, 1968), p. 125.

22. Norton, p. 59.

23. Ruth Nichols, *The Marrow of the World* (Toronto: Macmillan, 1977), p. 57.

24. Ibid., p. 100.

25. Curry, *Beneath the Hill,* p. 200.

26. Williams, p. 173.

27. Madeleine L'Engle, *A Swiftly Tilting Planet* (New York: Dell, 1979), p. 199.

28. Ibid., p. 200.

29. Penelope Lively, *The Whispering Knights* (London: Pan, 1973), p. 63.

30. Ibid., p. 147.

31. Gordon, p. 194.

32. Jane Louise Curry, *The Sleepers* (New York: Harcourt, Brace, 1968), p. 237.

33. Norton, p. 57.

34. Ibid., p. 154.

35. Le Guin, p. 191.

36. D. Harding, "Psychological Processes in the Reading of Fiction," in *The Cool Web: The Pattern of Children's Reading,* ed. Margaret Meek, Aidan Warlow, and Griselda Barton (New York: Atheneum, 1978), pp. 69–70.

37. Bruno Bettelheim, *The Uses of Enchantment: The Meaning and Importance of Fairy Tales* (New York: Alfred E. Knopf, 1976), p. 52.

38. John Shea, *Stories of God: An Unauthorized Biography* (Chicago: The Thomas More Press, 1978), p. 39.

39. Ibid., p. 56.

40. "Refashioning" is similar to Lloyd Alexander's view that the "pot of story" revitalizes worn-out plots. I discuss this similarity and other aspects of ethical fantasy in my essay, "The Earthsea Trilogy: Ethical Fantasy for Children," in *Ursula K. Le Guin,* ed. Joe DeBolt (Port Washington, N.Y.: Kennikat Press, 1979), pp. 128–49.

41. Shea, p. 74.

42. Ibid., p. 55.

43. John Cawelti, *Adventure, Mystery, and Romance: Formula Stories as Art and Popular Culture* (Chicago: University of Chicago Press, 1976), p. 4.

44. Ibid., pp. 8–38.

45. Ibid., p. 16.

And the World Became Strange: Realms of Literary Fantasy

George P. Landow

For the past two centuries fantasy has provided a capable and compelling alternative to the realistic novel. The recent attention to this literary mode, which comes in part from the new academic and intellectual respectability of popular culture, is a radical departure from standard views of nineteenth- and twentieth-century fiction. According to F. R. Leavis' extremely influential formulation of this usual view in *The Great Tradition* (1948), "The great English novelists are Jane Austen, George Eliot, Henry James and Joseph Conrad." Although Leavis willingly admits that there are many other novelists well worth reading, he believes that the four he has named constitute the major continuum of English fiction and that such fiction is great chiefly because it devotes itself to presenting human life in terms of social and societal realities. Like all such critical taxonomies, that popularized by Leavis valuably directs attention to major works while encouraging the neglect of others which are equally important. Although one might question his neglect of the Brontës, one perceives that it is Dickens, possibly *the* great English novelist, who most suffers from such definitions of major fiction in terms of realistic modes. In fact, traditional assessments of the art and literature of the period offer obvious similarities: students of the visual arts have considered fantastic representations, when they have considered them at all, as relatively unimportant, and they have devoted most scholarly and critical attention to the traditions of Realism, Impressionism, and

Post-Impressionism. Students of literature have similarly devoted themselves largely to the Great Tradition while neglecting that stream which runs from the German *Märchen* through Carlyle, MacDonald, Carroll, Meredith, and Morris to Lewis, Lindsay, and Tolkien.

Valuable insights that enable us to perceive the characteristic strengths and beauties of literary fantasy and thus redress this critical imbalance appear in Richard Chase's *The American Novel and Its Tradition.* Although this apparently unlikely source of insight into British fiction does not specifically concern itself with fantasy as a literary mode, its description of the American novel in terms of Romance provides us with several points of departure for our voyage through the lands of fantasy. As Chase points out, novel and romance differ primarily in the attitudes they take towards reality. The novel, which emphasizes plausible, possible events, "renders reality closely and in comprehensive detail. It takes a group of people and sets them going about the business of life. We come to see these people in their real complexity of temperament and motive. They are in explicable relation to nature, to each other, to their social class, to their own past." Whereas the novel (or realistic fiction) makes character more important than plot or action, romance, which distantly follows medieval example, prefers action to character and

> feels free to render reality in less volume and detail. . . . The romance can flourish without providing much intricacy of relation. The characters, probably rather two-dimensional types, will not be complexly related to each other or to society or to the past. Human beings will on the whole be shown in ideal relation—that is, they will share emotions only after these have become abstract or symbolic. . . . Astonishing events may occur, and these are likely to have a symbolic or ideological, rather than a realistic, plausibility. Being less committed to the immediate rendition of reality than the novel, the romance will more freely veer towards mythic, allegorical, and symbolistic form.[1]

Much of Chase's description of romance applies directly to fantasy, which would seem to be a more extreme form of this mode, one which emphasizes its antithetical relation to the real as we normally conceive it. Indeed, as Eric S. Rabkin suggests in *The Fantastic in Literature,* an emphasis upon this antithetical relation to reality continually appears in the individual work itself: "While fairy tales use the World of Enchantment as their location, and are therefore highly fantastic, a true fantasy such as *Alice* continues to reverse its ground rules time and time again. . . . Fantasies may be generically distinguished from other narratives by this: the very nature of ground rules, of how we know things, on what basis we make assumptions, in short, the problem of knowing infects Fantasies at all levels, in their settings, in their methods, in their characters, in their plots."[2]

Rabkin's useful working definition of literary fantasy leads us to several central points about this imaginative mode in both the visual and verbal arts. First, fantasy and our conception of what is fantastic depend upon our view of reality: what we find improbable and unexpected follows from what we find probable and likely, and the fantastic will therefore necessarily vary with the individual and the age. Many of the basic assumptions which the Middle Ages or the eighteenth century made about society, human nature, the external world and the laws that govern it appear bizarre today, while many of our century's attitudes towards body and spirit, like its technological, artistic, and political creations, would appear as pure fantasy to earlier times. Air travel, telecommunication, lasers, and creation of new elements were found only in the realms of magic and faerie but a short time ago. Nonetheless, obsolete ideas of reality in earlier works of painting and literature do not, by themselves, create in us today a sense of the fantastic—a second element is required. Something, whether the reactions of a character within a literary work or some other device, must signal us that we are to take certain elements as fantastic. Whereas literature possesses several such devices, they are far harder to employ in painting and book illustration—a fact which creates problems and fascinations for the student of fantasy in the visual arts. One does not, for example, perceive as fantastic a *sacra conversazione* because it contains saints who lived in different ages, just as one does not take as bizarre floating human figures whom we perceive to be angels, emblems of fame, or the Virgin Mary rising to heaven. And yet when one encounters the floating or flying people in Arthur Rackham's illustration for "The Young Giant" (Plate 1) or W. Heath Robinson's *Cosie Hokie*, one does take them as fantastic. Similarly, we take the fairy figures in Richard Doyle's *Feasting and fun among the fuchsias* (Plate 2) and John Simmons' illustration to *A Midsummer Night's Dream* (Plate 3) as fantastic, and the reason is that these works depend upon our conventions of reality, our commonplace, shared assumptions about what is real. Religious and mythological paintings, as well as those based on purely literary subjects, may have major elements of unreality; and yet because we accept them as conventional ways of embodying conventionally accessible ideas, we do not focus our attention upon their ontological status. For example, we do not react importantly to the potentially fantastic elements in Veronese's *Mars and Venus United by Love* in large part because we recognize both that mythological figures are a Renaissance painterly convention and that this particular image provides the artist with a culturally accepted way to make a statement about the way that love and fertility prevent conflict. This example suggests that fantastic art, art which is created to be perceived as fantastic, works under the great difficulty of employing conventions relied upon by nonfantastic art, and yet it must in some crucial way appear as improbable or bizarre—in other words, as unconventional. Since the signals that artists use to inform the audience that a work is to be taken as fantastic themselves become conventions, they are always in danger of failing to achieve their intended effect, which is to stimulate in the reader that sense of wonder at encountering something delightfully or fearfully strange. One common response to this problem, which is made by artists as different as Caldecott (Plate 4), Griset (Plate 5), Potter, and Sime, is to emphasize the element of whimsy.

Subject is one of the devices which artists, like writers, employ to immerse us in a fantastic world, for when coming upon a picture of the lands of faerie (Plate 2) or *The Arabian Nights* (Plate 6), the land beyond the Looking Glass, or that inhabited by Kate Greenaway's children (Plate 7), we immediately recognize that we have left our normal, everyday reality and entered another imaginative cosmos. Similarly, an encounter with grotesque or anthropomorphic forms, which we do not expect to encounter in our waking life, signals us that the artist is working with the fantastic. George Tinworth's *Steeplechase*, Beatrix Potter's *The Day's News*, and Randolph Caldecott's *A Frog he would awooing go* (Plate 4) present us with images of animals engaged in human activities, while Walter Crane's *While Tulips lift the banner red* (Plate 8) and Arthur Rackham's *There's a whispering from tree to tree* (Plate 9) animate the inanimate vegetable world to create a fantastic effect.

Essentially, fantastic subjects, like anthropomorphic renderings of objects and animals, are devices of transformation, and both art and literature possess the capacity to use many such devices, the most powerful of which change our usual means of perception. Such informing distortion, which Ruskin took to be one of the chief effects of high imagination, can be produced in many ways. The artist can, for instance, show us his subject from an unusual physical vantage point, revealing a bizarre aspect of the reality we believe we already know. Although E. J. Detmold's illustrations for *Fabre's Book of Insects* are in one sense merely precise entomological studies, the fact that he presents his *Praying Mantis* and *Field Cricket* from a point more closely than the human eye usually perceives them, and hence in larger scale, produces the effect of the strange and exotic.

Part of Detmold's effect derives from the great precision, the uncanny sharpness of outline and detail, which his insects now transformed into bizarre monsters possess. As both Ruskin and Tennyson well knew, rendering objects in more precise detail than that with which they are normally perceived can produce an hallucinatory effect, for such precision changes our relations to our world. The photographs of Wynn Bullock proffer such a fantastic vision of a shimmering, unnaturally precise reality which we never perceive with our waking eyes, and early Pre-Raphaelite works, such as Millais' *Ophelia* and Hunt's *The Awakening Conscience*, similarly convey a realistic description so heightened as to border upon the fantastic. But although markedly increasing the precision and detail of our perceptions of otherwise prosaic matters can create the sensation of the fantastic, it is the transforming of usual perception, and not the detail itself, which is crucial, for the artist can work in the opposite manner, as does Detmold in his *Arabian Nights* illustrations (Plate 6), rendering objects within a dreamlike haze; or, again, like Ruskin, another master of visual detail, the artist can surround a more or less precisely outlined object, as he does in his *View of Amalfi*, and thus produce a powerful suggestion of strange, unnatural movement.

As these works by Detmold and Ruskin remind us, fantasy occasionally appears in unexpected ways in the art of the last century and a half; and while literary and visual fantasy have much in common, not all important fantastic art derives from narrative or dramatic literature. Nonetheless, most of the greatest creations of strange and wondrous worlds do appear as illustrations—as visualizations of verbal fantasy. Such illustrations include pictures both for contemporary work and for work written long before, such as *A Midsummer Night's Dream* and *The Arabian Nights*. Martin

Timlin, Rudyard Kipling, Edward Lear, W. Heath Robinson, and Walter Crane all illustrated their own writings, while wonderful pairings of contemporaries appear in Arthur Hughes's work for George MacDonald's fictions and Sir John Tenniel's justly famous illustrations for the *Alice* books.

In order to examine the characteristics of literary fantasy since 1850 in the most economical manner, I propose in the following pages to survey this Victorian and modern literary mode in terms of one work by each of five major authors—John Ruskin (1819–1900), George MacDonald (1824–1905), George Meredith (1828–1909), William Morris (1834–1896), and William Hope Hodgson (1875–1918). These five works, each of which represents a particular form of fantastic fiction, will enable us to perceive the defining characteristics of this literary form while also permitting us to observe what the verbal and visual arts in this mode have in common.

John Ruskin's *The King of the Golden River* exemplifies the literary fairy tale, a form which, like the literary ballad, imitates the anonymous products of popular or folk tradition. Ruskin's tale, which he wrote in 1841, two years before he began *Modern Painters,* tells of Hans and Schwartz, two selfish, evil brothers whose greed costs them their Edenic Treasure Valley and then their lives, and of the third brother, Gluck, whose generosity and self-sacrifice restore the valley's fertility. One cold winter evening when Gluck is minding the house, a fairy visitor arrives and demands entrance:

> It was the most extraordinary looking little gentleman he had ever seen in his life. He had a very large nose, slightly brass-coloured, and expanding towards its termination into a development not unlike the lower extremity of a key bugle; his cheeks were very round, and very red, and might have warranted a supposition that he had been blowing a refractory fire for the last eight-and-forty hours; his eyes twinkled merrily through long silky eyelashes, his moustaches curled twice round like a corkscrew on each side of his mouth, and his hair, of a curious mixed pepper-and-salt colour, descended far over his shoulders. He was about four-feet-six in height, and wore a conical pointed cap of nearly the same altitude, decorated with a black feather some three feet long. His doublet was prolonged behind into something resembling a violent exaggeration of what is now termed a "swallow tail,"

PLATE 1

Arthur Rackham (1867-1939): *When her husband saw her, he shouted, "Hi! come to me here."* From "The Young Giant" in *Little Brother and Little Sister and other tales* by the Brothers Grimm. Pen, ink, and watercolor, 7 3/16″ x 6″. Museum of Art, Rhode Island School of Design, Gift of Mrs. Gustav Radeke.

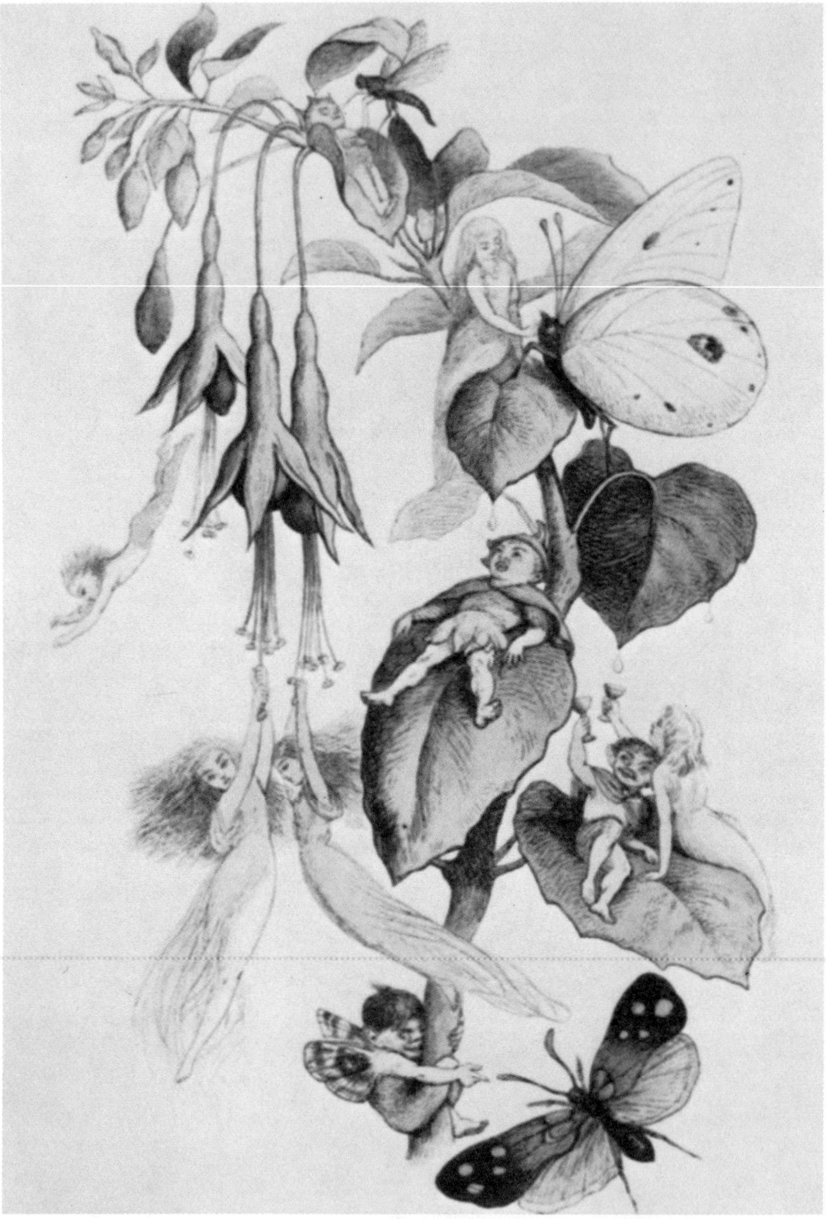

PLATE 2

Richard Doyle (1824-1883): *Feasting and fun among the fuchsias,* from *In Fairyland, A Series of Pictures from the Elf-World* (1870). Wood-engraved plate from bound volume, 8″ x 12″. Library of the Rhode Island School of Design, Bequest of Mrs. Henry G. Russell from the Library of Mrs. A. A. Ives.

PLATE 3

John Simmons (1832-1876): *The honey bugs steal from the humble bees,* Act III, Scene i, from *A Midsummer Night's Dream* (1866). Watercolor and bodycolor, 13½" x 10½" (arched top). City Museum & Art Gallery, Bristol.

PLATE 4

Randolph Caldecott (1846-1886): Dinner Scene from *A Frog he would a-wooing go* (1883). Pen, ink, and watercolor, 6⅜″ x 7¼″. By courtesy of the Victoria and Albert Museum.

PLATE 5

Ernest Henry Griset (1844-1907): *The Dream of the Fisherman*. Pen, ink, and watercolor, 6⅝″ x 10½″. By courtesy of the Victoria and Albert Museum.

PLATE 6

Edward Julius Detmold (1883-1957): *On this dome is a brazen horseman, mounted on a brazen horse* from "The Story of the Third Calendar" in *The Arabian Nights* (1922). Watercolor, 31″ x 22″. Robert Isaacson.

PLATE 7

Kate [Katherine] Greenaway (1846-1901): *Where waters gushed and fruit trees grew, and flowers put forth a fairer hue,* frontispiece to *The Pied Piper of Hamelin* by Robert Browning (1887). Pen, black ink, and watercolor, 8⅝" x 7⅝". The Pierpont Morgan Library, Gift of Mrs. George Nichols.

Plate 8

Walter Crane (1845-1915): *While Tulips lift the banner red* from *Flora's Feast: a Masque of Flowers* by Walter Crane (1889). Pen, ink, and watercolor, 8 1/16″ x 6″. Courtesy, Museum of Fine Arts, Boston, Gift of Mrs. John L. Gardner.

PLATE 9

Arthur Rackham (1867-1939): *There's a Whispering from Tree to Tree,* from *A Dish of Apples* by Eden Phillpots. Pen, ink, and watercolor, 15⅛″ x 10¼″. Photograph courtesy John Merriam.

> but was much obscured by the swelling folds of an enormous black, glossy-looking cloak, which must have been very much too long in calm weather, as the wind, whistling around the old house, carried it clear out from the wearer's shoulders to about four times his own length.[3]

When the cruel, avaricious brothers return home, they expectedly order their strange visitor, who turns out to be South West Wind Esquire, to leave. At the stroke of midnight, the brothers are awakened by a tremendous crash to discover that their room is flooded. "They could see in the midst of it an enormous foam globe, spinning round, and bobbing up and down like a cork, on which, as on a most luxurious cushion, reclined the little old gentleman, cap and all. There was plenty of room for it now, for the roof was off" (1.323). The morning light reveals that their precious valley, whose riches they never shared, has been transformed into a desert of red sand, and so, not having learned their lesson, they decamp for the nearest city where they set themselves up as cheating goldsmiths. Failing to prosper, they soon melt down all their hoarded gold until they have only Gluck's mug which an uncle had given the little boy. "The mug was a very odd mug to look at. The handle was formed of two wreaths of flowing golden hair, so finely spun that it looked more like silk than metal, and these wreaths descended into, and mixed with, a beard and whiskers of the same exquisite workmanship, which surrounded and decorated a very fierce little face, of the reddest gold imaginable, right in the front of the mug, with a pair of eyes in it which seemed to command its whole circumference" (1.326–27). Placing the mug in the melting pot, the brothers leave for the alehouse and instruct their younger brother to watch over the pot. While gazing out of a window at the desiccated remains of his beloved Treasure Valley, Gluck is astonished to hear the melted gold singing, and when on its orders he decants it, out jumps a golden dwarf a foot and a half high—the King of the Golden River, who had been enchanted by an evil spell. The grateful king thereupon rewards Gluck by telling him how to make his fortune: " 'Whoever shall climb to the top of that mountain from which you see the Golden River issue, and shall cast into the stream at its source three drops of holy water, for him, and for him only, the river shall turn to gold. But no one failing in his first, can succeed in a second attempt; and if any one shall cast unholy water into the river, it will overwhelm him, and he will become a black stone' " (1.331).

Predictably, the two brothers, who try to cheat each other, turn themselves into black stones, whereas Gluck, who gives his last holy water to an old man, a child, and a dog (all of whom turn out to be the dwarf king in magic guise), is rewarded again by the King of the Golden River with three drops of dew. When sprinkled on the source of the river, they transform the desert valley once again into an earthly paradise.

Although Ruskin uses the fairy tale to enforce the moral that selfishness is evil and destructive, its chief point is one central to his entire career as a critic of art and society—namely, as he put it in *Unto This Last* (1860), that "THERE IS NO WEALTH BUT LIFE. Life, including all its powers of love, of joy, and of admiration" (17.105). Nonetheless, his later statements about fantasy and imagination suggest that the understanding of these ideas is at most a secondary experience and not the primary one he intended. According to his lecture "Fairy Land" in *The Art of England* (1884), fantastic or fairy art is "the art which intends to address only childish imagination, and whose object is primarily to entertain with grace" (33.332). For him, such an aim is an extremely important one.

Ruskin has all too often been mistakenly thought to espouse a crude didacticism, in part because he advances so emphatically the notion that beginning artists should present visual truth. But, in fact, as he several times urges in *Modern Painters* and his other writings, the most valuable, most educational, most *moral* function of art is simply to be beautiful. He can take such an undidactic approach to the arts because his theories of beauty assume that beauty is a divinely intended pleasure the enjoyment of which is itself a moral and spiritual act. Similarly, when he writes of fairy literature and art for children, he opposes its vulgarization by didactic intent because he believes that exercising the young imagination is itself a most valuable purpose. Appropriately, Ruskin begins his lecture on fairy art by announcing that he will take on Dickens' Gradgrind, the archetypal utilitarian educator who wanted children to learn facts and suppress their imaginations. Like Dickens, Ruskin works within a moral and philosophical tradition which held that feeling and imagination play—and should play—crucial roles in moral decision; so that to develop the imagination is to develop a mature human mind. Ruskin therefore tells his audience that "it is quite an inexorable law of this poor human nature of ours, that in the development of its healthy infancy, it is put by Heaven under the absolute necessity of using its imagination as well as its lungs and its legs;—that it is forced to develop its power of invention, as a bird its feathers of flight" (33.329).

Although "Fairy Land" concerns itself largely with art and literature for children, his remarks decades before in *Modern Painters* make it abundantly clear that he conceives the fantastic imagination as one of the defining characteristics of humanity and its highest art. According to him, whereas the student artist and those of lesser imagination must concentrate upon topographical, realistic studies which store the mind with visual fact, the great artist, such as Turner, creates imaginative transformations of reality which most of his audience will receive as fantastic distortions—thus the need for criticism and for Ruskin to have begun *Modern Painters* in order to demonstrate to hostile critics that Turner's later visions of mist and fire were firmly based on reality. By creating such unusual and unexpected images of the world of matter and spirit, the great artist produces a work which enables us to perceive with his eyes and imagination. Each artist necessarily transforms the world according to the strengths and limitations of his own character, imagination, and age, and in the third volume of *Modern Painters* (1856), Ruskin endeavors to explain the various imaginative modes in which artists work. Purist art, for example, arises in the "unwillingness . . . to contemplate the various forms of definite evil which necessarily occur in . . . the world" (5.103–04). Artists, like Fra Angelico, "create for themselves an imaginary state, in which pain and imperfection either do not exist, or exist in some edgeless and enfeebled condition" (5.104). Turning to a lesser English example, he describes Thomas Stothard in terms strikingly like those with which he was later to describe Kate Greenaway (Plate 7):

> It seems as if Stothard could not conceive wickedness, coarseness, or baseness; every one of his figures looks as if it had been copied from some creature who had never harboured an unkind thought, or permitted itself an ignoble action. With this intense love of mental purity is joined, in Stothard, a love of mere physical smoothness and softness, so that he lived in a universe of soft grass and stainless fountains, tender trees, and stones at which no foot could stumble. (5.105)

Although such art can provide us some brief respite from the pains of this life, it is, finds Ruskin, essentially childish and incomplete.

A potentially higher art appears in the grotesque, which takes three forms. The central mode of the grotesque arises from the fact that the human imagination "in its mocking or playful moods . . . is apt to jest, sometimes bitterly, with under-current of sternest pathos, sometimes waywardly, sometimes slightly and wickedly, with death and sin; hence an enormous mass of grotesque art, some most noble and useful, as Holbein's *Dance of Death*, and Albrecht Dürer's *Knight, Death and the Devil*, going down gradually through various conditions of less and less seriousness into an art whose only end is that of mere excitement, or to amuse by terror" (5.131). In addition to this darker form of the grotesque, which includes work ranging from traditional religious images of death and the devil to satire and horrific art, there is a comparatively rare form which arises "from an entirely healthful and open play of the imagination, as in Shakespeare's Ariel and Titania, and in Scott's White Lady" (5.131). This delicate fairy art is so seldom achieved because "the moment we begin to contemplate sinless beauty we are apt to get serious; and moral fairy tales, and such other innocent work, are hardly ever truly, that is to say, naturally, imaginative; but for the most part laborious inductions and compositions. The moment any real vitality enters them, they are nearly sure to become satirical, or slightly gloomy, and so connect themselves with the evil-enjoying branch" (5.131–32).

The third form of the grotesque, which served as the basis for Ruskin's conception of a high art suited to the Victorian age, is the "thoroughly noble one . . . which arises out of the use or fancy of tangible signs to set forth an otherwise less expressible truth; including nearly the whole range of symbolical and allegorical art and poetry" (5.132). Ruskin's valuable perception that fantastic art and literature form part of a continuum which includes sublime, symbolic, grotesque, and satirical works is particularly useful to anyone interested in this mode, because fantastic art does, in fact, share much with satire and symbol, caricature and sublime. After all, much of the delight of Caldecott's courting frog (Plate 4), Griset's fisherman (Plate 5), and Rackham's witches arises in the way they caricature normal humanity, and similarly, when we receive pleasure from this last artist's wonderfully humanized trees (Plate 9), it is precisely because they are so human; because, in other words, they share so much of the human that they enable us to see ourselves better because we see ourselves in such guise.

Such delightful, and often unsettling presentation of aspects of our everyday reality in strange form is also a common feature of literary fantasy and appears in works as different as *Alice in Wonderland* and *Peter Pan in Kensington Gardens.* But the literary fantasy's primary method is to transform not single elements in our world but that entire world itself, thus immersing us in another reality whose laws are different, often disconcerting, and occasionally terrifying. George MacDonald's *Phantastes* (1858), which will serve as our second major example, takes as its province the world of fairyland. Although MacDonald's fairyland, like that of Lord Dunsany's *The King of Elfland's Daughter,* borrows many features from the fairy tale, this far more complex fictional world is essentially a new creation through which its inventor can explore adult themes.

MacDonald opens his tale in our world, but by the second chapter he has transformed it into a very strange place indeed. The morning after his twenty-first birthday, when the orphan Anodos has come into his estates, he is greeted by a tiny fairy-figure able to vary her size at will, who announces that she is his grandmother and that she has come to inform him that he is about to make a voyage to Fairy Land. Anodos, who does not even believe in Fairy Land, is astonished to awaken the next morning to

> the sound of running water near me; and, looking out of bed, I saw that a large green marble basin, in which I was wont to wash, and which stood on a low pedestal of the same material in a corner of my room, was overflowing like a spring; and that a stream of clear water was running over the carpet, all the length of the room, finding its outlet I knew not where. And, stranger still, where this carpet, which I had myself designed to imitate a field of grass and daisies, bordered the course of the little stream, the grass-blades and daisies seemed to wave in a tiny breeze that followed the water's flow; while under the rivulet they bent and swayed with every motion of the changeful current, as if they were about to dissolve with it, and, forsaking their fixed form, become fluent as the waters.
>
> My dressing-table was an old-fashioned piece of furniture of black oak, with drawers all down the front. These were elaborately carved in foliage, of which ivy formed the chief part. The nearer end of this table remained just as it had been, but on the further end a singular change had commenced. I happened to fix my eye on a little cluster of ivy-leaves. The first of these was evidently the work of the

> carver; the next looked curious; the third was unmistakably ivy; and just beyond it a tendril of clematis had twined itself about the gilt handle of one of the drawers. Hearing next a slight motion above me, I looked up, and saw that the branches and leaves designed upon the curtains of my bed were slightly in motion. Not knowing what change might follow next, I thought it high time to get up; and, springing from the bed, my bare feet alighted upon a cool green sward; and although I dressed in all haste, I found myself completing my toilet under the boughs of a great tree.[4]

This transformation of the main character's everyday reality into a far different one well exemplifies a central device of the literary fantasy.

Whereas the artist working with visual fantasy usually must place us immediately inside a fantastic kingdom, the creator of literary fantasy, who works with a narrative, sequential mode, has two choices. Like the artist he can open his work by immediately immersing us in his new world and such is the manner of proceeding adopted by William Morris in *The Water of the Wondrous Isles* and George Meredith in *The Shaving of Shagpat,* two works at which we shall soon look. The far more usual strategy is for the writer to employ some narrative device which displaces us from our everyday world into his created one. The most prosaic such device occurs in C. J. Cutliffe Hyne's *The Lost Continent* (1899), in which an adventurer discovers an ancient manuscript in a South American cave; when deciphered this manuscript turns out to contain the tale of Deucalion, the last survivor of Atlantis. A similar favorite device of this lost-world fiction so popular around 1900 is the discovery of a map which then leads the adventurous protagonists on a voyage of discovery which culminates in the fantastic world. In contrast, William Hope Hodgson's *The Night Land* (1912), William Morris' *The Dream of John Ball* (1888), and Lewis Carroll's *Alice* books (1865, 1871), use the device of the dream to move us into the fantastic realm, while the magic doorway or mirror, which appears in George MacDonald's *Lilith* (1895) and C. S. Lewis' Narnia books, is another effective means of transporting us to a fantastic world. Occasionally, as in *Through the Looking Glass,* an author may first employ a magical transformation and only later, at the story's end, reveal that the metamorphosis of reality actually occurred within a dream.

Since much of the fascination and delight which characterize the finest literary fantasies derive from their continual sharp contrast of fantastic and everyday existence, such devices of transformation are central to the form. Even Morris, who begins his narrative already within his imagined world, must find a means of displacing us from our usual conceptions of things, and so he employs a peculiar invented language and geography—a technique adopted by many subsequent authors—to insulate us from our world and its prosaic expectations. In the comparatively rare cases where the visual artist effects a transformation from our normal, prosaic world to his fantastic one within the picture itself he must similarly make use of formal devices. For example, in Rackham's *There's a whispering from tree to tree* (Plate 9) we perceive that the figures in the distance exist in a nonfantastic world, while the trees closest to the viewer become progressively more animated as they near the picture-plane. Rackham, in other words, has found a convincing means of showing how, as human beings withdraw from the forest, its hidden, fantastic life comes into being. To do so he has made use of devices of rational perspective to turn a potentially static image into a sequential, narrative one. Furthermore, by making the eye of the spectator effect this narrative or sequential progression, he has not only made him animate the picture himself but has also permitted him briefly to borrow the artist's vision and see, for a few moments, with his eyes.

Once we have entered the world of MacDonald's *Phantastes*, we soon discover that its laws, its principles of order, are completely different from those we know. As Anodos remarks, "it is no use trying to account for things in Fairy Land; and one who travels there soon learns to forget the very idea of doing so, and takes everything as it comes; like a child, who, being in a chronic condition of wonder, is surprised at nothing" (p. 33). In *Phantastes*, unlike more prosaic forms of fantastic fiction, such as that devoted to lost worlds, the principle of transformation continues to operate throughout the narrative, creating surprising incident and novel delight. Anodos finds a statue of a woman which springs to life; then he receives advice from an animated tree, finds a magic boat which takes him to a fairy palace, leaves it and finds himself in a wasteland, enters a cottage whose magic doors return him to his past, and so on. Such episodic narrative is entirely in keeping with the main drive of fantasy, which is to deny the primacy of our everyday laws of cause-and-effect.

Although *Phantastes* and similar works, such as David Lindsay's *A Voyage to Arcturus* (1920), deny the applicability of some of our basic facts of existence, these episodic plots are hardly random or chaotic, for as C. S. Lewis explains, "To construct plausible and moving 'other worlds,' you must draw on the only 'other world' we know, that of the spirit."[5] This fantastic world can take as many forms as the human spirit itself. For Lewis himself "the world of the spirit" is the world of Christian theology, and both his Perelandra and Narnia series, like MacDonald's *Lilith,* are allegorical embodiments of the Christian truths of redemption and spiritual growth. David Lindsay, who finds such belief irrelevent to human needs, presents an entirely different set of embodied human (and alien) possibilities. For Morris, also a secular thinker, the world of the spirit takes the form of an ideal of sexual and social development. In *Phantastes,* which relates Anodos' discovery of the moral truth that one cannot find oneself until one loses sight of oneself and one's desires, the spirit is largely moral, though imbued with theological overtones.

Following the German art fairy tale or *Märchen,* MacDonald employs a dream or dreamlike structure, revealing that to him the world of the spirit must be seen in terms of human psychology, the human inner world. In fact, a great many Victorian and later fantasies employ such dream structure, for the movement into the subjective world of the mind is the first step into fantasy. Essentially, there are two ways to claim that the world of everyday reality, the world of the realistic novel, is inadequate to human needs: the first is to claim that a higher world of religious or political ideas and ideals is more important, more relevant; while the second is to claim that the inner worlds of the human mind, its subjective experiences, have primary value. Lewis and MacDonald embody the first view; Kafka and Lovecraft the second.

Novel and fantasy touch upon each other in this matter of the inner world, and if one envisages a spectrum of fictions with the realistic novels of Eliot and Trollope at one end and the fantasies of MacDonald and Lindsay at the other, the novel of psychological realism occupies a middle position—and shares qualities of both. Thus, *Jane Eyre,* which purports to convey both the objective experiences and inner world of its orphan protagonist, has as much in common with the creations of MacDonald as it does with those of Thackeray, Trollope, and Gaskell. Modernist and later fiction which employs stream-of-consciousness and episodic, discontinuous structure often seems far closer to *Phantastes* than to *Middlemarch* or *The Way We Live Now.*

Although it is one of the most imaginative of fantastic tales in its rich incident, unexpected transformations, and completely imagined landscapes, *Phantastes* ends by returning us to this world. MacDonald chooses to have Anodos leave Fairy Land in part because the now wiser hero must learn to apply the lessons learned there in this world. An even more important reason is that excessive dwelling in the inner world is dangerous and destructive: *Phantastes,* which opens with an epigraph from Shelly's "Alastor," demonstrates that an excessive yearning for the ideals created by our imaginations can destroy the self and others, particularly when the self has a Pygmalionlike vision and attempts to possess another human being as a means of fulfillment. In contrast, some of the greatest authors of later fantasy, including H. P. Lovecraft, Clark Ashton Smith, and Lord Dunsany, have chosen the road MacDonald rejected and written of dreamworlds more "real" than the waking world. Whereas Hodgson and Morris use the dream as a way of entering a supposedly existent future world, whether it be hundreds or millions of years distant in time, these others have employed the dream as a way into an entirely subjective realm to which the power of desire gives a higher reality—though one which is almost always destructive and cruel.

MacDonald's *Phantastes,* which combines the worlds of the fairy tale and the *Märchen,* exemplifies one chief form of literary fantasy. Another major form is the exotic tale set in the magical universe of the *Arabian Nights,* and this form has always held great appeal for illustrators. Like Shakespeare's *The Tempest* and *A Midsummer Night's Dream, The Arabian Nights, or the Book of a Thousand and One Nights* has provided a great source of inspiration for artists including John Dickson Batten; Edward Julius Detmold (Plate 6); Edmund Dulac; Arthur Boyd Houghton; Henry Justice Ford; Charles, Tom, and William Heath Robinson; and Sir John Tenniel. Artists and writers conceive of this exotic realm as sensual, lush with heavy perfumes, strange vegetation, and bright intense colors—a world of fierce justice and bizarre adventure in which lamps contain djinns or genies and great risks can bring great success. The visual side of this fascination with the exotic, which is one of the important currents of European and British romanticism, appears not only in fantastic illustration but also in scenes of life in the Middle East painted by so many nineteenth-century artists, including W. J. Muller, David Roberts, J. F. Lewis, William Holman Hunt, Joseph Farquharson, and Andrew Geddes.

George Meredith's first work of extended fiction, *The Shaving of Shagpat* (1855), offers us a glimpse at the literary use of the exotic fantasy at its most delightful. Like Dulac, who later imitated the conventions of Persian, Chinese, and Japanese art for his illustrations, Meredith uses the exotic style known to readers of *The Arabian Nights* to displace us into his fantastic imagined world: "Now, the story of Shibli Bagarag, and of the ball he followed, and of the subterranean kingdom he came to, and of the enchanted palace he entered, and of the sleeping king he shaved, and of the two princesses he released, and of the Afrite held in subjection by the arts of one and bottled by her, is it not known as 'twere written on the finger-nails of men and traced in their corner-robes?"[6] This tale of a brave and adventurous, if vain, barber begins as a spoof of the genre, because it has such an unusual hero and even more unusual villain, who at first seems little more than an obese pile of black hair—"indeed a miracle of hairiness, black with hair as he had been muzzled with it, and his head as it were a berry in a bush by reason of it. . . . Now would he close an eye, or move two fingers, but of other motion made he none, yet the people gazed at him with eagerness" (pp. 8–9). Meredith turns this apparent parody of the adventure tale into a straightforward exotic fantasy when he reveals that Shibli's future wife, the good sorceress Noorna, had unwittingly created this apparently comical monster, who possesses strong supernatural powers, when she placed in Shagpat's scalp the magical hair of the Genie Karaz, from whom she was fleeing. To save the world, which is increasingly coming under Shagpat's power of illusion, Shibli must pass repeated tests, obtain a magic sword, and destroy the source of evil magic.

Like the art and poetry of Beardsley (and like Wallace Stevens in "The Comedian as the Letter C"), Meredith employs the barber as a grotesque figure of the artist in a fallen world—a man who attempts to establish order and beauty which time and nature continually destroy. In Meredith this conception of the artist —for Shibli, like his creator, is a teller of tales—is treated only half-seriously. Meredith similarly handles and much qualifies traditional notions of adventure, heroism, and masculine strength. As the clear-sighted Noorna tells her father, the good Vizier Feshnavat, "there is all in this youth . . . that's desirable for the undertaking. . . . 'Tis clear that vanity will trip him, but honesty is a strong upholder; and he is one that hath the spirit of enterprise and the mask of dissimulation" (p. 95). In this most unpuritanic, un-English, un-Victorian world, dissimulation is a virtue, for Meredith has caught the tone of all great adventurers who descend from Odysseus to entertain us with cunning and resourcefulness. But despite the fact that Shibli is well aware of the dangers of vanity, he continually succumbs to it and is victorious only because Noorna scolds and rescues him until he is finally able to rescue her in turn. Like MacDonald's almost exactly contemporaneous *Phantastes, The Shaving of Shagpat* uses its fantastic events to present serious themes of human illusion, the dangers of pride, and the nature of true heroic action. In fact, its guiding ideas much resemble those of the usual nineteenth-century *Bildungsroman,* but unlike the realistic novel of growth and self-discovery, *Shagpat* does not dramatize major changes in the main character. We are warned against his immature vanity, we see its dangerous effects, and we see him conquer it, but as we close the covers of the book, we do not find Shibli, the barber turned monarch, essentially changed. We wonder what would happen to him without Noorna and hope she will never be far from his side.

As delightfully as Meredith enacts these serious themes, which incidentally also inspired his far different novels of high comedy, he most impresses us with his depiction of magical weapons and an underground world. Escaping the wiles of the evil sorceress Rabesqurat by means of a lily rooted in a living heart, Shibli enters the underground lands and begins a series of tests which gain him the magic sword he needs to destroy Shagpat. He strikes a magic door

> and discovered an opening into a strange dusky land, as it seemed a valley, on one side of which was a ragged copper sun setting low, large as a warrior's battered shield, giving deep red lights to a brook that fell, and over a flat stream a red reflection, and to the sides of the hills a dark red glow. The sky was a brown colour; the earth a deeper brown, like the skins of tawny lions. Trees with reddened stems stood about the valley, scattered and in groups, showing between their leaves the cheeks of melancholy fruits swarthily tinged, and toward the centre of the valley a shining palace was visible, supported by massive columns of marble reddened by that copper sun. (p. 177)

Entering the palace, Shibli survives a series of tests characteristic of the romance to gain the magic sword at last. The book closes after his triumphant battle against Shagpat, the Genie Karaz, and the evil sorceress Rabesqurat, who rely upon magical weapons and strange transformations. *The Shaving of Shagpat* is thus an important nineteenth-century precursor of the so-called "Sword-and-Sorcery" school of fantasy literature. This form, which was inspired largely by Lord Dunsany in his "The Fortress Unvanquishable, Save for Sacnoth" and similar writings, combined the ancient materials of *The Arabian Nights* with chivalric legend and dragonlore of the North. In the twentieth century this kind of fantasy became a mainstay of pulp magazines and, like space operas with science fiction, did much to lower the reputation of fantasy as a serious form. These elements have been developed far more successfully in recent decades by J. R. R. Tolkien and the Americans Ursula K. Le Guin and Anne McCaffrey.

Ruskin and MacDonald have guided us into the fantasy world of Fairy Land, and Meredith has shown us the universe of the exotic fantasy. An historically more important imaginative cosmos appears in the prose romances of William Morris. According to Lin Carter, the author of fantasy literature whose paperback editions of the masters of this mode have done so much to popularize it in America, Morris is the true creator of heroic fantasy:

> Oriental tales like *Vathek* and *The Shaving of Shagpat* are set—not in completely imaginary worlds of their authors' invention, as are the romances of William Morris—but in "literary" versions of the actual Middle East. . . . No one ever tried to write another *Vathek* or *Shagpat*, and only a few books (such as the *Perelandra* trilogy of C. S. Lewis and David Lindsay's brilliant and astounding novel *A Voyage to Arcturus*) show to any extent the influence of *Lilith* and *Phantastes*. But the genre of heroic fantasy laid in an imaginary world descends from William Morris to Lord Dunsany and E. R. Eddison, and from thence to whole generations of writers such as James Branch Cabell, Fletcher Pratt (*The Blue Star*), Robert E. Howard, J. R. R. Tolkien, L. Sprague de Camp (*The Tritonian Ring* and *The Goblin Tower*), Fritz Leiber, Jack Vance, Jane Gaskell, [and] Lloyd Alexander. . . . From the world of the Wood and the world of the Well descend all the later worlds of fantastic fiction, Poictesme and Oz and Tormance, Barsoom and Narnia and Zothique, Gormenghast and Zimiamvia and Middle-Earth.[7]

Writers in the twentieth century have advanced farther down the road towards imagining alternate universes, for increasingly they have attempted, like de Camp, to people their worlds with new sentient creatures, societies, and entire congeries of legend, religion, and culture. Such movements of fantasy literature into the realm of speculative anthropology and theology make it clear that fantasy and romance create their imagined worlds as a means of exploring this one. It is important to emphasize once more the essential seriousness and potential humanistic contributions of such genres, since until recently their claims have been consistently scanted by academic critics and other advocates of "high" culture.

Similarly, students of Morris and Victorian culture have in general failed to see in his great prose romances anything more than escapist fiction. Although the obvious connections between his political beliefs and the propagandistic *A Dream of John Ball* (1888) and *News from Nowhere* (1891) have long been perceived, the equally important relation between these beliefs and the prose romances have not. One importance of the imagined world in *The Water of the Wondrous Isles* and similar writings is that it permits Morris to solve a basic problem confronting an author of political fiction—the problem of how to represent life in an ideal society which, by definition, does not exist under present conditions. The difficulty of dramatizing a positive political program is very great, and most successful political novels in fact take the form of satire or of a quasi-journalistic exposé of existing abuses. In contrast, Morris' romances take the more daring approach of creating the image of a better world for which man can strive. *A Dream of John Ball* is set in the fourteenth century and *News from Nowhere* takes place in the near future. In contrast, *The House of the Wolfings* (1888) and *The Roots of the Mountains* (1889) take place at that historical moment when Roman armies came into conflict with German tribal society, and although these works have major fantastic elements, their worlds are still largely historical reconstructions. Only with the great allegorical romances, *The Well at the World's End* (1896) and *The Water of the Wondrous Isles* (1897), does he bring to fruition his search for an ideal world in which to dramatize the problems of self and society which he had begun with his first prose fiction, *The Wood Beyond the World* (1894).

The Water of the Wondrous Isles, one of the finest as well as the most unusual of fantasies, well represents Morris' contribution to the genre. It is the tale of a young girl, Birdalone, who was kidnapped by a witch and raised in isolation. She escapes from her captor in the witch's magic Sending Boat and voyages to the Castle of the Quest by way of a series of fantastic islands. At the castle she falls in love with one of the knights, flees from him after she causes the death of another knight, and goes to live and work in a city. At last, she recognizes her duties to self, lover, and society, and she rescues her Arthur. As Barbara J. Bono, author of the most important study of Morris' fiction, points out:

> Birdalone's sojourn in and around the Water of the Wondrous Isles forms an extended allegory of sexual maturation. Her journey away from the Castle of the Quest to the City of the Five Crafts reverses this pattern as she gains experience of the world of societal relations. In her first journey across the lake she encounters many emblems of the destructive extremes of pure femaleness and pure maleness, beginning with the two offshore islets, Green Eyot and Rocky Eyot, and continued and developed in much more grotesque form in the isles of her later journey. If the witch's Isle of Increase Unsought is a Bower of Bliss of extreme female sensuality, the Isle of Nothing is the reductive expression of male sterility, while neither the lush beauty of the Isle of Queens nor the fierce stoniness of the Isle of Kings prevents these places from being essentially dead. . . . After Birdalone's journey across the water she has both the nature-derived power and the experience of sexual awakening which will enable her to love.[8]

She must now learn the proper social context for her love, Bono adds, and the second half of the book is occupied with this social education, which "culminates in Birdalone and Arthur's decisions to leave their idyll of love to be reunited with their friends." Although Morris always presents nature as the source of his characters' strength, he emphasizes that such strength can only be developed and fulfilled within a community of other human beings.

Like Rossetti and Burne-Jones, Morris creates an ideal quasi-medieval fantasy world whose keynote is a spiritualized eroticism. Dante Gabriel Rossetti, who early came under the spell of chivalric romance and Dante's *Vita Nuova,* set the tone for many of his associates when he placed his pensive, yearning lovers within medieval settings. In his early works Burne-Jones eagerly followed him into this fantasy world of passionate love and heroic rescues with *Clerk Saunders* (1861), *Iseult on the Ship* (1857), *The Knight's Farewell* (1858), and *Sir Galahad* (1858). Such Pre-Raphaelite visions of idealized romantic love in a medieval setting had an enormous influence on English Victorian fine and decorative arts. Painters as different as John William Waterhouse, J. R. Spencer Stanhope, John Melhuish Strudwick, and Walter Crane continued to paint in this mode for more than a half century after Rossetti began it, and its influence upon the decorative arts was as equally long-lived and interesting. The close association of this idealized medieval fantasy world and Pre-Raphaelite conceptions of ideal love had a particularly important effect on the decorative arts, for they gave a major impetus to the attempt by Morris and his associates to create a complete, aesthetically satisfying environment. They not only wanted to create well-designed implements and total settings for a full, humane existence, but they also wished to use them to transform their own living space into miniature fantasy worlds. The Victoria and Albert's *Saint George* Cabinet (1861), designed by Webb with scenes painted by Morris himself, and The *King René of Anjou's Honeymoon* Cabinet, designed by Seddon and decorated by Rossetti, Burne-Jones, Brown, and Prinsep for Morris, Marshall, Faulkner and Co., exemplify such use of Pre-Raphaelite themes to fantasize the implements of dairy life.

Nonetheless, although Morris resembles other members of the Pre-Raphaelite movement when he makes romantic love in a quasi-medieval setting central to his prose romances, his characterization of Birdalone as a heroic, active, sensual young woman sounds an entirely new note. Both the early Pre-Raphaelite Brotherhood and the later aesthetic Pre-Raphaelitism, which evolved under Rossetti's direction and influence, depicted love from the male point of view. As a result, both earlier and later forms of Pre-Raphaelitism tend to present a particularly masculine conception of woman. Their peculiarly Victorian notion of female nature conceives of it dividing quite sharply into two diametrically opposed categories—the active Lilith figure who devours men, and the passive, pensive maiden who waits for a man to awaken or complete her partially formed nature. The active woman, of whom Victorian men seemed so fearful, appears as Rossetti's *Lady Lilith* and *Astarte Syriaca* and as Swinburne's Delores and his Venus in "Laus Veneris." This conception of the fatal, devouring woman, which so inspired illustrators such as Aubrey Beardsley and Alastair, plays a comparatively minor role in Pre-Raphaelite work. Far more important is the other more central conception of woman as a passive, contemplative creature awaiting the lover for awakening, salvation, or even creation. Many of the most important paintings of the early Brotherhood form a series on the theme of romantic love and its frequently tragic aftermath: Millais' *The Woodsman's Daughter* (1851), which is an illustration of Patmore's poem on the unrequited love of a young country girl for a squire's son, presents the first act of a drama which ends with the seduced girl's death, while his *Mariana* (1851) presents a young woman from Tennyson's poem awaiting her lover who does not arrive. The paintings by Hunt and Millais of *The Eve of St. Agnes* (1848, 1863) follow Keats's poem in depicting a successful close to a tale of romantic love, while Millais' *Lorenzo and Isabella* (1849) and Hunt's *Isabella and the Pot of Basil* (1867) illustrate another poem by this poet which ends tragically. Hunt's *The Pilgrim's Return* (1847) and his illustration to Tennyson's "The Ballad of Oriana" (1857) represent the lover mourning over his dead beloved, but the most famous example of the "dead woman" theme is, of course, Millais' *Ophelia* (1851), though Arthur Hughes and many other artists and sculptors attempted the same subject.

Whereas these early works in the Pre-Raphaelite hard-edge style present a precise historically locatable world in sharp outline and bright colors, Burne-Jones' paintings, which represent the high point of the aesthetic Pre-Raphaelitism that descends from Rossetti, set their figures in a sensual, penumbral world. A large proportion of Burne-Jones' major works concern themselves with embodying his fascination, almost obsession, with the relations of men and women. Taken together, these works comprise a sexual myth that had great appeal for the artist and his contemporaries. *St. George and the Dragon* (1868), *Cupid Delivering Psyche* (c.1871), and the *Perseus* series (1875–1888), like Rossetti's "The Wedding of St. George and the Princess Sabra" (1857), present various stages in the dominant male's rescue of the helpless maiden. Similarly, in *The Briar Rose* series (1870–1890) the heroic prince pierces the forbidding enchanted thicket in order to awaken this sleeping beauty, thus restoring her and her entire world to life. *King Cophetua and the Beggar Maid* (1880), which appropriately repeats the disposition of figures employed in his *Annunciation* (1876–1879), depicts a powerful male character essentially creating his beloved—a subject Burne-Jones rendered most elaborately in the *Pygmalion* series (1868–1870), a work which can stand as the type of his sexual myth. Here the young man literally creates his own ideal beloved and is blessed when Venus vivifies her—a Victorian dream come true! MacDonald's Anodos learns all too painfully that such attempts to discover, capture, and possess one's ideal in another person are a self-destructive form of aggression. The Pre-Raphaelites, on the other hand, tended to see this as the ideal form of romantic love—and as one attainable both in art and life. As is well known, members and associates of the Pre-Raphaelite circle married relatively uncultured and even illiterate young women whom they then sought to remake according to a desired image. Although Holman Hunt ultimately failed to be either Cophetua or Pygmalion to Annie Miller, Brown, Rossetti, and Morris married their young women.

Many of Burne-Jones' major depictions of this sexual fantasy derive from Morris' own *Earthly Paradise,* for which they began as illustrations, and it is certainly tempting to see Morris' radically different women of the late prose romances as his mature reaction against the results of attempting to embody such attitudes in real life. At any rate, Birdalone is a development of Pre-Raphaelite conceptions of idealized womanhood which move far beyond the all-too-Victorian world of erotic reverie created by his friends and associates. Although Birdalone shares the innocent beauty and grace, as well as the rich inner life of the Pre-Raphaelite heroine, she is a strong, active figure who not only shapes her own destiny but who also rescues her beloved and restores him to self, sanity, and civilization.

In contrast to Morris' progressive use of the fantasy, William Hope Hodgson, whose *The Night Land* (1912) exemplifies the darker or horrific form of this mode, uses it to embody reactionary social and sexual belief. His vision of a sunless earth millions of years in the future inhabited by Boschian monsters and fearsome spiritual and physical horror clearly is the product of that major cultural anxiety which John A. Lester, Jr. has analyzed in *Journey Through Despair, 1880–1914.*[9] Hodgson's vision of "the Last Redoubt—that great Pyramid of grey metal which held the last millions of this world from the power of the Slayers"[10] well expresses the attitudes of those many thinkers who feared that Western civilization was drawing to a close.

Hodgson relates his bizarre tale of the dark future in an archaic, almost Morrisian diction, which serves, like that of his predecessor, to displace the reader into his imaginative world. The unnamed teller of the tale is an English landowner of some unspecified but pre-modern age who grieves for his dead wife, Mirdath the Beautiful. He discovers that "at night in my sleep [I] waked into the future of this world, and [have] seen strange things and utter marvels. . . . In this last time of my visions, of which I would tell, it was not as if I *dreamed*; but, as it were, that I *waked* into the dark, in the future of this world. And the sun had died" (p. 34). The narrator, who preserves a memory of his earlier identity, discovers that he is a telepathically gifted youth trained to help preserve the great Redoubt. The burden of the tale, which follows the pattern of medieval romance, takes the form of the young man's perilous adventures in the Night Land to save a telepathic girl from the Lesser Refuge, a smaller redoubt of which all knowledge had been lost for thousands of years until the hero makes mental contact with it. The young woman, Naani, discovers herself to be the reincarnation of Mirdath, and so the two lovers are reunited after millions of years—but first they must make the journey to safety, crawling for days through total darkness, avoiding giants, ab-humans, enormous spiders, and a spiritual evil which is far more terrifying than these physical dangers. Hodgson's archaic and often repulsive ideas of the ideal relations between man and woman are appropriate to a work derived from chivalric romance, but his disturbing mixture of chivalric devotion and brutality—he obviously takes great pleasure in having the hero physically punish his beloved—adds a bizarre dimension to an already strange work. The weird love interludes which punctuate the return journey nonetheless do serve as effective counterpoints to the characters' horrific adventures, the imagination of which provides the main appeal of *The Night Land.*

Introducing us to this nightmarish future, the protagonist explains that the monstrously evil beings surrounding the Great Redoubt had their origin in the

> Days of the Darkening (which I might liken to a story which was believed doubtfully, much as we of this day believe the story of the Creation). A dim record there was of olden sciences (that are as yet far off in *our* future) which, disturbing the unmeasurable Outward Powers, had allow [sic] to pass the Barrier of Life some of these Monsters and Ab-human creatures. . . . And thus there had materialised, and in other cases developed, grotesque and horrible Creatures, which

> now beset the humans of this world. And where there was no power to take on material form, there had been allowed to certain dreadful Forces to have power to affect the life of the human spirit. . . . As that Eternal Night lengthened itself upon the world, the power of terror grew and strengthened. (pp. 44, 46)

Like the American H. P. Lovecraft, whose work also was often marred by repetition, stilted writing, and reactionary ideas, Hodgson's great gift was the ability to communicate this "power of terror." Both in *The Night Land* and *The Boats of the "Glen Carrig"* (1907), a tale of men shipwrecked on a monstrous island, he embodies all the fears that haunt men sleeping and waking—fears of dissolution, loss of identity, and helplessness in the presence of hideous evil.

Horror fiction takes two basic forms, the most popular of which is the horror or ghost story which reveals the presence of often unexpected terrors within a realistically conceived world. Edgar Allan Poe, Sheridan Le Fanu, Algernon Blackwood, Charles Dickens, Arthur Machen, and many authors of recent years have excelled in writing this sensational cousin to the realistic novel. Frequently, the narrator or main character is a skeptical, even unimaginative person who, by the tale's end, is either convinced of the existence of fantastic horror breaking into his everyday world or punished for his skepticism by it. In contrast, the horrific fantasy—like the allegorical romances of Morris—takes place in either a fully created world or so emphasizes the hidden presence of such a world bordering on our own (or lying beneath it) that it subsumes the everyday world with which it began. Hodgson's books, Mervyn Peake's "Boy in Darkness," and Lovecraft's many tales exemplify such worlds of terrifying fantasy.

The evil which provides the horror in both forms of fiction—horror story and horrific fantasy—appears in a limited number of forms. First, there is the common use of Satanism and witchcraft, which obviously relies heavily on a Judaeo-Christian conception of evil that often receives a distinctly Manichean twist: the presence of Satanic evil in such overwhelming form makes the devil appear another deity of potency equal to God. Medieval grotesques, medieval and later representations of temptations and the Last Judgment, and the work of Bosch, Brueghel, and their imitators have provided powerful inspiration for artists and writers who work in this fantastic mode. In the period since 1850 it appears in illustration both in seriously horrific forms and in the more whimsical creations of Rackham's witches and Sime's "Devil with a Coal Scuttle." A second, closely-related source of evil, which presents the continued existence of older, all-but-forgotten divinities and forces, derives from classical and Northern mythology and the darker side of fairy lore. Arthur Machen's "The Lost Brother" (from *The Three Imposters,* 1890) and Lovecraft's "The Dunwich Horror" exemplify the use in horrific fantasy of these dangerous, destructive, and often hideously cruel forces which remain outside the Judaeo-Christian scheme of things, while Sime's drawings for *The Fantasy of Life* (1901) represent their appearance in fantastic art.

The third source of horror, which occasionally combines with the previous two, derives from man's fear of formlessness, chaos, and devolution. Machen's "Novel of the White Powder" (1901), Lovecraft's "The Dunwich Horror," and the giant slugs and other creatures of *The Night Land* draw upon both our normal antipathy to slimy, decaying substances and our instinctive revulsion at the way death and dissolution reduce living form to shapelessness. As Barton L. St. Armand has pointed out in his study of Lovecraft, the American writer's use of such horrifying dissolution, which use embodies his existential nausea and fear of universal corruption, derives largely from the classical example of such an image—Poe's "The Facts in the Case of M. Valdemar."[11] At the conclusion of Poe's tale, Valdemar, who had been hypnotized at the point of death, is awakened from his trance and "his whole frame— within the space of a single minute, or even less, shrunk—crumbled—absolutely *rotted* away beneath my hands. Upon the bed, before the whole company, there lay a nearly liquid mass of loathsome—of detestable putrescence."[12] In Harry Clark's wonderfully grisly illustration of this passage, the onlookers recoil in horror at the disintegrating body, from which part of an arm has detached itself and from whose eyes and mouth blood and gore run.

Although Hodgson's *The Night Land* relies frequently on such horrific sensationalism, it is equally concerned with emphasizing the ability to endure this horror possessed "by that lonely and mighty hill of humanity, facing its end—so near the Eternal, and yet so far deferred in the minds and to the senses of those humans. And thus it hath been ever" (p. 46). Hodgson frequently attempts to show that his nightmarish cosmos has a serious general significance, that it is relevant to human experience throughout the ages. His remarks about evolution, science, and spirituality suggest that he took these points quite seriously and they are not, as is often the case in such stories, merely attempts to establish the credibility of a fictional world. The miraculous intervention of a good divinity in this Manichean world at points when the hero has otherwise no chance of survival further suggests that Hodgson believed that if man strove heroically to preserve love and humanity against the forces of evil, he might expect to be rewarded by supernatural aid which, while it might not bring him final victory, would allow him to battle on equal terms.

In fact, all the examples of fantasy at which we have looked turn out to be vehicles by which their authors dramatize ideas of high seriousness rather than mere escapist fictions. The essential seriousness of much fine fantastic literature in the nineteenth and early twentieth centuries appears nowhere more clearly than in works such as Charles Kingsley's *The Water-Babies* (1863) and George MacDonald's "The Golden Key" and *At the Back of the North Wind* (1871), which employ the great potential of fantasy as a literary mode to convey Christian ideas of the afterlife. *At the Back of the North Wind,* for instance, relates how a young boy has magical adventures in the company of the mysterious North Wind who we gradually come to realize is Death itself. In the nineteenth century, when diseases carried away many children before they reached their teens, sermons, tracts, and fiction often sought to console parents and prepare children for an early death by removing its terrors. Fantasy is far better suited than the tract or sermon to convey the essentially paradoxical notion that earthly life (which is but a preparation for a higher, fuller eternal life) is a form of death, while death (which at first seems so fearful) is the only means to true life. In the Gospels Christ tells His disciples that a seed can only bear fruit if it dies—if it loses its initial state and develops into another. The Christian lives with this paradox and must learn to redefine death, ultimately finding in it a new, higher, and essentially fantastic meaning. Since the central principle of literary and visual fantasy is precisely such shifting of basic laws or meanings by which we experience the world, this artistic mode is well suited to embodying views which deny that everyday reality, the here and now, is either all-important or the only form of reality.

As the various works at which we have looked suggest, fantasy in fact comprises a second great tradition of English fiction. Even the Marxist critic Arnold Kettle, who despises the romance as the escapist fictions of a ruling class, recognizes that "all art is, in an important sense, an escape.... There is a sense in which the capacity to escape from his present experience ... is man's greatest and distinguishing ability.... This fantastic quality of art, that it takes us out of the real world so that, as Shelley put it, it 'awakens and enlarges the mind itself by rendering it the receptacle of a thousand unapprehended combinations of thought,' this quality is not a trivial or accidental by-product but the very essence of the value of art. If art did in fact—as the ultra-naturalistic school tends to assume—merely paint a picture of what is, it would be a much less valuable form of human activity, for it would not alter men's consciousness but merely confirm it."[13] Kettle's important recognition of the essential value of escape or withdrawal from everyday life and its assumptions is developed independently by Morse Peckham into a compelling theory of the arts. According to his *Man's Rage for Chaos: Biology, Behavior, and the Arts*, the arts are "an adaptational mechanism" which acts as a "rehearsal for those real situations in which it is vital for our survival to endure cognitive tension, to refuse the comforts of validation ... when such validation is inappropriate because too vital interests are at stake; art is the reinforcement of the capacity to endure disorientation so that a real and significant problem may emerge. Art is the exposure to the tensions and problems of a false world so that man may endure exposing himself to the tensions and problems of the real world."[14] Although neither Kettle nor Peckham concerns himself with fantastic literature and art, it seems probable that the strange worlds of such paintings and fictions have an equal if not greater capacity to return us to everyday life with our imaginations exercised and strengthened as do works of the realistic schools. Fantasy's essential abilities to entertain, instruct, and exercise the mind and spirit make it, in short, a major mode and one well worth serious, if delighted, attention.

NOTES

1. Richard Chase, *The American Novel and Its Tradition* (Garden City, N.Y.: Anchor/Doubleday, 1957), pp. 12–13.
2. Eric S. Rabkin, *The Fantastic in Literature* (Princeton: Princeton University Press, 1976), p. 37.

3. John Ruskin, *Works* (The Library Edition), eds. E. T. Cook and Alexander Wedderburn, 39 vols. (London: George Allen, 1903–1912), I, 316. Hereafter cited in the text by volume and page.

4. George MacDonald, *Phantastes* (Grand Rapids, Mich.: Eerdmans, 1964), pp. 19–20. Hereafter cited in the text.

5. C. S. Lewis, "On Stories," in *Of Other Worlds: Essays and Stories*, ed. Walter Hooper (New York: Harvest, 1975), p. 12.

6. George Meredith, *The Shaving of Shagpat* (New York: Ballantine, 1970), p. 1. Hereafter cited in the text.

7. Lin Carter, "About *The Well at the World's End* and William Morris," in *The Well at the World's End*, 2 vols. (New York: Ballantine, 1970), I, x–xi; II, [iii].

8. Barbara J. Bono, "The Prose Fictions of William Morris: A Study in the Literary Aesthetic of a Victorian Social Reformer," *Victorian Poetry*, 13, no. 3–4 (1975), 52.

9. John A. Lester, Jr., *Journey Through Despair, 1880–1914* (Princeton: Princeton University Press, 1968). See also Samuel Hynes, *The Edwardian Turn of Mind* (Princeton: Princeton University Press, 1968).

10. William Hope Hodgson, *The Night Land* (Westport, Conn.: Hyperion, 1976), p. 34. Hereafter cited in the text.

11. Barton L. St. Armand, *The Roots of Horror in the Fiction of H. P. Lovecraft* (Elizabethtown, N.Y.: Dragon Press, 1977), pp. 59–77.

12. Edgar Allan Poe, *The Complete Tales and Poems* (New York: Modern Library, 1938), p. 103.

13. Arnold Kettle, *An Introduction to the English Novel*, 2nd ed. (London: Hutchinson, 1967), I, 31.

14. Morse Peckham, *Man's Rage for Chaos: Biology, Behavior, and the Arts* (New York: Schocken, 1967), p. 314.

Fantastic Visions: Illustration of the *Arabian Nights*

Terry Reece Hackford

British illustrations of the *Arabian Nights* lead one directly to fundamental questions about the nature of the fantastic in the visual arts. In particular, the illustrations of this extremely popular fantasy text reveal the specific pictorial means by which the artist renders the intangible tangible and also permit us to understand how these pictorial methods relate to those conventions used to depict the world realistically.[1]

Scheherazade, that true enchantress, weaves her tales in *One Thousand and One Nights* each into the next to create a fantasy world of extraordinary breadth and complexity. The *Arabian Nights* coalesce into a vast but self-enclosed realm subject to the laws of an alien culture and of magic, an exotic world filled with caliphs and kings, demons of every description, and unearthly settings, which has held sway over the Western imagination from the moment the tales were first introduced to Europe in the early eighteenth century.[2] In England especially, the tales enjoyed immense popularity, giving rise to a multitude of British illustrated editions of the text; between 1800 and 1915 (to choose arbitrary guidelines) over forty different British illustrators interpreted the text, and of these editions the most popular were repeatedly reissued.

Moreover, this infatuation with the *Arabian Nights*, which influenced numerous other facets of British nineteenth-century culture, reveals the preoccupation with fantasy characteristic of the period as a whole. The fairy-tale text became a source of inspiration to poets, novelists, and artists. The oriental rhapsody (exemplified in the heated fantasies of William Beckford's *Vathek*) emerged as a form of literary genre modelled upon the *Nights*.[3] Tennyson, in his "Recollections of the Arabian Nights" (1830), paid tribute to the magical reverie of his first encounter with this exotic world. Frederick Lord Leighton, President of the Royal Academy between 1878 and 1896, realized an architectural fantasy out of the *Arabian Nights* when he built Arab Hall, a domed pavilion adorned with Eastern tiles and a murmuring fountain that he annexed to his Kensington home.[4] Individual tales, especially the favorite ones like Sindbad and Ali Baba, had appeared in crude chapbook form back in the early eighteenth century, and by the mid-nineteenth century, plays featuring these characters drew audiences in Drury Lane.[5] Thus the exotic realm of the *Arabian Nights* manifested itself in many guises in England during the nineteenth century, manifestations that can often be traced in turn back to the many different illustrated editions of the tales that gave visual form to this fantasy world.

Here I will be concerned with the work of four illustrators of *Arabian Nights* editions ranging in date from 1865 to 1915: Arthur Boyd Houghton, John D. Batten, Henry J. Ford, and Edmund Dulac. Formal analysis of the designs of these artists—a serious approach too often denied to the art of illustration—reveals that despite the variety of styles and processes used, one crucial characteristic of fantasy art emerges. The persuasive fantasy image—be it the cave of the forty thieves, a roc in flight, or the stone king of the Ebony Isles—depends in a complex manner upon the artistic conventions and semiotic codes associated with realism. The fantasy illustrator takes the pictorial conventions of realistic portrayal and then manipulates or inverts them to create marvelous worlds for which there can be no earthly analogy.

The period between 1855 and 1870 in England saw an unprecedented surge in both the quantity and the quality of book illustration. The enlarged reading public eagerly absorbed an influx of new periodicals, newspapers, and novels, the latter often in serialized form. Illustrations played a primary role in enhancing the appeal of this mass of printed material, and a generation of talented artists tried their hands at the popular art form. Many artists found illustration to be a source of steady support when their academic pursuits flagged; some found it genuinely more congenial than other media. These factors converged to create the golden age of British illustration known as "the Sixties."[6]

To keep pace with the acceleration of the commercial market, wood engraving, which was much faster and more efficient than copper engraving, became the preferred printing method. The illustrator would turn his design over to a professional engraver, who then cut it into a wood block; the finer the engraver, the more adeptly he could render the nuances of texture and each artist's line.[7] An impressive amount of the best illustration of the period was produced by one firm of wood engravers, the brothers Dalziel, who were artisans of unusual sensitivity and enterprise. They did not limit themselves to cutting blocks, but ventured into publishing, deciding in the early 1860s to make their London debut by publishing a series of popular works.[8] The send-off for the series, carefully calculated to win them an audience, was the *Dalziels' Illustrated Arabian Nights' Entertainments*.[9]

This book was contrived, quite deliberately, to serve as a showplace for the plentiful full and half-page illustrations. No single illustrator provided the drawings, but a cluster of artists ranging from established figures like Sir John Everett Millais and Sir John Tenniel, to inexperienced artists whom the Dalziels encouraged. Among this second group was the artist Arthur Boyd Houghton (1836–1875).[10] Ultimately, the success of the *Dalziels' Illustrated Arabian Nights* rests on the outstanding quality of the illustrations which Houghton contributed. The fantastic content apparently liberated him, for these illustrations far surpass his other graphic work. Therefore, his *Arabian Nights* illustrations are my first area of inquiry.

The first thing that strikes the viewer upon entering Houghton's fantasy world is the dominance of the human figure. This potent figure type was a radical departure from the typical illustration style of the preceding generation of the 1830s and 1840s, exemplified in a scene from the tale of Princess Badoura by the illustrator William Harvey (Plate 1).[11] Harvey's figures are usually tiny, schematized Orientals, all basically interchangeable. Compare Harvey's world to Houghton's representation of Aladdin refusing to surrender the lamp to the evil magician (Plate 2). In Houghton's illustration, not only the two figures, but even the spirit hovering overhead is burly and substantial. Houghton's characters command the scene and are capable of interacting with each other.

Moreover, Houghton, who possessed the sharp eye of a playwright or caricaturist, uses gesture and pose to suggest subtleties of emotion which far outstrip the text itself. Take, for example, his illustration for a scene from the story of the Second Calender (Plate 3); it shows a dervish (or Moslem friar) plucking seven white hairs from the tale of a cat in order to effect a miraculous cure. The dervish's feet are arched, his back is arched (the cat trapped in his lap) while he grabs the hairs between thumb and forefinger—his attitude one of complete, unself-conscious absorption in the task at hand. Often Houghton deliberately avoided illustrating the key dramatic scenes, choosing instead those which illuminated a character's state of mind. This human or psychological dimension in his figures inspires an instantaneous identification in the reader.

Houghton further encourages the reader's access to the fantasy world through the persuasive naturalism of his settings. Often he reveals his settings in partial views and accidental glimpses that impart an air of casual encounter. Then, by using an intense, raking light source from the side, he throws his foreground figures into high sculptural relief; the light plucks out texture and exaggerates volume, rendering the forms almost supernaturally distinct and tactile. Light also filters through open forms like hair, beards, and trees, suggesting spatial ambience. Houghton often silhouettes these fully modelled forms against rectangles of white wall or against the open sky that forms a radiant backdrop to so many of his images. The backgrounds, on the other hand, are often sketched in without the strengthened contours or the dramatic blasts of light which excavate space and carve out form in the foreground. However, these backgrounds—like the housetops and domes seen over the Dervish's shoulder in Plate 3—still appear steeped in sun. The prevalence of white light is a crucial means by which the disparate zones of the different spatial layers can be integrated.

Another reason why Houghton's designs seem to radiate light is that even in deep shadows his hatching rarely closes a field. Some light penetrates into the obscure corners, and reflected lights are suggested in areas like the hollow under the Dervish's lap. Not only do the shadows exhibit this quality of transparency, but shadows falling upon forms follow their volumetric contour, and more uniquely, shadows cast by forms appear to cling to, and "echo," the shape of the substance. Were Houghton being scientifically precise, the shadows thrown by such a brilliant light would be knife-edged and very dark. Instead, he combines different atmospheric conditions creating a wonderfully bright, but not harsh world.

A quality of motion contributes to the sense of palpable atmosphere pervading Houghton's world. For instance, in the tale of the enchanted horse (Plate 4), the artist uses flexible materials like hair, fringes, feathers, the horse's mane, and the sweeping clouds to convey the unearthly flight of the horse. Some of the clouds appear as lines of force—the swirling current of the air itself made visible. Even more remarkable is the way in which he uses similar lines of motion to evoke an undersea realm in the picture of Princess Gulnarè and her brother (Plate 5). Their hair undulates upon the currents of the water in a completely believable fashion, while fish circle about them. In slow motion these figures seem to meander through an impossible world.

In addition to the stature of his figures, the quality of light and space, and the energy with which he infuses his *Arabian Nights* universe, Houghton relies upon the inclusion of significant details to lend further weight to his vision. For instance, he brings the moment in Plate 3 alive with incidental observations: lizards sun themselves on the whitewashed walls, and townspeople converse in the far distance. Moreover, these things are not suspended in an ideal state—note the cracks in the wall and tatters in the old man's garb, notes of realism that lend credibility to the fantastic elements with which they are mixed.

This naturalism is, in effect, so magnetic that the viewer is apt to be initially unconscious of the guiding hand of the designer in these images.[12] In regard to principles of composition, Houghton was a classicist. He favored an architectonic structure and frequently employed a central vertical axis to organize the field and act as a stabilizing core for the design as a whole. Plate 5 provides a good example of this technique. Throughout all the designs, major forms and many of the minor details are aligned along vertical and horizontal axes, regardless of their relative position in depth. For example, the casual disposition of Gulnarè's head aligns with the branch of coral to the left, and the fish are arranged in horizontal zones. These pervasive alignments weave a tectonic grid in two dimensions which locks together elements shown in three dimensions. The voluminous garments and hair of Houghton was a classicist. He favored an architectonic structure rich the underlying grid with languid, decorative curves in the surface design. On the whole, Houghton's compositions are bold and satisfying in their lucidity, a characteristic especially admirable in view of the fact that he often drew swiftly on the block from rough preliminary designs.[13]

One final image from Houghton's contribution to the *Dalziels' Illustrated Arabian Nights* will demonstrate both his mastery of design and his exuberant response to the fantastic content of the tales. Plate 6 represents the embrace of two young lovers, Princess Badoura and Prince Camaralzaman, who were brought together for a single night through the meddling intervention of demons and then were forced to endure trials and imprisonment before being reunited. In this illustration the tectonic structure is easily recognized; the axie of Camaralzaman's stance fixes the design and is reinforced by the band of inscription on the wall behind. Yet the formal structure is completely submerged in the viewer's awareness by the sensual delight of the scene. Badoura's body curves in towards Camaralzaman (note how the slipper drops from her foot), and the two embrace obliviously. The ceramic vases flanking them repeat and amplify the curves of Badoura's gown; her body is compact and has a childlike roundness. The weight of her hair is tangibly different from that of Camaralzaman. The moment is transient and infused with life—the hem of her skirt is still waving in the air after her impulsive rush to meet her lover. The rich curves, the interlocking of their bodies on the picture plane, the repetition of shapes in the surrounding setting—all these factors reveal masterful design, but design thoroughly bonded to the expression of a very personal vision of love in an oriental paradise.

On the whole, Houghton's treatment of the fantasy world of the *Arabian Nights* is remarkable for the way in which he encourages the reader towards participation, even bodily identification, with these spirited, emotional people. He uses the pictorial conventions one associates with realism: atmospheric lighting conditions; sharply focused sculptural form; specific details and insightful characterization. There is nothing dreamlike or removed about his treatment of the exotic, except perhaps for the weight and grace of his figures, which impart a certain sense of slow, relaxed time. For the most part, he treats a nonexistent world with startling immediacy, creating a world in which magic is a potent force and fantasy full-blooded and convincing.

Since no canonical standards determine appropriate form and content in the field of fantasy art, each artist's vision carries its own authority. Therefore, although Arthur Boyd Houghton's explorations of the *Arabian Nights* would provide later artists with points of departure, his work in no way circumscribed future efforts at visualizing this fantastic narrative. The illustrators of the 1890s, who drew heavily upon the legacy of Houghton and others active in the 1860s, brought to the text an intensified aesthetic awareness and self-consciousness; within the license of fantasy, they created highly wrought, ornamental tableaus. The two works I have selected as representative of both '90s fantasy illustration and of '90s illustration in general are John D. Batten's (1860–1932) *Fairy Tales from the Arabian Nights* (ed. E. Dixon, London: J. M. Dent, 1893) and H. J. Ford's (1860–1941) *The Arabian Nights Entertainments* (ed. Andrew Lang, New York, London and Bombay: Longmans, Green, 1898).

The intervening thirty years between the publication of the *Dalziels' Illustrated Arabian Nights* and these two 1890s editions witnessed a revolution in book illustration. The exacting craft of wood engraving perfected by the Dalziels was rendered obsolete by photographic reproduction methods on the commercial market.[14] At the same time, private presses (such as William Morris' Kelmscott Press) began to produce books conceived from cover to cover as exquisite art objects. This new book format reflected a metamorphosis in the aesthetic climate in England; the cumbersome trappings of the Victorian era were shed in pursuit of a new purity of design.[15]

During these intervening years appeared new English translations of the *Nights* far more extensive and sophisticated than those preceding,[16] and at the same time the market for children's books was thriving. Thus the character of the various editions of the *Arabian Nights* became more stratified; the elaborate, multivolume adult versions were complemented by a flood of children's editions, such as Ford's and Batten's, boasting gay and plentiful illustrations. Ford and Batten were both professionals in the field of fantasy; they illustrated the *Arabian Nights* as part of a whole series of children's tales set in distant, or non-existent, lands.[17]

The flavor of these exotic worlds differs markedly from the robust magic of Houghton. An aura of tension, which finds its source in their formal manipulations, charges them with energy and adds greatly to their drama. Fear, excitement, and the allure of Eastern adventure are enhanced by pictorial means, especially the use of a strong, containing border.

Consider *The Giant Enters* (Plate 7), an illustration by Ford from the story of Sindbad the Sailor that presents the moment when the giant discovers the luckless voyagers in his lair. Ford

PLATE 1

William Harvey, vignette from the story of the Prince Kamar Ez-Zemàn and the Princess Budoor, from E. W. Lane, trans., *The Thousand and One Nights* (London: C. Knight, 1839-41), II, 115.

PLATE 2

Arthur Boyd Houghton, *The Magician commanding Aladdin to give up the Lamp,* from *Dalziels' Illustrated Arabian Nights' Entertainments* (London: Ward, Lock and Tyler, 1863-65), p. 585. Courtesy, Houghton Library, Harvard University.

PLATE 3

Arthur Boyd Houghton, *The Envious Man plucks the hairs out of the cat's tail,* from *Dalziels' Illustrated Arabian Nights' Entertainments* (London: Ward, Lock and Tyler, 1863-65), p. 69.

PLATE 4

Arthur Boyd Houghton, *The Journey of Prince Firouz Schah and the Princess of Bengal,* from *Dalziel's Illustrated Arabian Nights' Entertainments* (London: Ward, Lock and Tyler, 1863-65), p. 737.

Plate 5

Arthur Boyd Houghton, Trial proof in the collection of the British Museum of *The Brother and Sister* from *Dalziels' Illustrated Arabian Nights' Entertainments* (London: Ward, Lock and Tyler, 1863-65), p. 417.

PLATE 6

Arthur Boyd Houghton, *The Meeting of the Prince and Badoura,* from *Dalziels' Illustrated Arabian Nights' Entertainments* (London: Ward, Lock and Tyler, 1863-65), p. 328.

PLATE 7

Henry J. Ford, *The Giant Enters,* from *The Arabian Nights Entertainments* (New York, London and Bombay: Longmans, Green, 1898), p. 143.

PLATE 8

John D. Batten, *Sindbad's Ship is pursued by the Rocs,* from *Fairy Tales from the Arabian Nights* (London: J. M. Dent, 1893), opposite p. 246.

PLATE 9

John D. Batten, *Danhasch carries off the Princess Badoura*, from *Fairy Tales from the Arabian Nights* (London: J. M. Dent, 1893), opposite p. 122.

PLATE 10

Henry J. Ford, *The Prince and Princess arrive at the capital of Persia on the Enchanted Horse,* from *The Arabian Nights Entertainments* (New York, London and Bombay: Longmans, Green, 1898), p. 375.

Plate 11

Henry J. Ford, *Sindbad in the Valley of the Serpents,* from *The Arabian Nights Entertainments* (New York, London and Bombay: Longmans, Green, 1898), p. 137.

PLATE 12

Edmund Dulac, *The cup of wine which she gives him each night contains a sleeping draught,* from *Stories from the Arabian Nights* (London: Hodder & Stoughton, 1907), precedes p. 19.

PLATE 13

Edmund Dulac, *Dahnash and Meymooneh,* from *Princess Badoura* (London: Hodder & Stoughton, 1913), p. 16.

PLATE 14

Edmund Dulac, *Camaralzaman cures Badoura,* from *Princess Badoura* (London: Hodder & Stoughton, 1913), opposite p. 48.

Plate 15

Edmund Dulac, *Aladdin finds the Magic Lamp,* from *Sindbad the Sailor and Other Stories from the Arabian Nights* (London: Hodder & Stoughton, 1914), opposite p. 64.

Plate 16

Edmund Dulac, *And there in its midst stood a mighty Genie,* from *Stories from the Arabian Nights* (London: Hodder & Stoughton, 1907), opposite p. 2.

silhouettes the body of the monster from behind, inside a narrow door which echoes the shape of the image as a whole. Although this cyclopean giant enters stooped, his huge frame hardly fits within the available opening. Down in the lower right-hand corner of the design, the sailors recoil and collapse, seemingly trapped by the border itself. This border is no mere outline, but it actively constrains and compresses the image, leaving neither the victims, nor the viewer, any avenue of escape.

Houghton employed partial views, but his borders rarely sliced into the substance of his images to the extent cultivated by Ford and Batten. In a scene by John Batten that illustrates a later episode in Sindbad's tale (Plate 8)—his flight from the great birds, the rocs—one roc hovers just beyond the reader's vision, the talons menacingly close. Ford, too, favored this use of the border to fragment the image in order to suggest unlimited scale.

The border also forcibly separates the world of common reality from that governed by magic. Within its guidelines, our familiar conventions of perspective are used both to involve and disorient the viewer. For example, in Plate 8 by Batten, one looks down upon Sindbad's ship from the impossible viewpoint of another roc. Conventional schema are employed first to establish expectations and second to reverse them, here quite literally pulling the ground out from under the viewer's feet.

Thus, what especially sets the work of the '90s artists apart from their predecessors is the way in which aesthetic considerations, like the framing edge, become the shaping force behind their fantastic conceptions. These images are highly patterned and flattened against the picture—meant to be looked at, but not entered into. Batten, to a greater extent than Ford, created pictures of such exciting ornamental intensity.

Batten's most spellbinding image occurs in the tale of Camaralzaman and Badoura, in which he portrays the demon Danhasch abducting the sleeping princess (Plate 9). He conceives of Danhasch as a monumental, reptilian monster, a composite of recognizable animal characteristics, who cuts an astonishing profile. All the sharp forms—horns, brow, nose and chin—find echoes elsewhere, creating a tight internal rhythm and resonance. The border straps in the image. Danhasch's arms are rigidly posed to create a rectangle on the picture plane through which the princess is threaded like a slip of silk. Batten lays in long, unbroken contours that are thick and cordlike around the demon, but give way to faint lines reminiscent of silverpoint to describe the princess. She glows with an incandescent light brighter than that of the crescent moon. Forced up against the picture plane and compressed within the confines of the border, these two dramatically contrasted figures overwhelm the reader's vision; they lack all plastic form and do not occupy tangible space—captivating, but forever fixed in two dimensions.

Looking at this image, one also realizes how cool and completely un-Eastern Batten's female figures are. Ford shares this essentially Celtic mode of feminine beauty, a diluted, streamlined rendition of the Pre-Raphaelite ideal. Batten, who makes no attempt to reproduce the physiognomy of the East, simply thrusts the heroine of Northern folklore onto the Arabian stage. Such inconsistency does not disturb the realm of fantasy in which the rules of logic need not apply.

Reference was made earlier to the influence of the illustrators of the 1860s upon those of the 1890s; for example, illustrators of the *Arabian Nights* could look to past editions as a reservoir of successful schemes to be sustained or reinterpreted. Sometimes one encounters unabashed quotations, deliberate "lifts" from other artists, such as Ford's illustration to the tale of the magic horse (Plate 10), which is an overt adaptation of Houghton's picture for the same tale (Plate 4). The differences between these two illustrations are telling: Ford places more distance between us and the figures, abolishing the tremendous personal presence of the Houghton image, and he shrinks his figures, centering them evenly from the page boundaries. Uncomfortable with the expanses of white lavished by Houghton, Ford embroiders all his garments and stray surfaces with pattern. His line, choppy and irregular, remains consistently open throughout and also asserts the flat quality of the picture plane. Houghton, on the other hand, lays in rich shadows and carves out the foreground figures.

This comparison also illuminates how the two artists chose to select from the conventions of realism. Houghton wove a world that had a psychological verity, for however bizarre his characters (even those as strange as Prince Beder transformed into a bird), they sway us with an uncanny human presence. To this consistent undercurrent, he added selective naturalistic details and placed his sculptural figures within convincing spaces. Ford, who relies much more upon detail, explicitly delineates the variety of costume, furniture, and intricacies of a given setting, incorporating more Eastern garb and accoutrements. His human figures, like Houghton's, have naturalistic proportions; yet the dimension of psychological realism has vanished. Instead, the abundance of almost scientifically observed detail persuades the reader that this fantasy realm must be tangible.

In one of Ford's finest illustrations, *Sindbad in the Valley of the Serpents* (Plate 11), an exciting metamorphosis of the ordinary into the extraordinary occurs. The coiling den of snakes is described with meticulous attention paid to the details of the head contours, the fangs, and the hot vapor from the nostrils, as if Ford were recording a biological specimen. Yet, hidden in the lower right corner is the tiny figure of intrepid Sindbad, and this juxtaposition that explodes our normal expectations of scale transforms a mundane garter snake into a full-fledged monster. Such a proliferation of realistic detail and jarring departures from realistic scale make Ford's fantasy world both tantalizingly close and altogether alien to the world of reality.[18]

Thus, the *Arabian Nights* illustrations of these two artists of the 1890s add new dimensions to the tales by using aesthetic tensions to heighten the narrative tension. Their compression of the frame, emphasis upon the taut integrity of the two-dimensional picture plane, and the decorative vitality of their designs escalates the drama of fantastic events. While these aesthetically self-conscious maneuvers remove the work from the realm of daily reality, their selective fidelity to realistic details still provides essential points of contact with our world. Flashes of recognition occur in the reader when encountering Ford's serpents, or the half-human, half-reptile Danhasch of Batten's. These flashes activate the fantasy realm, providing crucial bridges between the realm of the material and the immaterial—which is always one characteristic of fantasy art.

The final phase of this survey of the fantastic world of the *Arabian Nights,* which will discuss the work of Edmund Dulac (1883–1957), moves out of the realm of black and white and enters a magical world of intense color. During the last decades of the nineteenth century, technical advances in printing enabled accurate color reproduction for the first time, and this breakthrough revolutionized fantasy illustration.[19] No one exploited the new techniques in as breathtaking a manner as the illustrator Edmund Dulac.

Dulac, by birth a Frenchman and by preference an Englishman,[20] pursued a lifelong fascination with Eastern tales in a series of sumptuous gift books, including *Stories from the Arabian Nights* (1907), *Princess Badoura* (1913), and *Sindbad the Sailor and Other Stories from the Arabian Nights* (1914).[21] In addition to his adventurous use of color in these illustrations to Eastern tales, the eclectic Dulac experimented with Eastern art forms. His images, which bear the strong impress of Japanese prints and Persian miniatures, thereby evoke a wondrous, hybrid world in which the familiar stories have been recast in a form alien to the Western eye. His two concerns—exploitation of color for expressive purposes and reliance upon the formal characteristics of Eastern art—were the key means by which Dulac conjured up his unique fantasy world.

Dulac's earliest *Arabian Nights* illustrations, those in the 1907 volume which secured his reputation in London, have a striking dominance of blue. Prussian blue, midnight and indigo hues swirl together, creating a world of almost submarine mystery; in his original watercolors, Dulac often over-damped the foreground to achieve this fusion of color.[22] These approaches to color create a hushed world in which the Queen of the Ebony Isles slips a sleeping draught into her husband's evening glass of wine (Plate 12). Here the bronze sheen of the lamp, the orange of the woman's scarf, and the rust hue of the pillows float within the field of blue that hovers in pale lozenges behind the sorceress and becomes soft and indeterminate at her feet. Not a single object found in this fantastic world can cast a shadow into the palpable atmosphere of color. However, dense as the color is, it remains bound to these objects and does not dissolve their form. The pitcher, the table, and the woman herself remain oddly self-contained, fixed within their distinct contours.

This unusual balance between color and integrity of contour evolved out of Dulac's working method. Using preliminary sketches made on tracing paper, Dulac continually retraced his forms, incorporating changes, and eventually assembled the composition by layering the transparent images and shifting them in relation to one another. As a result, the solid forms appear suspended like cutouts in a lush ambience.[23]

In this early "blue" phase of his style, Dulac recognized that a palette limited in hue, particularly one dominated by blue with its connotations of twilight and dreams, endowed his fantasy world with an atmosphere completely removed from real life. Later, he abandoned this almost monochrome mode in search of further expressive options through color. Turning, for instance, to Plate 13, the confrontation of two demons in *Princess Badoura* of six years later, note how Dulac frames the silver body of the demon Meymooneh against a mandorla rendered all the more intense by the gloom surrounding her and Danhasch. Here Dulac employed tiny points of light in the sky, the wings, and the ropes of pearl and jewelry; these leap to the eye. Dulac employs color as a vehicle to disorient his viewer, by juxtaposing hues of such strangeness or intensity that they could only exist in an order outside nature.

Dulac further disorients the viewer by choosing stylistic prototypes foreign to Western artistic convention. In the early 1907 *Arabian Nights,* he had drawn freely upon Japanese prints, and their influence upon his style became all-pervasive by the 1913 *Princess Badoura.* This tale, which took place in the Princess' homeland of China, was a fitting one for Dulac's strongly orientalizing treatment.

The love story climaxes in the reunion of Badoura and her lover Camaralzaman, a popular scene which had inspired one of Houghton's loveliest designs fifty years earlier (Plates 14 and 6). Dulac's version of this same moment could not be further removed from that of Houghton. In Dulac's rendition, economy of means, balance, and lightness prevail, for a delicate grid formed by the oriental architecture anchors the design. Lacking all depth, the image seems paper-thin, almost translucent, and the opalescent blue of the early period has disappeared to be replaced by frosted colors reminiscent of the seashore. By these technical means, Dulac has drained of all physicality a scene of tempestuous reunion. The curved, lapping train of Badoura's gown suggests that she drifted into her lover's embrace; a book open on the floor and an overturned lamp hint at past motion. All is serene. Perhaps in no other design is it so evident how Dulac brought his elements into formal harmony one by one, echoing the shape of the lovers in the green vase and mirroring their gestures in one another, creating a world as exquisitely balanced and as artificial as a Haiku.

After a trip to the East in 1913, Dulac's newly awakened enthusiasm for Persian miniatures superseded his earlier interest in Japanese prints. Manuscripts like the sixteenth-century works created for the Safavid rulers revealed to him untapped potential for fantastic effects in his own work.[24] The Persian artists juxtaposed pastels with fields of pure gold, and by painting with brushes only a single hair in thickness, they built up forms of indescribably soft texture. Contrary to artists working with the Western concept of deep pictorial space, these masters scattered their designs upon the flat plane, like a tapestry. Dulac enthusiastically began to seek similar effects with the means he had at hand.

His efforts led directly to the illustrations for *Sindbad the Sailor and Other Stories,* best exemplified in his picture of Aladdin tiptoeing, spellbound, into a fairy-tale garden (Plate 15). Trees and plants of all colors—purple and pink, ochre, crimson, and turquoise—border his path up to the lamp, while the tangerine sky overhead recalls the precious gilding of the miniatures. The rounded forms of the plants interlock edge to edge without a shadow to puncture the pure sheet of pattern. Pinpoints of color shimmer throughout. It is clear that contact with Eastern art awakened Dulac to novel juxtapositions of hue that make his pages glow with uncanny intensity. Dulac also shrunk his human figures, making them less accessible as they wander about in their jewel-like settings.

Dulac's earlier preoccupation with Japanese design conferred a remarkable air of tranquility and silence upon his fantasy world. Persian models inspired a new palette and daringly flat compositions. The attentive artifice of Dulac's style, drawing upon these models so alien to our Western expectations of perspectival depth and volume, removes these realms from the flux of ordinary time, and in their crystalline stillness the reader finds repose.

However, as I have suggested in exploring the work of Houghton, Batten, and Ford, some points of contact with the natural world are essential for a fantasy world to engage the reader. Likewise, the success of even Dulac's most dreamlike illustrations depends on the tension caused by the intrusion of familiar details into the exotic domain. Dulac's scene of the fisherman releasing the genie from the jar (Plate 16) epitomizes this interplay. Here is an impossibly small island in the midst of a sapphire sea. Dulac has purified the setting of all but a few subsidiary details: the jar and its lid resting on the fisherman's net and a handful of round pebbles. He concentrates his realistic touches in the figures. The genie is glowering—an absurd, cross-eyed scowl. The skin across his chest is withered and slack, and one wonders whether the hands are curled to be menacing or whether he is stretching out cramped fists after his long confinement. Dulac had a marvelous ability to capture perplexity and to caricature the foibles of men and women—observe the terrified little fisherman bowled over backwards at the apparition of the genie.

This illustration demonstrates how (in a manner reminiscent of Houghton) Dulac animated his *Arabian Nights* worlds with humor and insight that force us to recognize ourselves in his droll figures. His wit is not satirical, but affectionate; it does not dispel the exotic mood of the tales but provides a counterpoint to the sense of removal.

Ultimately, it is this fusion of the familiar and the magical (which can take countless forms) that animates the best fantasy art. I have touched upon just a small sampling of nineteenth-century and early twentieth-century illustration concerned with a single fantastic text to demonstrate the scope of techniques. The technical means available and the prevailing artistic trends of the period shape each artist's attempt—but within these restrictions the expressive possibilities of fantasy art are extraordinary.

To conclude, all these very different artists share a reliance upon the pictorial conventions associated with realism: gesture and human expression, spatial depth and natural light, the inclusion of detail, logical scale relationships, and so on. Such conventions do not curtail the imagination and creativity of the fantasy artist; instead, he can manipulate, invert, or reject outright each formal property. By disrupting our expectation of normal scale relationships, Ford creates his menacing giant serpents, when at the same time he brings them to life with an alarming precision of detail. Houghton intensifies a realistic treatment of light and space to create a tangible, supernatural universe; Edmund Dulac intensified his palette to create a mysterious, glowing universe. All these artists incorporate the attention to detail that one expects from first-hand observation but which when applied to monsters or imaginary cities dupe the eye into accepting the existence of a dream. Likewise, they integrate witty observations of human gesture and facial expression—which we automatically recognize as belonging to the world of daily reality—into their fantasy worlds and thus lend them psychological verity. Each artist develops distinctive means for manipulating, intensifying or departing from the conventions of realism. As we have seen in these four illustrators of the *Arabian Nights*, the finest fantasy art is a liberation from reality that never loses sight of its point of departure.

NOTES

1. I wish to acknowledge the assistance of Prof. George P. Landow of Brown University, whose ideas inspired this exploration and whose guidance saw it to completion. The catalogue of the exhibition, *Fan-*

tastic Illustration and Design in Britain, 1850–1930 (Providence, R.I.: Museum of Art, Rhode Island School of Design, 1979) by Diana L. Johnson with an introduction by Prof. Landow, provides an excellent handbook for the study of English fantasy art in many media. For an overview of fantasy illustration in England between 1860 and 1920, consult Brigid Peppin, *Fantasy: The Golden Age of Fantastic Illustration* (New York: Watson-Guptill [1975]).

2. Mia I. Gerhardt, *The Art of Story-Telling: A Literary Study of the Thousand and One Nights* (Leiden: E. J. Brill, 1963) provides detailed background on the appearance of this text in the West, and a complete bibliography of translations.

3. Robert J. Gemmett, *William Beckford* (Boston: Twayne Publishers, 1977), pp. 17–28; Martha Pike Conant, *The Oriental Tale in England in the Eighteenth Century* (New York: Columbia University Press, 1908), pp. 1–72.

4. Patricia Baker, "London's Arab Hall," *Aramco World Magazine,* 29 (November/December, 1978), 9–15. Also see Terry Reece Hackford, "Lord Leighton's Arab Hall," M.A. thesis, Brown University, 1981.

5. Percy Muir, *Victorian Illustrated Books* (New York and Washington: Praeger Publishers, 1971), p. 30. Listings of numerous English plays based on themes from the *Arabian Nights* are included in Allardyce Nicoll, *A History of English Drama 1660–1900* (Cambridge: At the University Press, 1969), VI, pp. 7–8, 10, 20, 364, 408, 463.

6. Gleeson White, *English Illustration "The Sixties": 1855–70* (Bath: Kingsmead Reprints, 1970); reprint of first edition of 1897. White's pioneering study defined this period of British illustration. It was followed by a second key source: Forrest Reid, *Illustrators of the Eighteen Sixties* (New York: Dover Publications, 1975), originally published in London in 1928.

7. To make a wood engraving, the engraver employs a graver or burin to cut into the dense end grain of the wood. The incised grooves then appear as white lines, while the raised ridges create black lines in the final print. For a good contemporary account of the process, see W. J. Linton, *Wood-Engraving: A Manual of Instruction* (London: George Bell and Sons, 1884).

8. George and Edward Dalziel, *The Brothers Dalziel—A Record of Fifty Years' Work—1840–1890* (London: Methuen and Co., 1901), pp. 226ff.; Muir, *Victorian Illustrated Books,* pp. 129–48.

9. H. W. Dulcken, ed., *Dalziels' Illustrated Arabian Nights' Entertainments,* 2 vols. (London: Ward, Lock and Tyler, [1863–65]). The volumes, issued in parts between 1863 and 1865, include illustrations by Sir John Everett Millais, John Dawson Watson, Sir John Tenniel, George John Pinwell, Thomas Morten, Thomas Dalziel, and Arthur Boyd Houghton.

10. Houghton (1836–1875) was born in 1836 in Kotagiri, Madras, and returned with his family to England in 1837. He began his study of art at Leigh's and then entered the Royal Academy Schools in 1854. Financially unsuccessful as a painter, Houghton turned to illustration through collaboration with the Dalziels. He contributed to numerous books and periodicals and spent a few months in America in 1869 producing a special set of journalistic drawings for *The Graphic*. Houghton died in 1875 at the age of thirty-nine. He was a powerful and gifted artist who remains little known to this day. See Paul Hogarth, *Arthur Boyd Houghton* [exhibition catalogue] (London: Victoria and Albert Museum, 1975); Simon Houfe, *The Dictionary of British Book Illustrators and Caricaturists 1800–1914* (Woodbridge, Suffolk: Baron Publishing, 1978), p. 345; and Paul Hogarth, *Arthur Boyd Houghton* (London: Gordon Fraser, 1981).

11. E. W. Lane, trans., *The Thousand and One Nights,* 3 vols. (London: C. Knight and Co., 1839–41); issued in parts with "many hundred engravings on wood, from original designs by William Harvey." For further information on this very popular edition, consult Muir, *Victorian Illustrated Books,* pp. 30–33.

12. Laurence Housman, *Arthur Boyd Houghton* (London: Kegan Paul, Trench, Trübner, 1896), pp. 18ff. This excellent monograph on Houghton's work, written by an illustrator and critic of the 1890s, is also the main source available for reproductions of Houghton's work.

13. Hogarth, *Arthur Boyd Houghton,* p. 11.

14. The development of numerous photographic reproduction processes eliminated the intervention of a professional engraver in the printing process. In the "line block" process exemplified in these works by Ford and Batten, the original drawing was photographed onto a sensitized zinc plate and then acid was used to etch away the white parts of the design. The resulting block printed every nuance of the original line drawing. See James Thorpe, *English Illustration: The Nineties* (New York: Hacker Art Books, 1975), pp. 10ff.

15. Elizabeth Aslin, *The Aesthetic Movement: Prelude to Art Nouveau* (London: Elek, 1969), pp. 160–74; John Russell Taylor, *The Art Nouveau Book in Britain* (London: Methuen and Co., Ltd., 1966).

16. The three significant nineteenth-century English translations of the *Arabian Nights* are E. W. Lane's three-volume translation of 1839–41, John Payne's nine-volume translation of 1882–84, and Richard Burton's ten-volume translation of 1885.

17. John Dixon Batten (1860–1932) was born at Plymouth in 1860. He studied at the Slade School. Batten, who was much influenced by the Pre-Raphaelites, participated in the revival of tempera painting and also executed a wall painting for Christ Church, Lichfield. He specialized in illustrating children's books with mythological and fairytale subjects.

Henry Justice Ford (1860–1941) studied at the Slade School and also at Bushey. In 1889 he entered into collaboration with Andrew Lang for whom he executed numerous illustrations and cover designs for fairy tales and folklore. See Johnson, *Fantastic Illustration,* p. 66.

For additional biographical information and bibliography of the works of Batten and Ford, consult R. E. D. Sketchley, *English Book-Illustration of To-day* (London: Kegan Paul, Trench, Trübner, 1903), pp. 109–112; Houfe, *Dictionary . . . ,* pp. 228–306.

18. Another master of this technique of over-scaled microscopic vision was the British illustrator Edward Julius Detmold (1883–1957); see David Larkin, ed., *The Fantastic Creatures of Edward Julius Detmold* (London and Sydney: Pan Books, 1976) and Johnson, *Fantastic Illustration,* pp. 61ff.

19. By photographing through colored filters, the printer could make half-tone blocks that reproduced the yellow, blue, and red areas of the artist's original design. These color blocks were then printed over a key block made from a black and white negative. The technique permitted accurate reproduction of water-color originals and preserved great subtlety of tone. White, *Edmund Dulac,* p. 23.

20. Edmund Dulac (1882–1953) was born in Toulouse in 1882, where he later studied law and art. After an abortive enrollment in the Académie Julien, he turned his main efforts to book illustration. In 1905 he settled in London and thereafter earned an outstanding reputation for his illustrations for books and periodicals. In addition he produced caricatures, costume designs, and commercial art. I am indebted to Colin White's superb monograph *Edmund Dulac* (New York: Charles Scribner's Sons, 1976) as the basis for this portion of my essay.

21. All the Christmas gift books were published in London by Hodder and Stoughton. Dulac's color illustrations were tipped in.

22. White, *Edmund Dulac,* pp. 28ff.

23. Ibid., pp. 24ff.

24. A similar influence of Persian miniatures upon *Arabian Nights* illustration is evident in the work of E. J. Detmold's *The Arabian Nights* (London: Hodder and Stoughton, [1924]).

Pure and Applied Fantasy, or From Faerie to Utopia

Robert Crossley

HERE IS THE OPENING of the purest fantasy I know:

> Once upon a time there lived in a certain city of China an impoverished tailor who had a son called Aladdin. From his earliest years this Aladdin was a headstrong and incorrigible good-for-nothing. When he was ten, his father wished to teach him a decent trade; but as he lacked the means to pay for his training he took him into his own shop to teach him the trade of a tailor. Being accustomed to pass his time playing with the urchins of the quarter, however, Aladdin never stayed in a single day. Whenever his father went out of the shop or was attending to a customer, he would run off to the parks and gardens with little ruffians of his own age. He thus persisted in his idle and unruly ways until his father, grieving over the perverseness of his son, fell into an illness and died.[1]

"Aladdin and the Enchanted Lamp" is a story in which wish effortlessly becomes fact and in which enormous success glorifies one of the most undeserving characters imaginable. At the outset Aladdin is a juvenile delinquent and a dedicated escapist, skipping out of work to hang out at the playground with his neighborhood gang. He is an unlovely, unloving figure whose singular accomplishment consists in giving his father so much grief that it kills him. In pure fantasy the powerful old domestic metaphor—

"If you keep that up, it'll kill your father"—becames literal and exact. Yet, for his perverseness Aladdin is rewarded with nearly limitless power and heroic status; he wins wealth, a spouse, and a throne without ever exercising a single moral virtue. Aladdin's is a story of luck rather than merit, a story in which a sow's ear is transformed—magically and entirely—into a silk purse. Anyone who believes that literary fantasy traffics in ethical sentimentalities about good and evil would do well to take a careful look at this classic and thoroughly amoral segment of *The Thousand and One Nights*.

Now consider the ending of one of the great utopian romances of the industrial era. The narrator, having been a guest in a neo-pastoral, pleasantly anarchic society of the twenty-first century, finds himself suddenly back in his own nineteenth-century bed; lying there, he hears the voice of a utopian woman from the future insisting on the importance of his return to the present:

> "No, it will not do; you cannot be of us; you belong so entirely to the unhappiness of the past that our happiness even would weary you. Go back again, now you have seen us, and your outward eyes have learned that in spite of all the infallible maxims of your day there is yet a time of rest in store for the world, when mastery has changed into fellowship—but not before. Go back again, then, and while you live you will see all round you people engaged in making others live lives which are not their own, while they themselves care nothing for their own real lives—men who hate life though they fear death. Go back and be the happier for having seen us, for having added a little hope to your struggle. Go on living while you may, striving, with whatsoever pain and labour needs must be, to build up little by little the new day of fellowship, and rest, and happiness."[2]

In *News from Nowhere* William Morris envisions a transformation as miraculous as the one effected by Aladdin's lamp. England, "a country of huge and foul workshops and fouler gambling-dens" as the Guest knew it, is entirely renovated as "a garden, where nothing is wasted and nothing is spoilt."[3] But this change is not magical or instantaneous, and it does not exalt a lucky individual over the other "ruffians of his own age." Nineteenth-century wish becomes twenty-first century fact only at the cost of generations of struggle, suffering, disappointment, and bloodshed. Because Utopia is an achievement of the social imagination—of applied fantasy—no jinnee can bypass the revolutionary process and offer Morris' Guest permanent residency in Nowhere. The explicit message conveyed by the voice from the future is that one may not inhabit an unearned utopia, that utopia can neither be experienced vicariously nor attained without merit nor enjoyed at the expense of social conscience. Anyone who believes fantasy is basically self-indulgent, escapist, or politically irresponsible would do well to look carefully at the program for change imagined in *News from Nowhere*.

The opening of "Aladdin" and the close of *News from Nowhere* make serviceable bookends for bracketing the spectrum of literary fantasy.[4] They are not, I should hurry to add, "representative" or "typical" fantasies; the longer I study the fantastic mode, the less sure I am of what *is* typical of this very heterogeneous kind of fiction.[5] There are "pure" fantasies of the magical type that *are* morally charged and deal impressively with issues of individual merit and social justice; H. G. Wells's modern Aladdin story, "The Man Who Could Work Miracles" and Ursula Le Guin's Earthsea novels belong in such a grouping. And there are "applied" fantasies of the utopian type that are little more than homages to applied science—to technological wizardry isolated from moral or social conscience. Edward Bellamy's American utopia *Looking Backward* (to which *News from Nowhere* was a reply) and H. G. Wells's 1935 utopian film *Things to Come* are among the most problematic utopian fantasies of the last one-hundred years. Nevertheless, if "Aladdin" and *Nowhere* are inadequate or misleading representatives of the nature of fairy story and the nature of utopian romance, they are emblematic of a clear and persistent tension within the fantastic mode.[6] That tension is between private gratification and social obligation, between the seductions of enchantment and the challenges of reformation, between the perilous realm of Faerie and the paradoxical perfection of Utopia.

The whole of the Aladdin story is directed to the satisfaction of the hero's private whims, lusts, aspirations. It encourages the reader's vicarious pleasure in Aladdin's success precisely because, as in a lottery, the success is arbitrary and gratuitous. If good fortune can strike even a bum like Aladdin, then there's no reason why it may not come to us too. Aladdin begins his career as a proletarian malcontent, poor, rebellious, and politically unaware. He swiftly becomes rich, comfortable, and renowned, but remains inert politically. The tale does not invite a social perspective, and Aladdin never applies his good fortune to the *condition* of poverty out of which he arose. In one triumphal procession he does scatter gold to the masses, but this is a self-aggrandizing gesture that simply distracts the poor from their own misery long enough to gawk at the lucky few who catch a coin. Bejeweled, brocaded, and unassessably wealthy, Aladdin is a mesmerizing figure and the crowds adore him because he allows them the vicarious thrill of hitting the jackpot. They embrace him as their hero because he fulfills their dreams; they impute to him a merit he doesn't have because they must perceive him as deserving to explain to themselves why he has succeeded and they have not.[7] In fairy stories chance is treated as if it were design, communal aspirations are embodied in a surrogate, and the heroic ethos serves to nullify social inquiry or analysis. Aladdin is the apt governor of a kingdom of Faerie and his magnetic heroism is an effective deterrent to Utopia.

In the-good-place-which-is-no-place-at-all, to deploy the paradox Thomas More enforced when he coined the punning term Utopia, imagination is applied to an entire community rather than distilled in a single hero.[8] A literary form whose very name provokes skepticism about wish-fulfillment is diffident toward the romantic ideal of heroism. Instead of personal, isolated, lucky successes, Morris' utopian country of Nowhere manifests the good life as lived by a variety of artists, artisans, and agriculturalists in a future green world. Although Nowhere has little of the planned and regulated goodness often (and not always accurately) associated with Utopia,[9] Morris is clearly writing applied fantasy; imagination is in the service of social welfare. Where "Aladdin" depicts the extravagant indulgence of a personal appetite for luxury, *News from Nowhere* abolishes the "organized misery."[10] that underlies a consumer society by encouraging the universal exercise of creative imagination. The first two men Morris' Guest meets in Nowhere are a "dustman" (that is, trash collector) and a weaver, both of whom are fantastically dressed in rich fabrics and accessories they themselves designed and made. In Nowhere all men and women become artists and enjoy the pleasure of artifacts created by their own—or their neighbors'—hands. One cannot imagine Aladdin picking out his own clothes, let alone sewing a shirt.

In fairy story adventure takes precedence over ideas; the reader's attention is engaged in the fortunes (both narrative and economic) of a hero. Utopian fantasy focuses on what Morris calls "the arrangements of life": how do the inhabitants of an ideal society get along with each other, make community decisions, exchange goods and services, deal with transgressions, conduct foreign policy, raise their children, apportion their time? Such questions, at the heart of utopian romances, are peripheral in Faerie, because pure fantasy is "pure" precisely in the degree to which it foregoes issues for images and abandons daily, domestic life to embrace wonders and perils. Had Tolkien kept his hobbits in the Shire and explored the arrangements of their pastoral life, while relegating the history of the war with Sauron to the appendices, *The Lord of the Rings* would belong to utopian literature. In sending the hobbits out on the road, to contend with an external enemy, he moved his narrative out of Utopia and into Faerie.

The term Faerie, used to designate the locale of fairy stories, is one of Tolkien's contributions to the modern theory of fantasy. But Tolkien's notorious hostility to technological romances, his almost Luddite arcadianism, has obscured some of the likenesses between Faerie and Utopia. In his essay "On Fairy-Stories" Tolkien created a terminology for fantastic art by proposing that fairy stories create "secondary worlds," alternative kingdoms of desire, separate from the "primary world" of our daily, waking experience.[11] But what Tolkien says of the imaginative integrity of the secondary world of Faerie holds as well for Utopia. A utopia also projects an alternative reality meant to be distinct from the primary world. A utopia too has its internal rules and laws that give it completeness and self-sufficiency. And the utopographer's art consists in laying out an entire world into which, as Tolkien says of fairy story, "your mind can enter"—a world which demands not simply the suspension of disbelief but the activation of desire. Both Faerie and Utopia are situated in a wishful landscape, though Faerie is more likely to be represented as a nostalgically authoritarian *kingdom* of desire and Utopia—in principle if not always in execution—a more egalitarian community.

The author of utopias enjoys drawing blueprints for an imaginary society for some of the same reasons Tolkien labored over his maps of Middle Earth: both are explorers of the topography of desire. The utopographer—surveyor of desirable noplaces—does not necessarily have a greater commitment to the practicability of his fantasies than the author of fairy tales. The utopian attitude may be more playful than practical; the application of fantasy in

Utopia is chiefly internal, within the ideal world, rather than metafictional.[12] In an important essay called "How to Play Utopia," Michael Holquist proposes that as soon as utopia moves from the realm of imaginative play to the realm of implementation it becomes the police-state.[13] The famous dystopian satires of the twentieth century—Zamiatin's *We*, Huxley's *Brave New World*, Orwell's *1984*, Vonnegut's *Player Piano*—are all fearful responses to implemented utopian fantasies. But it isn't necessary to consult the anti-utopians on this matter. Many utopographers have been explicitly uninterested in settling in the utopian worlds they have designed; they maintain an aloof, amused, playful relationship to their fictional worlds.

B. F. Skinner, for instance, admires from afar the experiment at Twin Oaks, Virginia, modeled on his fictional *Walden Two*.[14] In his *Utopia*, More creates a fictional self named Thomas More who reacts to the ideal society described by the traveler Raphael. The fictional More remains studiously uncommitted to the end of the narrative: "Well, I must think it over," he says at the end of Book II. "Then perhaps we can meet again and discuss it at greater length."[15] Utopia prompts not assent—or, in Tolkien's term, "primary belief"—but reflection and discussion. It demands reconsideration and debate, a spirit of intellectual game rather than zealous activity. H. G. Wells's effort to accommodate Plato and More to the twentieth century in *A Modern Utopia* is a celebration of the impracticable. Utopia, he suggests near the end of his narrative, cannot bear very much reality: "a Utopia is a thing of the imagination that becomes more fragile with every added circumstance."[16] In a fascinating article called "How I Came to Write *Looking Backward*," published the year after his utopian novel appeared, Edward Bellamy reflects more extensively on the paradox of Utopia. As artist, Bellamy claims, he never thought his utopian ideas might be implemented; in fact, in his original conception of *Looking Backward*, his fictional Utopia was not an extension of the primary world but was located in the secondary world of Faerie:

> I had, at the outset, no idea of attempting a serious contribution to the movement of social reform. The idea was of a mere literary fantasy, a fairy tale of social felicity. There was no thought of contriving a house which practical men might live in, but merely of hanging in mid-air, far out of reach of

> the sordid and material world of the present, a cloud-palace for an ideal humanity.[17]

Like these utopian writers, Tolkien attempts to keep his primary and secondary worlds distinct; he cherishes a dual stance of imaginative engagement with and physical detachment from Faerie. As utopographers prefer to live in an imperfect world where they may continue to compose utopian speculations about a perfect one, so Tolkien realizes that dragons can only be desirable from the vantage of a reader situated securely in the dull primary world:

> I desired dragons with a profound desire. Of course, I in my timid body did not wish to have them in the neighbourhood, intruding into my relatively safe world, in which it was, for instance, possible to read stories in peace of mind, free from fear.[18]

As the subtitle of *The Hobbit* advertises and as the whole essay on fairy stories recommends, the purpose of Tolkienian fantasy is to take us "There and Back Again," refreshed and purified. The pure fantasy of fairy story does not alter the primary world; it simply changes how we see familiar reality. We return from the secondary world to the spot from which we started with renewed appreciation. Utopian fiction affects us differently. We visit a more rational, more humane society and return to our world troubled and discontent with things as they are. We want to change *what* we see. Unable to inhabit the utopia we have imagined, we are encouraged to make the world in which we must exist more livable. Thus the insistent refrain, "Go back again," heard by William Morris' Guest as he wakes from his dream-vision of Nowhere.

Although Bellamy and Morris offer antagonistic utopian versions of the twenty-first century, both stress the nightmarish quality of their protagonists' returns to late nineteenth-century society. After his stay in the future Boston, Julian West of Bellamy's *Looking Backward* dreams he has returned to 1888 and is horrified to move once more through his city's neighborhoods. He observes the frenzied consumerism of the retail district on Washington Street, the "throbbing" of the financial "abscess" in the banks of State Street, the industrial melancholy of the factories of South Boston, and the "Inferno" of the wretched slums of the South Cove district. Sensing his impotence to change the corrupt world of his origins, West gratefully reawakens in the year 2000 like "an escaped convict who dreams he has been recaptured and brought back to his dark and reeking dungeon and opens his eyes to see the heaven's vault spread above him."[19] The Guest in *News from Nowhere* is not given West's lucky break; instead, he discovers that the twenty-first century, not the nineteenth, is the dream world and he wakes up an exile in his own era. Under stormy skies, "like a nightmare of my childish days,"[20] the Guest returns to 1890 dismayed but eager to change the world he sees around him. With a rededicated sense of political purpose, he decides to change dream into prophecy, to help make possible the renovated world he will not live to inhabit. In traveling to the future, Morris' Guest escapes into freedom, escapes in order to return.

"Go back again." The exhortation of nearly all fantasists, pure and applied, is that you *must* go home again. But the trip to an alternative world of desire is never simply a vacation. To go there and back again entails, necessarily, some change either in the nature of the place or the nature of the person. Ursula K. Le Guin's physicist Shevek, propounder of a new theory of time, offers the essential fantastic qualification to an old platitude: "You *can* go home again, the General Temporal Theory asserts, so long as you understand that home is a place where you have never been."[21]

The recurrent language of escape and return, of journeys through time and space and memory and dream in both fairy stories and utopian romances, is a reminder of how emphatically the fantastic mode belongs to the literature of travel. But the reader who travels to Faerie is likely to have a different sort of trip than the visitor to Utopia. In "On Fairy-Stories" Tolkien suggests that the sojourner in Faerie is largely passive and receptive, will be—or should be—at a loss for words to name or report his experience:

> In that realm a man may, perhaps, count himself fortunate to have wandered, but its very richness and strangeness tie the tongue of the traveller who would report them. And while he is there it is dangerous for him to ask too many questions, lest the gates should be shut and the keys be lost.[22]

The visitor to Utopia, on the other hand, is properly a tourist rather than an adventurer, often guided on the journey by one who has been there before or by an inhabitant of the alternative world. The guide may, in fact, have a carefully planned itinerary, a sequence of attractions designed to elicit questions in a climactic order. Exploration yields to exposition, and the dialogue form that has attracted utopian writers from Plato to B. F. Skinner is as plain a rhetorical sign as one could ask for that utopian fantasy thrives on discussion, inquiry, analysis. When one visits Utopia, it is impossible to ask too many questions.

Consider the arrival of two characters into two rather different locales. First, in *The Dispossessed,* the entrance of Le Guin's Shevek into the utopian city of Abbenay on the world of Anarres:

> The dirigible came down at a cargo depot at the south end of town, and Shevek set off into the streets of the biggest city in the world.
>
> They were wide, clean streets. They were shadowless, for Abbenay lay less than thirty degrees north of the equator, and all the buildings were low, except the strong, spare towers of the wind turbines. The sun shone white in a hard, dark, blue-violet sky. The air was clear and clean, without smoke or moisture. There was a vividness to things, a hardness of edge and corner, a clarity. Everything stood out separate, itself.[23]

There are two notable features of this arrival in Utopia: the mode of travel and the language of description. One does not enter Faerie by dirigible. Although L. Frank Baum had Dorothy Gale attempt to *leave* Oz by balloon, she arrived by tornado and ended up leaving in enchanted shoes. In *A Voyage to Arcturus* David Lindsay has his traveler fly to the planet Tormance in a crystal torpedo, and in *Perelandra* C. S. Lewis sends Elwin Ransom to Venus in an angel-powered coffin. Travel in utopian fiction tends to the more orthodox: James Hilton takes his characters to *Lost Horizon*'s Shangri-La by airplane, Thomas More—like the many authors of island-utopias—uses a boat, and science-fiction utopias favor conventional star-ships (if I may use such a fantastic term) rather than crystal torpedoes.

But even more significant than his conveyance is the quality of the landscape Shevek sees in Abbenay. The clarity, hardness of edge, vividness, distinctness of the locale Shevek finds himself in comprise the essential vocabulary of utopian description. Travels to Utopia are narrated in lucid, exact words that render the alter-
meant to be exhibited, inspected, and evaluated, the reader can,
native world with almost photographic artistry. Because Utopia is

meant to be exhibited, inspected, and evaluated, the reader can, as Le Guin says of Abbenay, "see it all, laid out as plain as spilt salt."[24] Just before he dreams himself into Utopia, Morris' Guest wishes he could visualize a more perfect society: " 'If I could but see a day of it,' he said to himself; 'if I could but see it!' "[25] The utopographer tries to bridge the abyss between Utopia and our own imperfect society by making the world of imagination as accessible to the eye as possible. If Utopia is to be an impetus to reform, to the social application of private fantasy, it needs to be seen as clearly as we see the primary world. This requirement does not mean, however, that utopian prose is necessarily flat or stylistically graceless or unenlivened by image or metaphor. In her recently rediscovered 1915 utopian fantasy *Herland,* Charlotte Perkins Gilman has her narrator use a vividly evocative language that succeeds in realizing the fantastic locale. Here is the narrator's view of the first town he sees in the foothills of Herland:

> You see, I come from California, and there's no country lovelier, but when it comes to towns!—I have often groaned at home to see the offensive mess man made in the face of nature . . . . But this place! It was built mostly of a sort of dull rose-colored stone, with here and there some clear white houses; and it lay abroad among the green groves and gardens like a broken rosary of pink coral.[26]

That the figurative language of *Herland* is basically spare and functional, rather than decorative or atmospheric language can best be appreciated by examining it alongside some verbal specimens from fairy stories. Consider, next, this entrance into another secondary world. When the protagonist of George MacDonald's *Lilith* first stumbles into a preternatural world inhabited by Adam and his two wives Eve and Lilith, he attempts to identify his surroundings and finds that words fail him:

> I beg my reader to aid me in the endeavour to make myself intelligible—if here understanding be indeed possible between us. I was in a world, or call it a state of things, an economy of conditions, an idea of existence, so little correspondent with the ways and modes of this world—which we are apt to think the only world, that the best choice I can make of word or phrase is but an adumbration of what I would convey. I begin indeed to fear that I have undertaken an impos-

> sibility, undertaken to tell what I cannot tell because no speech at my command will fit the forms in my mind.[27]

Having arrived in the secondary world through a mirror in his attic—a method of entry that clearly marks the locale as Faerie—MacDonald's hero uses an elaborately imprecise language that enforces an impressionistic rather than photographic view of the landscape. The language of fairy story favors such suggestive imprecision which makes description connotative, not denotative. Images are rich, complex, highly colored, and multiple—and nevertheless shadowy and blurred. The reader is given choices (call it a world, a state, an economy, an idea) and is urged to complete the picture that the narrator can only sketch. The clear, hard lines of Abbenay dissolve into an adumbration. The traveler in Faerie can tell us how he felt but cannot always tell us, in terms that will call forth an exact visual representation for the reader, what he saw.

Readers of fairy stories may associate certain concrete, sensuous images with particular texts—the heaped platters of jewels and cups of coffee spiced with amber in "Aladdin," the tunnels and towers, abysses and rivers that make up the physical and mental landscape of Tolkien's Middle Earth, the throne of rainbow and ice and the twilight barrier between the primary and secondary worlds in Lord Dunsany's *The King of Elfland's Daughter*. But such images seldom have much representational value. What we perceive with the mind's eye often cannot be seen with the corporeal eye. An extreme, but by no means atypical, instance of this phenomenon occurs in *A Voyage to Arcturus* when David Lindsay invents two new primary colors, ulfire and jale. Despite Lindsay's effort to construct sensory analogues to enable us to "see" these colors, ulfire and jale remain fantastic abstractions visible only in Faerie and only to our inner eye.[28] Hence the common feeling of disappointment readers have on viewing cinematic versions of fairy stories like *The Lord of the Rings*, Roald Dahl's *Charlie and the Chocolate Factory*, and C. S. Lewis' *The Lion, The Witch and the Wardrobe*. When such a viewer complains, "That's not the way I saw it," he may be commenting not on a failure of the cinematographer's talent but on the very nature of verbal art in fairy stories, an art not essentially pictorial but abstract or impressionistic.

The most dramatic illustration of the abstract imagery of

Faerie may be, paradoxically, one of the most gorgeously sensuous modern fairy stories, C. S. Lewis' *Out of the Silent Planet*. Lewis throughout emphasizes the difficulty of verbalizing unprecedented sights on an alien world. On his planet Malacandra (Mars), terrain, flora, and anatomy are all so foreign to earthly experience that he resorts to multiple similes to create composite images by which the human reader might grasp the singularity of the Malacandrian environment. The encounter of Lewis' hero Ransom with the intelligent species of *hross* is a representative example:

> Suddenly the water heaved and a round, shining, black thing like a cannon-ball came into sight. Then he saw eyes and mouth—a puffing mouth bearded with bubbles. More of the thing came up out of the water. It was gleaming black. Finally it splashed and wallowed to the shore and rose, steaming, on its hind legs—six or seven feet high and too thin for its height, like everything in Malacandra. It had a coat of thick black hair, lucid as seal-skin, very short legs with webbed feet, a broad beaver-like or fish-like tail, strong forelimbs with webbed claws or fingers, and some complication half-way up the belly which Ransom took to be its genitals. It was something like a penguin, something like an otter, something like a seal; the slenderness and flexibility of the body suggested a giant stoat. The great round head, heavily whiskered, was mainly responsible for the suggestion of seal; but it was higher in the forehead than a seal's and the mouth was smaller.[29]

Can the reader really *see* a *hross* by the end of this passage? I suspect that the more detailed Lewis' language becomes, the more he tells us what a *hross* is like, the less we are able to visualize the creature. The analogues accumulate until the description becomes a compact bestiary; the picture of the *hross* blurs; the similes and epithets suggest, at last, an image too dazzling for camera to record, too wondrous for words to denote. The *hross* can be seen only with the mind's eye. And properly so. The passage does not reveal a failure of Lewis' descriptive art but demonstrates a stylistic principle in the aesthetic of fairy story.[30] Only in Faerie would such a creature be described in this way.

Perhaps. Unless Malacandra turns out to be Utopia as well as Faerie. *Out of the Silent Planet,* projecting as it does a complete and ideal society of three sapient species under theocratic rule, has some claims to be considered among the important Christian utopias. Other critics have debated whether *Out of the Silent Planet* is fantasy or science fiction; I cannot assert with any confidence whether it is more accurately classified as a fairy story or utopian romance. The truth is, of course, it would be a foolish error to insist on a rigid boundary between Faerie and Utopia. They are, after all, not political units whose territorial sovereignty needs to be defended, but tendencies of the fantastic imagination. Pure and applied fantasy spring from the same creative impulse and make use of many overlapping principles and literary conventions to take their readers to somewhat different destinations.

Some of the most splendid modern fantasies elude the neatness of ingenious critical categories. *The Lord of the Rings* is the pre-eminent fairy story of this century, but no one should be fooled by Tolkien's political disclaimers into assuming that it lacks an ideology that is plainly, if somewhat eccentrically, utopian. In many salient features Middle Earth is related to the arcadian green world of *News from Nowhere*—minus Morris' anarchism, which Tolkien has replaced with an authoritarian and patriarchal social structure familiar in classical and Christian utopias. And Gilman's extraordinary utopia *Herland* is as much an exercise in pure fantasy as it is an excursion of the applied imagination, a tale of enchantment as much as a satiric speculation on gender and society. In fact, a reader may fitly and bemusedly ask herself whether a country inhabited for two millennia only by women who have developed a religion of maternity, an ethos of sorority, and powers of parthenogenesis, belongs in Faerie or Utopia. The answer is not obvious. As Ursula Le Guin has suggested in the title of one of her essays on the nature of fantasy, it is a long way from Elfland to Poughkeepsie.[31] But Faerie and Utopia are two points on the same underground railway of imagination.

NOTES

1. *Tales from the Thousand and One Nights*, trans. N. J. Dawood (Baltimore: Penguin, 1973), p. 165.

2. William Morris, *News from Nowhere, or An Epoch of Rest,*

ed. James Redmond (London: Routledge and Kegan Paul, 1970), p. 182. *News from Nowhere* was first published in 1890.

3. Morris, *News from Nowhere,* p. 61.

4. Important recent efforts to name, describe, and assess the various types of literary fantasy are Tzvetan Todorov's *The Fantastic: A Structural Approach to a Literary Genre,* trans. Richard Howard (Ithaca, N.Y.: Cornell University Press, 1975) and Eric S. Rabkin's more readable *The Fantastic in Literature* (Princeton: Princeton University Press, 1976), especially chapter 4.

5. An earlier essay of mine brashly divides all fantasy into the rational and the numinous types, a distinction I now find naïve: "Education and Fantasy," *College English,* 37 (November 1975), 281–93.

6. Not everyone will agree with my placement of utopian romance alongside fairy story, or my insistence on seeing utopia as a form of fantasy rather than a version of science fiction. Perhaps the most concise justification for my approach is David Ketterer's observation: "To say that utopia is a place where everybody lives happily ever after, points to the true place of the genre: beside the fairy tale, as a branch of fantasy." See his *New Worlds for Old: The Apocalyptic Imagination, Science Fiction, and American Literature* (New York: Doubleday/Anchor, 1974), p. 98.

7. Notice how Aladdin's fans respond to him as a local boy who has made it into the big time, not as a political messiah: "The people marvelled at Aladdin's generosity and surpassing munificence; they were amazed at his good looks, his politeness and dignified bearing. They praised the Merciful for such a noble creature, and called down blessings upon him, although they knew him to be the son of a humble tailor. No one envied him: they all swore that he deserved it" (*Thousand and One Nights,* p. 205).

8. The pun on ou-topia (no-place) and eu-topia (good-place) has often been observed by utopian scholars. For a full account of utopian terminology and its shifting, sometimes confusing history, see Frank and Fritzie Manuel, *Utopian Thought in the Western World* (Cambridge, Mass.: Belknap Press of Harvard University, 1979), especially pp. 1–29.

9. The essential study of the problem of "conditioned virtue" in utopias is George Kateb's *Utopia and Its Enemies* (1963; rpt. New York: Schocken, 1972), chap. 6. In general, Kateb provides the most stimulating commentary available on the various offenses with which utopian thinking and fiction is usually charged.

10. Old Hammond, the crusty historian of Nowhere, defines civilization in its nineteenth-century form as "organized misery" (*News from Nowhere,* p. 80).

11. First presented as a lecture in 1938, Tolkien's "On Fairy-Stories" was published in *Essays Presented to Charles Williams,* ed.

C. S. Lewis (London: Oxford University Press, 1947). I have used the slightly revised version of the essay Tolkien reprinted in *Tree and Leaf* (Boston: Houghton Mifflin, 1965). Although not a conventionally well-ordered academic essay and often fuzzily argued and irritatingly allusive, "On Fairy-Stories" remains the one irreplaceable contribution to a modern aesthetics of fantasy.

12. Arguing against the notion of utopianism as the self-defeating pursuit of perfection, W. Warren Wagar defines utopography beautifully: "The value of the utopian impulse lies rather in its power to set men free from their apathetic or suffering acceptance of the world-as-it-is, and to give them self-transcending purposes. In this sense utopography becomes the picturing in detail of a preferred world; not a world that is necessarily perfect or ideal, but preferable to the present world, and consistent at the same time with one's definition of man. It may or may not be practically attainable in all respects, but it serves as a target for thought and action." See his passionately-argued *Building the City of Man: Outlines of a World Civilization* (New York: Grossman Publishers, 1971), p. 73.

13. Michael Holquist, "How to Play Utopia: Some Brief Notes on the Distinctiveness of Utopian Fiction," *Yale French Studies*, 41 (1968), 106–23; reprinted in *Science Fiction: A Collection of Critical Essays*, ed. Mark Rose (Englewood Cliffs, N.J.: Prentice-Hall, 1976), 132–46. In a similar vein, W. R. Irwin proposes naming utopias "impossible societies" because even when a social fantasy includes practicable ideas, the utopist's primary imaginative commitment is to intellectual and rhetorical play. See his *The Game of the Impossible: A Rhetoric of Fantasy* (Urbana, Ill.: University of Illinois Press, 1976), p. 109.

14. See Skinner's appreciative, but definitely spectatorial, preface to Kathleen Kinkade, *A Walden Two Experiment: The First Five Years of Twin Oaks Community* (New York: William Morrow, 1973), pp. v–x.

15. Thomas More, *Utopia*, trans. Paul Turner (Baltimore: Penguin, 1965), p. 132.

16. H. G. Wells, *A Modern Utopia*, intro. Mark Hillegas (Lincoln, Neb.: University of Nebraska Press, 1967), p. 352. The Nebraska text is a facsimile of the original 1905 edition.

17. Bellamy's 1889 article, originally in the May issue of *The Nationalist*, has been reprinted in *Science-Fiction Studies*, 4 (1977), 194–95.

18. "On Fairy-Stories," *Tree and Leaf*, p. 41.

19. Edward Bellamy, *Looking Backward 2000–1887*, intro. Erich Fromm (New York: Signet, 1960), p. 218. *Looking Backward* was first published in 1888.

20. *News from Nowhere*, p. 182.

21. Ursula K. Le Guin, *The Dispossessed: An Ambiguous Utopia*

(1974; rpt. New York: Avon, 1975), p. 44.

22. *Tree and Leaf,* p. 3.

23. *The Dispossessed,* p. 79.

24. Ibid., p. 80.

25. *News from Nowhere,* p. 2.

26. Charlotte Perkins Gilman, *Herland,* intro. Ann J. Lane (New York: Pantheon, 1979), p. 18. *Herland* was first published in six installments in Gilman's magazine *The Forerunner* in 1915.

27. George MacDonald, *Lilith* in *Phantastes and Lilith,* intro. C. S. Lewis (Grand Rapids, Mich.: Wm. B. Eerdmans Co., 1964), p. 194. *Lilith* was first published in 1895.

28. "Just as blue is delicate and mysterious, yellow clear and unsubtle, and red sanguine and passionate, so he felt ulfire to be wild and painful, and jale dreamlike, feverish, and voluptuous." David Lindsay, *A Voyage to Arcturus* (1920; rpt. New York: Ballantine, 1968), p. 53. Eric Rabkin comments on the interior logic of Lindsay's color scheme despite its perceptual impossibility for the human eye in his valuable essay, "Conflation of Genres and Myths in David Lindsay's *A Voyage to Arcturus,*" *Journal of Narrative Technique,* 7 (Spring 1977), 149–55.

29. C. S. Lewis, *Out of the Silent Planet* (1938; rpt. New York: Macmillan, 1965), p. 54.

30. With self-conscious playfulness, Lewis points to the nonrepresentational effect of his technique when he parodies the use of multiple similes in a description of the Malacandrian species of *pfifltrigg*: "It was rather like a grasshopper, rather like one of Arthur Rackham's dwarfs, rather like a frog, and rather like a little old taxidermist whom Ransom knew in London" (*Out of the Silent Planet,* pp. 112–13). The last item in the series comically subverts pictorial possibilities. Since the London taxidermist is known only to a fictional character and not to us, the simile cannot help us visualize a *pfifltrigg*; it does, of course, reinforce the *impression* of oddity, spryness, and smallness that Lewis has been seeking throughout the description.

31. Ursula K. Le Guin, "From Elfland to Poughkeepsie," in *The Languages of the Night: Essays on Fantasy and Science Fiction,* ed. Susan Wood (New York: Perigee/G. P. Putnam's Sons, 1979).

Aspects of Fantasy in Literary Myths about Lost Civilizations

Samuel H. Vasbinder

IN SCIENCE FICTION and fantasy, the sub-genre known as the Lost Civilization provides special access to periods of the past through the activities of contemporary characters. I am making a distinction between the historical novel and the novel set in the past in which the protagonist discovers a civilization set in an even more remote time. The feeling the reader has in a novel of the second type mentioned here is that the protagonist, though a man of the past, is still the reader's contemporary. It seems legitimate to consider lost civilizations presented in this way as part of this sub-genre.

The hypothesis that fragments of cultures or civilizations from remote antiquity could survive the general destruction of their worlds has often provided writers with a variety of possibilities in this special area of literary creation. Although the tales and stories readers most often associate with this genre date back only to H. Rider Haggard's *She,* written in the nineteenth century, the lost civilization story is not without its historical antecedents. It will be the purpose of this essay to analyze the Lost Civilization tale as it adapts itself to the requirements of fantasy, rather than of science fiction. To do this, I will undertake: (1) a brief discussion of the Lost Civilization tale in general with attempts to set the approximate limits of its boundaries, (2) a brief look at the historic antecedents of this type of story, and (3) a detailed examination of the Lost Civilization as it appears in modern fantasy fiction. This latter section will examine in turn the types of humans who discover the Lost Civilization and the metaphysical powers that govern the story.

The Lost Civilization tale develops its special ambience from several contributing factors that are usually present in every story. The first of these is that both the investigative team and the civilization that comes to light are either human or, at least, hominid. The persistence of the idea that a civilization or culture has survived from the most remote antiquity carries with it the idea that the civilization is in an obvious way human. All of the Lost Civilization novels of Haggard are peopled with humans. In *King Solomon's Mines,* Alan Quartermain discovers the remnants of an ancient culture guarded by contemporary black Africans who seem to be thoroughly Zulu. In *Alan Quartermain,* the city of Zu-Vendi is inhabited by a race of humans ruled by sister queens. *She* and *The Return of She* employ ordinary humans: black Africans in Kor and Mongolian racial types in the fastnesses of interior Asia for *Ayesha.* Burroughs too, who eventually pictured more than twenty civilizations of the "Lost" type in the African interior, used humans exclusively as the basis for each culture. Opar has a race of bestial men and beautiful women. Pal-ul-don utilizes tailed, but human, citizens; even the empire of the Antmen is populated by humans, although of lilliputian dimensions. In John Beynon Harris' *The Secret People,* a race of pygmy humans is discovered beneath the earth's surface.[1] Because they are so physically different from humans and repulsively shaped as well, the question arises whether they are, in fact, human:

> All folk-beliefs have a rational beginning somewhere if you can find it. Men didn't invent the tales of gnomes and trolls, nor the idea of giant toadstools. Someone had the tale from a man who had actually seen them—several men, perhaps, for the legends are widespread. In the course of time the stories became garbled, and at the hands of painters our pygmies underwent a transformation, but they were still dwarfs. . . .[2]

In Jack Vance's "DP!" the reader is introduced to a human type whose "milk-blue eyes" were "blank as clam shells. When they chanced into patches of sunlight, they cried out in hurt voices and clutched at their naked scalps, which were white as ivory netted with pale blue veins."[3] It is eventually announced that the "troglodytes," as these creatures are styled, are indeed human. Although they are issuing in alarming numbers from an opening in the earth, evidently evacuating their underground cities for a reason that is never made clear, the scientists in the story decide that "trogs are physiologically identical with surface humanity, and sexual intercourse between man and trog might well be fertile."[4] Edmund Hamilton's *A Yank at Valhalla* brings to light a civilization of the Norse gods who are all, despite their gigantic size, human:

> "Outlander, who call yourself Jarl Keith," Odin replied, "we Aesir are men, not gods. But we have lived for many centuries in Asgard, and many legends have arisen about us in the outer world."[5]

Richard Shaver's tale "Of Gods and Goats" shows the Grecian gods in all their beautiful, human forms—particularly Venus, whose human charms are described with loving care.[6] So too in the Shaverian novel *Prometheus II,* by S. J. Byrne, the human form is utilized for the gods who are, once again, at war.[7] In fact, no story that bears a resemblance to the Lost Civilization story that I have been able to discover has not in some manner utilized and relied upon the human form as the basis for the people of the tale.

Occasionally one discovers non-human civilizations, but they are so rare that they cannot be said to represent the type or even be a part of it. Such cultures, as the arachnid civilization in H. Warner Munn's "City of Spiders" or the sentient worms of Robert E. Howard's Bran Mak Morn tales, or the other worm shapes utilized by Howard in his "Valley of the Worm," are exceptions to a rather broadly human bias in the tales of Lost Civilizations.[8]

A second characteristic of the Lost Civilization is the Earth setting. Science fiction and fantasy fiction are filled with hominid and non-hominid civilizations set on other planets, on parallel worlds, and in other dimensions. Certainly John Norman's Tarnsman of Gor series, Burroughs' John Carter on Mars tales, Clark Ashton Smith's Zothique and Xiccarph series all have strong overtones of the Lost Civilization. Strange cities, lost or decadent races, ancient sorceries, the protagonist traveling back in time to a lost age, and heroic humans withstanding and often conquering the evil of those places are all present. But, it must be stated emphatically, these settings are not of this earth and should not be included in the Lost Civilization sub-genre. These fall more properly into the sub-genres of space travel, the discovery of alien cultures, and peoples in the outer reaches of space inhabiting interstellar worlds. The proper setting for the Lost Civilization is on the Earth itself. One exception here that should be mentioned is the story that sees earth as an outpost or colony of a human, galactic empire. Larry Niven peoples his Ringworld with variations of the human species who are the descendents of a human racial type who come from the galactic core. In *Ringworld* and *The Ringworld Engineers,* Niven presents a clever variation of the Garden of Eden myth. A similar motif is used in the Battlestar Galactica television series, where the human species is seen as capable of interstellar flight and has colonized the worlds of the galaxy. Earth itself has become a lost civilization to this advanced race. But this variation is too far away from the general type of Lost Civilization story to be considered here.

The third and last criterion of the Lost Civilization story is its association with beings (not necessarily of the hominid type) who possess supra-normal powers and as a consequence handle the laws of reality in a supernatural or occult manner. This will be discussed at length in the last section of the essay. It is, however, appropriate here to examine briefly the historical antecedents of the Lost Civilization story, since these sources have added some special nuances to the consideration of the Lost Civilization species.

Certainly the Lost Civilization is no stranger to the literature of the past. In *The Thousand and One Nights,* there are several references to the strange city cut off from the rest of the world. "The City of Many-Columned Iram," the source of the city of Irem mentioned by Lovecraft, is described with loving care:[9]

> It is related that Abdullah bin Abi Kilabah went forth in quest of a she-camel which had strayed from him, and as he was wandering in the deserts of Al-Yaman and the district of Saba, behold, he came upon a great city girt by a vast castle around which were palaces and pavilions that rose high into middle air. He made for the place thinking to find there folk of whom he might ask concerning his she-camel. But when he reached it, he found it desolate, without a living soul in it.[10]

In "The Ebony Horse," a man rides a flying artificial horse to a strange city. In the "City of Brass," a city similar to the one in the Iram tale is used as the setting for one of Scheherazade's exotic stories: "As the Commander of the Faithful was seated one day in his palace, conversing with his Sultans and Kings and Grandees of his empire, the talk turned upon the legends of past peoples and the traditions of our Lord Solomon, David's son." The subsequent discussions reveal that one of the court's grandfathers had sailed to a distant land where there were strange marvels. The Caliph sends out an expedition that eventually reaches this strange city:

> . . . it was a high castle, firm of foundations and great and gruesome, as it were a towering mountain, builded all of black stone, with frowning crenelles and a door of gleaming China steel that dazzled the eyes and dazed the wits. Round about it were a thousand steps, and that which appeared afar off as it were smoke was a central dome of lead a hundred cubits high.[11]

Similarly, the tales of Prester John are of ancient origin and recur with tantalizing frequency in the literature of pre-medieval and medieval Europe. Mentioned by Marco Polo and others, the empire of Prester John was believed to have existed somewhere in the interior of Asia or in Africa in what today is Abyssinia. This tradition was used by Norvell W. Page in his two novels *Flame Winds* and *Sons of the Bear-God,* as well as in a story by H. Bedford-Jones, "The Singing Sands of Prester John."[12]

The Matter of Britain is rich in stories of strange castles and lost kingdoms. The Lady of the Lake had a castle in a rock beneath the water of a British mere. One senses the constant shadow of another world and faery mounds in the motif of the Siege Perilous and in the remote location where the Sangreal is eventually revealed to the chosen. *Gawain and the Grene Knight* depicts that member of the Round Table making his way to an unknown kingdom to the castle of the strange, green man with whom he has made a deadly appointment. Sir John Mandeville in his *Travels* records tales of far-distant Cathay and the fabled land of Prester John.[13] In this tradition also is More's *Utopia,* which depicts people living in the uttermost parts of the earth, a tale that contributed ideas to the more modern *Lost Horizon* by Hilton and *The Island* by Huxley. It is clear that man's fascination with strange places and forgotten peoples of the earth has exercised its charm for centuries.

The Lost Civilization story falls into two general categories:

(1) that which is purely a tale of discovery and adventure and (2) that which is filled with discovery and adventure with an added metaphysical aspect that informs the civilization with a special dimension of feeling and atmosphere. In the remainder of this essay, the works discussed will be taken from this second category.

One of the first important aspects of the Lost Civilization fantasy is the choice of protagonist who discovers the civilization or by chance comes upon it. Like the Lost Civilization tale itself, this aspect falls into two categories of people: they are either drawn from the scholarly community or else they are adventurers, soldiers of fortune whose sole reason for existence is the excitement that strange places and races can offer.

The academics who figure largely in the story are university-trained scholars with an expertise in archaeology, language, or hard science. Trelawney, the British aristocrat of *The Jewel of Seven Stars* who discovers the tomb of the Egyptian Queen Tera, is a learned archaeologist. There is also included in the opening chapters a learned discourse about this queen and the discovery of her tomb by "one Nicholas van Huyn of Hoorn:"

> In the preface he told how, attracted by the work of John Greaves of Merton College, *Pyramidographia,* he himself visited Egypt, where he became so interested in its wonders that he devoted some years of his life to visiting strange places, and exploring the ruins of many temples and tombs. He had come across many variants of the story of the building of the Pyramids as told by the Arabian historian, Ibn Abd Alhokin, some of which he set down. . . . The narrative went on to tell how, after passing for several days through the mountains to the east of Aswan, the explorer came to a certain place.[14]

The exploratory party in the novel learns that the "certain place" is called the "Valley of the Sorcerer" because of the legend about the ancient magician who was entombed in the cliff side. In *Elaine's Tomb,* G. Peyton Wurtenbaker pictures his hero, who will participate in a tale of suspended animation via magic formulas, as Dr. Alan Frazer, a professor of chemistry.[15] Robert Bloch's "The Faceless God" depicts a certain "Dr. Stugatche," who, ruthless and cunning, had "come out to Egypt many years ago as an attache on an archaeological expedition, from which he had been summarily dismissed" for stealing "expeditionary trophies."[16] The unnamed hero of Dermot O'Byrne's "Ancient Dominions" is a trained artist and poet who, in the course of the story, reveals an intimate knowledge of literature and the past.[17] August Derleth and Mark Schorer's "The Lair of the Star-Spawn" purports to have been "found among the private documents of the late Eric Marsh, whose death followed so suddenly upon his return from that mysterious expedition into Burma, from which only he returned alive almost three decades ago."[18] Marsh is no soldier but a serious scholar able to converse with ease with "the philosopher and scientist, Doctor Fo-Lan, once far-famed among the scholars of the world. . . ."[19] Sir Hugh Willett, the main character in G. G. Pendarves' "The Altar of Melek Taos," is a trained archaeologist who has spent much time in the East; when the story opens, he is "superintending the excavation of the Daarb Temple."[20] H. Rider Haggard's *She* and *Ayesha, the Return of She* feature L. Horace Holly, a mathematical scholar at Cambridge, and his adopted son Leo Vincey, who is university-trained as well and a master of languages ancient and modern.[21] S. J. Byrne's *Prometheus II*, mentioned above, shows its hero Michael Kent to be a virile officer in the army, but he is, nevertheless, a trained mind who is not in any way a mere soldier of fortune. James Schuyler Grim, familiar to so many Talbot Mundy readers as "Jimgrim" in the novel of the same name, is a sophisticated member of the British Intelligence Service.[22]

A. Merritt utilized this type of character almost exclusively for his novels of lost-civilization fantasy. Nicholas Graydon in A. Merritt's *The Moon Pool* is a trained "first-class mining engineer."[23] Learning of the highest academic order is presented in many places in *The Moon Pool*. The story opens with a long tale of death and destruction told by Dr. David Throckmartin, a world-renowned archaeologist. Dr. Walter Goodwin, a world-famous botanist, tells the reader at the beginning of the novel that Throckmartin

> had planned to spend at least a year among these ruins, not only of Ponape but of Lele—twin centres of a colossal riddle of humanity, a weird flower of civilization that blossomed ages before the seeds of Egypt were sown; of whose arts we know little enough and of whose science nothing. He had carried with him unusually complete equipment for the work he had expected to do and which, he hoped, would be his monument.[24]

The book is dotted here and there with erudite references to science, particularly botany and archaeology. Merritt's *Dwellers in the Mirage,* one of the great achievements in Lost Civilization fantasy novels, introduces the reader to Leif Langdon, a graduate of Dartmouth and a mining engineer. Leif had gone

> into Mongolia with the Fairchild expedition. Part of its work was a mineral survey for certain British interests, part of it ethnographic and archeological research for the British Museum and the University of Pennsylvania. . . .[25]

It is clear that a great number of important novels of this genre give the explorer the most learned credentials. This is so because the scientist represents a special type of training that demands a rational mind, a mind not easily influenced by unseen powers and which will in all probability scoff at or reject the idea that such things could exist. So much the better. When the supernatural makes itself felt in the story, often with devastating results that leave the resources of the scientists helpless before it, the artistic effect is much more pronounced. A scientist makes a brilliant choice for a protagonist of fantasy fiction because of the intellectual tension thereby produced.

On the other hand, the muscular, daring adventurer is also favored as another appropriate main character in fantasy novels about Lost Civilizations. Robert E. Howard's Jason Brill, King Kull, Solomon Kane, and Conan are all types who are more physical than intellectual. They rely on the cutting edge of their swords rather than the cutting edge of their minds to get themselves out of the various predicaments they often find themselves in. Kane, for example, is "a tall man, long-armed and iron-muscled."[26] In "The Moon of Skulls," Kane, nearly exhausted after a journey of a thousand miles, finds it necessary to climb a nearly vertical cliff to reach his destination. The climb "would try his powers to the utmost":

> On up he struggled, and now to make his way harder, the cliff bulged outward near its summit, and the strain on nerve and muscle became heartbreaking. Time and again a hold slipped and he escaped falling by a hair's breadth. But every fiber in his lean hard body was perfectly coordinated, and his fingers were like steel talons with the grip of a vise.[27]

In Howard's "The Blonde Goddess of Bal-Sagoth," another of his lusty heroes is presented, a Gael named Turlogh O'Brien. Both he and a companion, Athelstane the Saxon, are described in heroic terms:

> Turlogh stared at the man who stood before him, feet braced to the lifting of the deck. He was of huge stature, a good half head taller than Turlogh who stood well above six feet. His legs were like columns, his arms like oak and iron.[28]

"Nekht Semerkeht," a story of Howard's finished posthumously by Andrew J. Offutt, tells the story of a Spanish warrior, Hernando de Guzman, who makes his way across the plains of the New World "like a grim god of steel, implacable and unconquerable, with bleak and pitiless eyes," with sword and wheel-lock pistols as his weapons.[29] Conan the Cimmerian, the best known of Howard's heroes, is noted for his physical prowess and his fighting ability. In "The Slithering Shadow," he is described in typical fashion:

> He stood like a bronze image in the sand, apparently impervious to the murderous sun, though his only garment was a silk loincloth, girdled by a wide gold-buckled belt from which hung a saber and a broad-bladed poiniard. On his cleancut limbs were evidences of scarcely healed wounds.[30]

The hero with muscles of iron and an indomitable fighting spirit offers the writer a different approach to the presentation of the supernatural forces within the story. Just as the scientists are helpless before the powers they face, so the barbarian and the soldier of fortune is apparently helpless as well. No figure, however physically powerful, seems able to stand up to the evil forces of the universe as they are levelled in full strength against him. The story develops power as the adventurer, armed only with a sword, is shown defeating, often at terrible cost to himself, the supra-normal powers that have crossed his path. That he is victorious is a tribute to the physical prowess of the hero that transcends even the incredible weapons of sorcerers[31]—and to fantasy's general tendency toward an emphasis on the effectiveness of the individual.

The last aspect of the Lost Civilization fantasy tale to be considered is the strange elemental and supernatural forces commanded by or ruling the peoples of the story. It is the presence of a supernatural force as an integral part of the Lost Civilization that projects it into the realm of fantasy. Harold Lamb's *March-*

ing Sands is an exemplary novel of the science-fiction Lost Civilization type, but there is no sorcery, magic cosmic force, or ancient Evil to be encountered. Generally speaking, the fantasy novel that utilizes the Lost Civilization motif develops the idea from three main areas of the supernatural: (1) the weird science of a past time that seems more akin to magic than to modern science, (2) the Being, in whatever shape it appears, that possesses strange powers, and (3) the Strange Force whose presence in an earthly setting sometimes causes much trouble and difficulty for the human beings with whom it comes into contact.

It was A. Merritt who stated the case for the appearance of otherworldly forces with the greatest eloquence. In the first chapter of *The Metal Monster,* he wrote:

> In this great crucible of life we call the world—in the vaster one we call the universe—the mysteries lie close packed, uncountable as grains of sand on ocean's shores. They thread gigantic, the star-flung spaces; they creep, atomic, beneath the microscope's peering eye. They walk beside us, unseen and unheard, calling out to us, asking why we are deaf to their crying, blind to their wonder.
>
> Sometimes the veils drop from a man's eyes, and he sees —and speaks of his vision. . . . Earth is a ship, plowing her way through uncharted oceans of space wherein are strange currents, hidden shoals and reefs, and where blow the unknown winds of Cosmos.[32]

Out of this idea springs the fantasy of the Lost Civilization. Certainly one of the first areas to be considered is that of the "lost science" whose methods are closer to magic than they are to present-day scientific method. In *A Yank at Valhalla,* Keith Masters reaches a hidden land in the far north that conceals what we have come to regard as the Norse gods. This land is warmer than the surrounding Arctic wastes, and "the air was informed with an eldritch glow," a "faint green radiance."[33] He learns that this land possesses "an ancient science, deeper and different than . . . outland science." Although there is a great deal of discussion about atomic radiation, it is coupled with myth in such a way as to project the story on the level of fantasy rather than pure science fiction. At the outset of the story, a dredge brings up a golden cylinder with runic writing on it. These runes explain that this cylinder is a "key" that chains "dark evil,/Midgard snake, Fenris,/

and Loki, arch devil./While I lie far/the Aesir safe are."[34] The story is a rational explanation of the Norse myths, but it is told in the style of high adventure coupled with sorcery.

"Elaine's Tomb," by G. Peyton Wurtenbaker, rediscovers a lost civilization that has come upon a substance that causes a kind of suspended animation to fall upon any person who takes it. As in the story above, the discovery of this substance is coupled with tombs and forgotten crypts.

> The room, in the lamplight, was simple and small. The walls and floor—even the ceiling—were covered with inscriptions in small letters of the strange alphabet I had seen before, carved into the stone with delicate precision.[35]

In this room is an ancient pharaoh, asleep. Like Queen Tera, the body is soft, cold, and alive. There is no attempt here to be coldly objective; the tone of the story is one of mystery and wonder. *Jimgrim* utilizes this tone to a great degree also. The evil magician, Dorje, "found a buried city in the Gobi Desert, where the Atlantean secrets are all preserved in synthetic gold tablets in chests of the same metal—chemical formulae—everything."[36] Dorje learns the secret of mind control and telepathy. The story is cloaked in mystery and overwhelming evil. It is unlike a straightforward "mad scientist" tale, where the technology is simply beyond our present ability, but is, rather, associated with monasteries in Tibet, the "Maitreya Legend," and other trappings of a supernatural force manifesting itself in the modern world to the consternation of all concerned. There are numerous stories that walk this fine line between science fiction and fantasy, that deal with the science of the past as though it were a special kind of magic.

A second type of Lost Civilization fantasy involves the being with strange, cosmic powers that man has difficulty understanding or dealing with. In Derleth and Schorer's "The Lair of the Star-Spawn," there are a number of alien forms, the most frequent of which "was a living mass of shuddering horror, a ghastly mountain of sensate, quivering flesh, whose tentacles, far-flung in the dim reaches of the subterranean cavern, emitted a strange humming sound."[37] This is the Lloigor ultimately defeated with the help of the Old Ones who return from the "stars of Orion" to battle the repulsive beings. Dr. Fo-Lan tells Eric Marsh:

> They are the Star-Warriors sent by the Ancient Ones from

> Orion. Up there they listened to my plea, for they know that Lloigor and Zhar and their evil spawn are deathless to man; they know that only the ancient weapons of the Elder Gods can punish and destroy.[38]

Tentacled beasts also appear in *Dwellers in the Mirage* in the form of ancient Khalk'ru, the Kraken. It is imprisoned in a triangular block of "yellow translucent stone," but with the appropriate ceremony and sacrifice, the "stone" dissolves and the tentacle of Khalk'ru reaches through another dimension into this world and feeds.[39] But its release depends entirely on the ritual and the sacrifice to permit it to enter this space-time continuum and thus raises this novel into the realm of fantasy. Similarly, Bloch's "The Faceless God," a pastiche of H. P. Lovecraft's Cthulhu mythos, revolves around Nyarlathotep, "the oldest god of all Egypt; of all the world":[40]

> It resembled a miniature sphinx—a life-sized sphinx with the body of a hyena. There were talons and claws, and upon the squatting, bestial body rested a massive, anthropomorphic head, bearing the ominous triple crown whose dread designs had so singularly excited the natives. But the worst and by far the most hideous feature was the lack of a face upon the ghastly thing. It was a faceless god; the winged, faceless god of ancient myth—Nyarlathotep, Mighty Messenger, Stalker among the Stars, and Lord of the Desert.[41]

Dr. Stugatche breaks into the world of ancient Egypt, still present and potent. The ancient gods still exercise their sovereign power over the present, and thus Egypt, as a lost civilization, makes its ghostly presence felt by eliminating a treacherous human who has violated its sanctity.

Robert E. Howard pictures several similar strange beings who preside over strange cities lost in the nethermost parts of the earth. Turlogh O'Brien is shipwrecked on a lost island where he sees a strange city "high in the air with fleecy clouds hovering about them." In this city lives Gothan the conjurer:

> "In the caves deep in the hills to which his tunnels lead, he [Gothan] works fearful and unholy magic. His subjects are beasts— serpents, spiders, and great apes; and men—red captives and wretches of his own race. . . . He has at least brought

> into foul life one creature that even he fears, the gibbering, mowing, nameless Thing he keeps chained in the furtherest cavern that no human foot save his has trod.[42]

Howard's "The Vale of Lost Women" incorporates forms not completely bestial; rather they are "slender brown women, lithe, naked, with blossoms in their night-black hair."[43] But these women are the soul-slaves of "some *thing*" that "would come to her [Livia] as it had come long ago to make these naked brown women the soulless beings they now were." And come it does to feed on the offered sacrifice:

> Its wings were bat-like; but its body and the dim face that gazed down upon her were like nothing of sea or earth or air; she knew she looked upon ultimate horror, upon black cosmic foulness born in night-black gulfs beyond the reach of a madman's wildest dreams.[44]

Conan kills it after a terrific battle with his sword and characterizes it as "a devil from the Outer Dark."[45]

A similar being is imagined in A. Merritt's *The Face in the Abyss.* This is by far the most complex usage of the being with supra-normal powers yet written. Filled with a number of races both human and human-animal (the Snake-woman), it develops at great length and with great power the idea of the being who commands supernatural forces. This being, called Nimir, is chained with what amount to enchantments in a hidden cavern by an ancient race. Nimir has escaped in a way by learning to fashion his will and his ego as a Shadow, a being as intangible as smoke seeking a human body to inhabit so that it may once again work and move in this world, yet be able to control the strange and outré powers it has at its command. Nimir is described thus:

> The face looked at him from the far side of the cavern. Bodiless, its chin rested upon the floor. Colossal, its eyes of pale blue crystals were level with his. It was a man's face and the face of a fallen angel's in one; Luciferean; imperious; ruthless— beautiful. Upon its broad brows power was enthroned —power which could have been godlike in beneficence, had it so willed, but which had chosen instead the lot of Satan.[46]

Merritt creates a sentient creature of metal in *The Metal Monster* that draws its arcane powers from regions normally closed off to humans. This monster, described throughout the novel with the greatest care in poetic prose of the highest order, is electrical in nature, "a prodigious magnet—or rather, a prodigious dynamo. By magnetism or electricity, it had lived and had been activated."[47] Yet it was an "enigmatic organism which while many still was one and which, retaining its integrity as a whole could dissociate manifold parts yet still as a whole maintain an unseen contact and direction over them."[48] Not science, really, but a kind of magic that is supernatural in origin and power.

The third and largest category of supernatural entity that is associated with the Lost Civilization fantasy is the disembodied force. Of inscrutable and inhuman power, it inhabits the earth or is called to the earth from regions beyond space and time. Although many of these stories are fantasy horror—that is, they show the helplessness of man before the onslaught of its power (most of the Cthulhu Mythos is of this variety)—there are also stories in which the power of the individual man, scholar or hero, prevails against it. The survival of the ancient, arcane powers from civilizations such as Egypt, various as these powers are, have been pictured numerous times. One of the first of which there is a literary record is Stoker's *The Jewel of Seven Stars*. Here, a mummified queen, a sorceress in command of the most strange and arcane forces, hopes for resurrection through the application of these magical forces:

> There is another belief of the ancient Egyptians which you must bear in mind; that regarding the ushaptiu figures of Osiris, which were placed with the dead to do its work in the Under World. The enlargement of this idea came to a belief that it was possible to transmit, by magical formulae, the soul and qualities of any living creature to a figure made in its image. This would give a terrible extension of power to one who held the gift of magic.
>
> It is from a union of these various beliefs, and their natural corollaries, that I have come to the conclusion that Queen Tera expected to be able to effect her own resurrection, when, and where, and how, she would.[49]

The jewel of seven stars by which means, among others, she will effect this resuscitation is developed in the novel as a special force. And side by side with this is the civilization of Egypt still existing and affecting the citizens of this world in the here and now. Tera, the sole survivor of this civilization is thus, in a supernatural manner, still alive and present although she is "asleep" in a strange coma. The British people of the story act for her as the people of Kor for Ayesha, special servants who carry out her orders.

It is tempting to regard Haggard's *She* and *The Return of She* as a kind of outgrowth of this earlier work by Stoker. Certainly the fire of life in which Ayesha bathes is related in theme. Ayesha's fire of life is a "revolving pillar of flame," but it is no earthly fire. It is the fire of existence, capable of rejuvenating human flesh or destroying it utterly.

> The mysterious fire played up and down her dark and rolling locks, twining and twisting itself through and around them like threads of golden lace; it gleamed upon her ivory breast and shoulders, from which the ahir had slipped aside; it slid along her pillared throat and delicate features, and seemed to find a home in the glorious eyes that shone and shone more brightly even than the spiritual essence.[50]

This time the flame displays its negative effects and dissolves Ayesha into an unthinkable old age. Yet she returns in the sequel as ineffably beautiful as before. Holly asks Leo "Are you sure that she was so born? . . . Like the visions on the fire, may not that hideous shape have been but an illusion of our minds? May she not be still the same Ayesha whom we knew in Kor, not re-born, but wafted higher by some mysterious agency?"[51]

G. G. Pendarves' "The Altar of Melek Taos" also uses fire as the agency of supernatural force. Here, a magician styled as Prince Dena ibn Zodh is "High Priest of the tribe known as the Yezidees." He has discovered the secret of the Zoroastrian fire, a "secret and occult force" which governs. This is the "Astral Fluid that radiates from every sphere in the universe" and is called the "Voice of Fire."[52] This prince rules over a people from a hidden city. But this fire too is ultimately destructive to its evil masters, killing them at the end of the story and releasing the morally upright. Merritt too utilizes a fiery force in *The Moon Pool*:

> There is an energy beyond and above ether, a purposeful, sentient force that laps like an ocean the furthest-flung star, that transfuses all that ether bears, that sees and speaks and

> feels in us and in you, that is incorporate in beast and bird and reptile, in tree and grass and all living things, that sleeps in rock and stone, that finds sparkling tongue in jewel and star and in all dwellers within the firmament. And this ye call consciousness.[53]

This energy is tapped by an enigmatic being called The Shining One and enables the ancient race discovered by Dr. Goodwin to utilize its inhuman powers for themselves.

Howard's Conan discovers several lost civilizations that gain their power from magical or supernatural forces. One of the types of inimical powers he meets is chronicled in "The Pool of the Black One" in which the being is a sentient pool of water that feeds upon the life force of those who are unlucky enough to be immersed in it. It has a race of beings who bring it food. When thwarted, it turns into a raging geyser, an elemental Force, which only the cunning of Conan is able to overcome. Related to this is the strange cloud that kills, observed by Hernando de Guzman in Howard's "Nekht Semerkeht."

Finally, there are the strange elemental and supernatural forces commanded by the King of the World in S. J. Byrne's *Prometheus II*. With war in every part of the inhabited globe (even the underground civilizations of the Deros are making war against the gods of space), ordinary solutions and heroes are of no value. Within this scientific and technologically advanced civilization, there appears a supernatural manifestation in which the hero, Michael Kent, is subjected to a training session on another plane of existence by the King of the World. Taken to the Himalayas, Kent is told to "prepare for a psychic experience."[54] He then becomes a "privileged visitor to the Seven Towers."

> He stood as though in another world or dimension. It was beyond his full comprehension. . . . Before him, beside the first gigantic step, was a massive looking tower, windowless, uninviting. Its soaring top was on a level with the first step, and up on that first step he saw another tower, which began where the first had left off, and its top, in turn, reached the second step of the mountain. Above these two he counted five more. . . . They faded upward into mists of distance.[55]

In these towers, on the earth yet somewhere else as well, Kent is subjected to a variety of unearthly visions and experiences, all of which show him and him alone the true situation that the world is in. Only in this supra-normal way is this information able to be imparted to him.

All of these forces, beings, and sciences are closely attached to civilizations that are generally regarded as "lost." Without these powers, the form would not and could not exist. With them, the reader is given a special experience that operates both on the plan of the familiar world and in a different manner—incredibly ancient. On a different scale and with different laws, it is this supernatural aspect that sets the Lost Civilization as fantasy quite apart from its science-fiction counterpart.

NOTES

1. John Beynon Harris, *The Secret People* (New York: Lancer, 1967). Other editions appeared under the pseudonym of John Wyndham.

2. Ibid., p. 53.

3. Jack Vance, "DP!" *Avon Science Fiction and Fantasy Reader*, 1 (April 1953), 3.

4. Ibid., p. 9.

5. Edmund Hamilton, *A Yank at Valhalla, Fantastic Story Magazine*, (January 1953), 22.

6. Richard Shaver, "Of Gods and Goats," *Amazing Stories Quarterly*, 21 (Summer 1948), 66–67 of Section I. This issue has three separate parts, each one paginated separately.

7. S. J. Byrne, *Prometheus II, Amazing Stories Quarterly*, 21 (Summer 1948), 8 of Section III. See note 6 above.

8. For distinctions in this matter, see the introductory essay in Roger C. Schlobin's *The Literature of Fantasy: A Comprehensive, Annotated Bibliography of Modern Fantasy Fiction* (New York: Garland, 1979).

9. H. P. Lovecraft uses the lost city situated in the Arabian desert regions a number of times. It is mentioned by name in his "The Lamp of Alhazred."

10. There are a variety of editions on the market. This quotation is taken from Sir Richard Burton's translation: *The Arabian Nights* (New York: Halcyon House, 1948), p. 139.

11. Ibid., pp. 478–79.

12. H. Bedford-Jones, "The Singing Sands of Prester John," *Fantastic Stories of Imagination*, 12, no. 9 (September 1963), 52.

13. For extensive, learned essays on both Mandeville and Prester John, see the *Encyclopaedia Britannica,* ninth edition. Later editions of the Britannica use facts from the same essay, much watered down.

14. Bram Stoker, *The Jewel of Seven Stars* (London: William Rider and Sons, 1912), pp. 139–40.

15. G. Peyton Wurtenbaker, "Elaine's Tomb," *Amazing Stories,* 40 (June 1966), 111.

16. Robert Bloch, "The Faceless God," *Magazine of Horror,* 2 (Winter 1965–66), 5.

17. Dermot O'Byrne, "Ancient Dominions," *Owl's Watch,* ed. George Brandon Saul (New York: Fawcett, 1965), p. 214.

18. August Derleth and Mark Schorer, "The Lair of the Star-Spawn," *Magazine of Horror,* 3 (Winter 1966–67), 8.

19. Ibid., p. 8.

20. G. G. Pendarves, "The Altar of Melek Taos," *Magazine of Horror,* 6 (February 1971), 13.

21. H. Rider Haggard, *She* (New York: Hurst and Co., n.d.) and *Ayesha, The Return of She* (North Hollywood, Calif.: Newcastle, 1977).

22. Talbot Mundy, *Jimgrim* (New York: Avon, 1968).

23. A. Merritt, *The Moon Pool* (New York: Avon, n.d.), p. 11.

24. Merritt, *The Moon Pool,* p. 4.

25. A. Merritt, *Dwellers in the Mirage* (New York: Avon, 1952), p. 11.

26. Robert E. Howard, "The Moon of Skulls," *The Moon of Skulls,* Time Lost Series (New York: Centaur Press, 1968), p. 10.

27. Ibid.

28. Robert E. Howard, "The Blonde Goddess of Bal-Sagoth," in *The Second Avon Fantasy Reader,* ed. Donald A. Wollheim and George Ernsberger (New York: Avon, 1969), p. 12.

29. Robert E. Howard, "Nekht Semerkeht," in *Swords Against Darkness,* ed. Andrew J. Offutt (New York: Zebra, 1977), p. 17.

30. Robert E. Howard, "The Slithering Shadow," in *Conan the Adventurer* (New York: Lancer, 1968), p. 103.

31. For other views on this subject, see Diana Waggoner's *The Hills of Faraway: A Guide to Fantasy* (New York: Atheneum, 1978).

32. A. Merritt, *The Metal Monster* (New York: Avon, 1945), p. 9.

33. Edmund Hamilton, p. 16.

34. Ibid., pp. 12, 29.

35. Wurtenbaker, p. 121.

36. Mundy, p. 254.

37. Derleth and Schorer, "The Lair of the Star-Spawn," p. 21.

38. Ibid., p. 26.

39. Merritt, *Dwellers in the Mirage,* p. 32.

40. Bloch, p. 10.

41. Ibid., p. 11.

42. Howard, "The Blond Goddess of Bal-Sagoth," pp. 33–34.

43. Robert E. Howard, "The Vale of Lost Women," *Magazine of Horror,* 3 (Spring 1967), 60.

44. Ibid., p. 62.

45. Ibid., p. 63.

46. Merritt, *The Face in the Abyss,* p. 53.

47. Merritt, *The Metal Monster,* p. 220.

48. Ibid.

49. Stoker, pp. 223–24.

50. Haggard, *She,* p. 232.

51. Haggard, *Ayesha, the Return of She,* p. 249.

52. Pendarves, p. 20.

53. Merritt, *The Moon Pool,* p. 24.

54. Byrne, p. 60.

55. Ibid., p. 61.

Modern Fantasy and Medieval Romance: A Comparative Study

Raymond H. Thompson

One of the first obstacles that confronts a serious study of fantasy is that of definition: how can we fully understand what we are reading if we do not know exactly what it is? This is a problem of deeper concern to critics and literary theorists than to ordinary readers, who are usually content to enjoy a book unperplexed by such esoteric questions. Nevertheless, the impulse is more than just a manifestation of the innate human desire to impose order upon the surrounding universe. If we are to avoid the dangers that arise out of misunderstanding what fantasy is trying to achieve and consequently judging it by inapplicable criteria, then we need some idea of its nature. The problem is illustrated in *The Hills of Faraway*, where Diana Waggoner praises William Morris because his characters are more than "mere representatives, in human form, of unhumanly ideal behavior, puppets without personality to be analyzed. . . . He added a dimension of intimacy to the old romances and epics, being more careful to describe the feelings and hopes of his characters."[1] Morris' characters may indeed be more realistically depicted than their counterparts in the earlier literature that he used as models, but is it legitimate to expect realistic characterization in fantasy?

Despite numerous attempts to reach a comprehensive definition of fantasy,[2] the results have continued to prompt grumbling from critics when they actually analyze a work of fantasy. In a recent article on Beagle's *The Last Unicorn* (1968), R. E. Foust complains that "existing theories of fantasy are clearly inadequate."[3] This problem is not, however, unique to fantasy, and we should feel reassured by the cautioning words of A. C. Gibbs in his examination of another genre within the romance mode: "when we talk in general terms about a phenomenon called 'The Medieval Romance' we are only too likely to find that its essential nature escapes from all our formulations."[4] Indeed, general definitions of medieval romance, like those of fantasy, tend to a vagueness that obscures as much as it clarifies, and this situation should help allay any defensiveness that we may feel about fantasy and attempts to describe it. However, similarities between the two genres extend beyond confusion over definitions. Critics frequently assume a relationship and trace the line of descent from medieval romance through William Morris' recreations of the Middle Ages and into modern fantasy where it remains most evident in that branch known as heroic or sword-and-sorcery fantasy.[5] This suggests that a more careful comparison of the two genres should further our understanding of fantasy and should reveal the extent to which we can apply the same critical techniques as have served to demonstrate the greatness of such medieval romancers as Chrétien de Troyes, Geoffrey Chaucer, the Gawain-poet, and Sir Thomas Malory.

Despite the difficulties that hinder attempts to define medieval romance, certain recurring features can be discerned. George Kane maintains, "The essential characteristics are that the story should be treated in terms of chivalry, and that it should not be naturalistic, but that instead its setting, characters and action should be heightened to enable the escape from the limitations of actuality which the romances were designed to afford."[6] However, these two essential characteristics do entail others, which Kane describes as "*accidents* rather than *essentials* of the *genre*" (p. 1). In dealing with their subject in terms of chivalry, writers translate it into a medieval cultural environment; in heightening settings, characters and actions, they set the boundaries of probability wide enough to include the marvellous, while tending to lapse into mere exaggeration, and showing their fondness for happy endings.

It is important to realize that the great theme of medieval romance is self-realization: "in the best work, the adventures are not there for their own sake, but to call forth the very essence of the knight's ideal of manhood."[7] Thus Charles Muscatine notes that the choice of an exotic setting, divorced from the real world, favors the presentation of adventure in the nearly abstract: "Freed from the exigencies of time and place, the hero can concentrate on his courtly quest. To cross over on a sword-bridge into a land whence no stranger has ever returned—for the love of a lady—is an act of gratuitous valour that no-one can quibble about."[8] Since the ideal of manhood in the Middle Ages was dominated by the aristocratic concepts of chivalry, the standards put to the test in the adventures encountered in medieval romance are those of knighthood. However, "there is no one attitude toward, or canonic form of, the individual chivalric career. Only its existence and centrality are universally accepted."[9] Despite differences, however, a basis of shared standards does remain: prowess, courage, loyalty, courtesy (in the sense of consideration for others), and wisdom are all to varying degrees admired.[10]

Proving the hero's values is as important to modern fantasy as it is to medieval romance. The dangers inherent in the ambitious pursuit of power are the subject of J. R. R. Tolkien's *The Lord of the Rings* (1954–55) and T. H. White's *The Once and Future King* (1958), as well as of the medieval romances of Alexander and the fourteenth-century English alliterative *Awntyrs off Arthure*; the problems imposed by conflicting responsibilities are explored in C. S. Lewis' *The Magician's Nephew* (1955), when Digory must choose whether to give the healing apple to Aslan or keep it for his sick mother, and in Malory's *Le Morte D'Arthur* (1470), when Lancelot finds himself forced to fight against King Arthur to save the life of his lady, Queen Guenevere; the related conflict between broader social responsibilities and the demands of personal love poses serious questions in H. Rider Haggard's *She* (1886), Lord Dunsany's *The King of Elfland's Daughter* (1924), and Patricia McKillip's *Heir of Sea and Fire* (1977), as it does in the twelfth-century romances of Marie de France and Chrétien de Troyes; and heroic values are ironically undercut in Mark Twain's *A Connecticut Yankee in King Arthur's Court* (1889), James Branch Cabell's massive Life of Manuel series, and the Incomplete Enchanter series by L. Sprague de Camp and Fletcher Pratt, as they are in Raoul de Houdenc's *La Vengeance Raguidel* from the early thirteenth century, the late fourteenth-century *Sir Gawain and the Green Knight,* and Miguel de Cervantes' *Don Quixote* (1604).

Moreover, the same combination of diversity and similarity of heroic ideals marks both medieval romance and modern fantasy. Clearly a wide gulf separates Conan the Barbarian, hero of a series of stories (c. 1930–36) by Robert Howard, from Ged, one of the two heroes in Ursula Le Guin's *The Farthest Shore* (1972). The former is violent and aggressive, hastening restlessly from one adventure to the next; whereas Ged, voyaging slowly, almost aimlessly, through the South and West Reaches of Earthsea, advises Arren, his young companion, "do nothing because it is righteous, or praiseworthy, or noble to do so; do nothing because it seems good to do so; do only that which you must do, and which you cannot do in any other way."[11] Yet both possess a code of values that is put to the test by their experiences. Conan "is amoral, brutal, violent, ruthless, tough and warlike but has a sort of barbaric nobility based on the brotherhood of the sword,"[12] in which prowess, courage, and loyalty to a companion are important. Despite his preference for inaction, Ged too possesses power that he wields to defeat his enemy when challenged; and he and Arren need both courage and loyalty to pursue this enemy into the realm of death, then return to the world of life again. Even Kenneth Grahame's humorous fantasy for children, *The Wind in the Willows* (1908), is concerned with heroic values: it warns of the dangers of vanity and self-indulgence while it delights us with the comic misadventures of the irrepressible Mr. Toad; and it too demonstrates the virtues of prowess, courage, and loyalty as Toad's friends help him recapture Toad Hall from the stoats. Moreover, both Grahame's and Le Guin's books also praise the virtues of consideration for others and wisdom, be it wiliness in outwitting an adversary, common sense in handling awkward problems, or more awesome powers of insight and understanding.

Nevertheless, the number of medieval romances that go beyond the mere assertion of a particular standard of behavior to explore meaningfully the problems and dangers posed by trying to maintain that standard was always a minority. For every romance like *Sir Gawain and the Green Knight*, a dozen have survived like the prose *Tristan* and *Guy of Warwick*, from the early thirteenth and the fourteenth centuries respectively, where the knightly champion's adherence to a frequently callous code of values is stamped with the approval of monotonous success. The same can be said of modern fantasy, where fine works like Tolkien's *The Lord of the Rings* are heavily outnumbered by the outpourings of Lin Carter, John Jakes, Gardner F. Fox, and many others who comprise the school of writing known as adventure or sword-and-sorcery fantasy.[13]

In medieval romance the testing of the chivalric ideal takes place in a medieval setting, regardless of the historical context of the original material. Thus in Geoffrey Chaucer's "The Knight's Tale" from the late fourteenth century, Theseus, the hero of ancient Greek legend, is transformed into a feudal duke who rides to war in full armor and tries to resolve a dispute between two courtly lovers by means of a tournament. Other heroes from classical legend, such as Alexander the Great and Hector of Troy, are similarly changed, while Arthur, the leader of the British struggle against the Germanic invaders in post-Roman Britain, grows to become the noble monarch whose reputation for valor and courtesy attracts to his Round Table the finest knights of Europe.

Of the various types of fantasy, heroic fantasy shows the greatest enthusiasm for recreating a quasi-medieval setting, thanks largely to William Morris, the earliest practitioner of this form, who consciously sought to revive the world of medieval romance. However, the setting is not confined to that of the High Middle Ages as in the romances, but included the world of the Early Middle Ages or the "Dark Ages" as they are often described. Thus while some fantasists, like Lord Dunsany in *The Charwoman's Shadow* (1926) and T. H. White in *The Once and Future King*, retain Morris' interest in the era of knighthood and chivalry, many others prefer the primitive barbarian culture of the tribes who migrated across Europe after the fall of the Western Roman Empire. The most influential of these was Robert Howard, whose stories of Conan the Barbarian initiated many imitations, including de Camp's stories of the Pusadian Age and Fritz Leiber's adventures of the Gray Mouser and Fafhrd. Some of the barbarian cultures portrayed clearly predate even the Early Middle Ages, but since the basic elements of these cultures changed relatively little over the centuries, to all intents and purposes they can be considered part of the quasi-medieval setting. The most obvious examples are stories set in a version of pre-Roman Celtic Britain, notably Lloyd Alexander's Chronicles of Prydain (1964–68) and the retellings of parts of *The Mabinogion* by Kenneth Morris and Evangeline Walton. Thomas Burnett Swann's fantasies also reach back to the primitive society of early legend.

Ironically, however, this revival of the Middle Ages goes against the spirit of medieval romance, which integrates the past into its own culture. Indeed the careful reconstruction of a world that satisfies our expectations of the past probably owes more to the tradition of the historical romance popularized by Sir Walter

Scott and results from the need of fantasy to create a believable and internally consistent world for readers who have a keener sense of the span of history than did their medieval predecessors.[14] Some fantasy writers, however, do adapt earlier material to a modern setting as did the medieval romancers. Two striking examples of this are Alan Garner and Susan Cooper. In *The Weirdstone of Brisingamen* (1960) and its sequel, *The Moon of Gomrath* (1963), Garner integrates elements of Norse, Welsh, and English tradition into the contemporary world; another Garner fantasy, *The Owl Service* (1967), relates how three young people in the twentieth century are compelled to re-enact the ancient Welsh legend of Blodeuedd, the woman made of flowers who betrayed her husband and conspired with her lover to murder him. Cooper's The Dark is Rising Series (1965–77) also revives Celtic, Welsh, and Arthurian legends in the modern period as part of an elemental struggle between good and evil that transcends the ages. The return of the Holy Grail, in fantasies like Charles W. S. Williams' *War in Heaven* (1930) and Sanders Anne Laubenthal's *Excalibur* (1973), is another example of adapting traditional material to a modern setting.

Yet even when the setting is not a reflection of the modern world, in successful fantasy it is usually highly distinctive, weaving traditional elements to form a fresh vision. Indeed the effectiveness with which traditional elements are combined to produce a new secondary world has become a critical criterion of modern fantasy: Patricia McKillip's Hed Trilogy (1976–79) is highly praised for its originality, whereas Terry Brook's *The Sword of Shannara* (1977) suffers from being too Tolkien-like. The danger of imitation lies not in the actual borrowing of traditional features—all writers do that—but in how they are used. Medieval romances borrow heavily from Celtic legend, but as Gibbs points out, "much of it seems to have been taken over for the specific purpose of providing *aventures* which would illustrate the ideal values of chivalry" (p. 10). Borrowings must therefore be carefully integrated into this pattern if they are to avoid straining the thematic structure of the work. Thus *Sir Gawain and the Green Knight* borrows from Celtic legend the figure of the shape-shifter with the power of surviving decapitation and the motif of the beheading game to examine the qualities of courage, loyalty, courtesy, and discretion, which together with prowess make up the ideal of knight-errantry in King Arthur's court. The borrowings consequently become an integral part of a testing process that is not only far more subtle and complex than any found in earlier uses of these elements, but also designed to probe a combination of qualities that are of special interest to a medieval audience.

The finest practitioners of modern fantasy demonstrate similar techniques. In Tolkien's The Lord of the Rings such creatures as the Ringwraiths, Elves, Tom Bombadil and the Barrow-wight, most of whose features are adapted from traditional folk-belief, are integrated into a series of encounters which develop in Frodo the qualities of courage, fortitude, loyalty, initiative, and self-discipline. These are all necessary if he is to undertake the quest to destroy the One Ring, the symbol of a power that it is vital the twentieth century learn to control.[15] In Le Guin's *A Wizard of Earthsea* (1968), the treachery, craftiness, and selfish greed traditionally associated with dragons serve to test Ged's principles when the Dragon of Pendor tempts the young wizard to betray his duty to protect the people entrusted to his care in return for a secret that may save his life. The conflict between selfishness and duty is age-old, but interpreting it in terms of the Jungian shadow as the author has chosen to do in this book is a modern approach.[16]

Even in a lesser work, like Nancy Springer's *The White Hart* (1979), borrowings can be well integrated into the fantasy's distinctive vision: the magical stone that pronounces Bevan the rightful king and so forces him to confront his responsibilities to the realm can, like both the Siege Perilous in accounts of the Grail Quest and the Holy Grail itself in the early thirteenth-century German *Parzival* by Wolfram von Eschenbach, be traced back to *Lia Fáil,* the Stone of Destiny in ancient Irish legend which roars out under the feet of the rightful king;[17] Coradel Orre, the magical cauldron that revives the dead, is derived from the cauldron of rebirth in the Welsh tale of "Branwen Daughter of Llŷr,"[18] but Springer causes its destruction to deprive the older race (themselves based on the Tuatha de Danaan of Celtic myth) of immortality as part of the fantasy's pattern of change from the old to the new order. *The White Hart* is thus a successful fantasy because it adapts traditional elements to its own thematic purpose. Although the fantasy's themes are by no means unique to the twentieth century, such concerns as the passing of the old way of life and the need to accept responsibility are as valid and as pressing today as they were a thousand years ago. It is important not that the themes explored be exclusive to our era, but that they be relevant to it.

The second essential of medieval romance is the process of

heightening the elements of setting, character and action. This is facilitated by placing events at a distance in time or space: ancient Greece or Rome; King Arthur's half-legendary Britain; perhaps some distant oriental realm, as in Chaucer's "The Squire's Tale"; or even, as Gibbs notes, "a dreamland quite outside geography" (p. 10). The world of fantasy is equally remote: Howard's tales of Conan are set in an ancient "Hyborean" age, Jack Vance's *The Dying Earth* (1950) in the far future; H. Rider Haggard's *She* (1886) takes the reader to darkest Africa, E. R. Eddison's *The Worm Ouroboros* (1922) to Mercury. As our knowledge of the world and the solar system continues to grow, fantasists have been forced to create their secondary world on even more distant planets, as is the case in John Norman's Gor series (begun in 1966), or in parallel worlds as in C. S. Lewis' Narnia series (1950–56); other secondary worlds are vaguely located, if at all.

In medieval romance this remoteness allows freedom in the treatment of the physical environment. This usually means splendid furnishings, fine clothing and armor, and sumptuous banquets, the richness of which, the writer assures us, lies beyond his modest talents to describe. By contrast, topographic detail is hazy: knights ride through forests, encounter challenges at fords, and joust in open meadows, but description of these places is often lacking. The writers of medieval romance concentrate the heightening process upon features of civilization, such as castles, chapels, and enclosed gardens, rather than the surrounding countryside, although when they choose they can utilize descriptions of the latter to striking effect, as Marie de France, Chaucer, and the Gawain-poet prove. The society portrayed is aristocratic: other classes of society appear but rarely, as occasional guides, minor enemies or objects of charity.

Although more democratic in its social range, as witnessed by Diana Wynne Jones's *Cart and Cwidder* (1975), modern fantasy often focuses upon aristocratic society also. Tolkien's *The Hobbit* (1937) and The Lord of the Rings both open and close in the Shire which recreates rustic England, but the major action takes place elsewhere and involves the nobly born. The same pattern reappears in the large group of fantasies that move their protagonists from a world that is ordinary, often mundane, to one that is fantastic, as in George MacDonald's *Lilith* (1895), Poul Anderson's *Three Hearts and Three Lions* (1961), Dean R. Koontz's *The Crimson Witch* (1971), and Gordon R. Dickson's *The Dragon and the George* (1976). The splendor of the new surroundings consequently gains from the wonder it inspires in these travellers from less exotic regions. In literary terms this device has the same effect as the romance writer's modest disclaimer. However, it possesses two additional advantages. Firstly, it emphasizes the spiritual and imaginative poverty of the ordinary world, from which the reader seeks respite and "recovery" in the realm of fantasy.[19] Secondly, it helps the reader identify with the protagonist from whose point of view the narrative is told, as Waggoner observes of the Hobbits in Tolkien's stories of Middle Earth: "They, with their modest abilities, self-doubts, and preference for the practical over the 'heroic,' provided him [Tolkien] with the means to make his heroic characters and events plausible beyond the confines of the narrative" (p. 41).

This concern for the credibility of the secondary world created in modern fantasy likewise accounts for the care over topography which is largely lacking in medieval romance. Geography is more precise today than it was in the Middle Ages, as a comparison of maps demonstrates, and a modern audience correspondingly is less willing to accept vagueness and inconsistency in this area. Skilled modern fantasists, like Tolkien, Le Guin, and Stephen R. Donaldson remedy this situation not only by providing maps of their secondary worlds, but also by making use of a greater range of physical settings to create atmosphere and suspense than do their medieval predecessors: Mirkwood in *The Hobbit* is as sinister and confusing as the dangers it contains; the subterranean labyrinth in Le Guin's *The Tombs of Atuan* (1971) symbolizes the mind-numbing destructiveness of the powers of darkness; the red stain on the moon in Donaldson's *Lord Foul's Bane* (1977) reflects the corruption of the land. As Gary K. Wolfe notes, the setting in fantasy "is more than a backdrop; it is integral to the events themselves, a kind of spiritual landscape in which even the least element might carry a moral meaning."[20]

Just as setting is heightened, so are both character and action. Northrop Frye describes "the typical hero of romance" as "superior in degree to other men and to his environment . . . whose actions are marvellous but who is himself viewed as a human being."[21] The ability of the knights of medieval romance to fight all day ankle-deep in their own blood, and to slay large numbers of opponents—in the English *Sir Perceval of Gales* from early in the fourteenth century the hero slaughters a sultan and his entire army—has been passed on to such mighty-thewed descendants as Howard's Conan the Barbarian and Fritz Leiber's Fafhrd, as well as some highly skilled swordswomen like C. L. Moore's Jirel of Joiry and Andrew J. Offut and Richard K. Lyon's more licentious creation, Tiana of Reme.[22]

In medieval romance the heroes rarely possess supernatural powers, and when they do it is usually a minor feature that survives from sources in legend, like the strength of Gawain, the nephew of King Arthur, which fluctuates with the movement of the sun, or the enchantments and prophesies of Merlin. Supernatural powers are more frequently encountered in the heroes and heroines of fantasy, e.g., Simon Tregarth and his family in Andre Norton's Witch World series (1963–68), the wizard Ged in Le Guin's Earthsea trilogy, and Morgan and Raederle in McKillip's Hed trilogy.

However, the true superiority of the champion in medieval romance rests upon his ability to adhere to his exacting set of values with greater success than most of his companions, and his physical superiority is largely a manifestation of this fact. Essentially, he is a hero because he tries harder. When he commits a mistake, as does Erec in *Erec et Enide* by Chrétien de Troyes, he suffers grievous remorse and redoubles his efforts to do better. It is this dedication to his ideals that enables Lancelot to win the love of the beautiful Guenevere, Perceval and Galahad to achieve the Grail quest, and Gawain to win the praise of the Green Knight as "the fautlest freke that ever on fote yede" (the most faultless man who ever walked, v. 2363) in *Sir Gawain and the Green Knight.* The same resolute commitment sustains the Fellowship of the Ring through physical and spiritual hardship "beyond hope" to defeat Sauron in Tolkien's *The Lord of the Rings*; it carries Ged and Arren into the realm of death and beyond in Le Guin's *The Farthest Shore* (1972); it leads Michael Moorcock's Eternal Champion through various planes of existence to fight for the virtues of Law against the Lords of Chaos; it prompts Oliver's self-sacrifice in Joy Chant's *Red Moon and Black Mountain* (1971); and it earns Hazel the leadership of the epic migration of the rabbits in Richard Adams' *Watership Down* (1973). This heightening of character and action focuses attention upon the heroic code of values which is subjected to such exacting tests.

The element of the marvellous is defined as one of the "accidental" features of medieval romance,[23] but when used skillfully it can reinforce thematic development. Marie de France develops a contrast between the beautiful world of faery and the ordinary mundane world to reinforce the conflict between tender love and an unsympathetic feudal society; Chaucer, in "The Franklin's Tale," uses the magical disappearance of the rocks not only to put the characters' ideals of behavior to the proof, but also as the symbol of that love itself. However, it is significant that these examples are all Breton lais, a sub-genre of romance closely linked with Celtic legend. Other than in the Grail romances, the element of the marvellous tends to be incidental to main thematic concerns, though it can provide very effective adventures that probe the qualities of the knights. Certainly the sword-bridge in Chrétien's *Lancelot* is a formidable test of the hero's devotion to his lady, and the Green Knight's ability to survive decapitation without ill effect puts considerable pressure upon Gawain who has agreed to play the beheading game with him in *Sir Gawain and the Green Knight*. Since the hero has no such ability, as he himself sourly points out (vv. 2282-3), he feels more strongly the temptation to withdraw from so unfair an encounter and so break his word.

Whereas in medieval romance the element of the marvellous is usually incidental, albeit both useful and popular, most theorists agree that "the literature that can be identified as fantasy is that corpus in which the impossible is primary in its quantity or centrality."[24] Quite simply there would be no story without Ged's Shadow in Le Guin's *The Wizard of Earthsea,* without Merlin's magical powers in White's *The Sword in the Stone,* without talking animals in Grahame's *The Wind in the Willows,* without the macabre environment of Tormance in David Lindsay's *A Voyage to Arcturus* (1920).

Another "accident" of medieval romance is the tendency for the heightening process to lapse into mere exaggeration. The astonishing numbers slain in battle by a Lancelot in the war against Galehaut in the Vulgate *Lancelot,* or a Gawain in the Vulgate *Merlin,* were surpassed in later romances such as *Guy of Warwick* and *Beves of Hampton* in an effort to impress the audience with the superiority of the new champions over earlier competitors. Adventure fantasy strikingly exhibits the same tendency, as writers like Norman in his Gor series and Chris Carlsen in his Berserker series, strive to outdo competing series in gore and brutality. Exaggeration also leads to repetition, in that adventure is piled upon adventure in an attempt to overwhelm the reader with evidence of a champion's superiority. The result, however, is structural weakness. Edgar Rice Burroughs' Barsoom series (1912–42) is as episodic and rambling as the thirteenth-century

Prose *Tristan.* Exaggeration is a tempting and deceptively easy device for the writer who wishes to assert the merits of his own hero over others, but it rapidly palls upon the reader, losing its effectiveness through excess. Moreover, it seriously undermines the sense of wonder which fantasy *must* inspire in its readers, for it reduces the marvellous to the commonplace.

The final "accident" of treatment in medieval romance is the fondness for a happy ending. More thoughtful works of both medieval romance and modern fantasy conclude with their characters learning an often bitter lesson through their experiences. Marie de France's Lanval can find fulfilment in love only in the realm of faery, for the feudal world is too hostile; Chrétien's heroes learn that high standards of conduct can be maintained only through ceaseless vigilance; in *Sir Gawain and the Green Knight,* Gawain discovers that even his best is not good enough, that he is no more capable of perfection than any human being. Frodo in Tolkien's The Lord of the Rings returns from the Mount of Doom knowing that he too had failed the final test and that disaster had been averted as much by the tendency of evil to confound itself as by good to overcome evil; in Le Guin's *A Wizard of Earthsea,* Ged discovers that the Shadow beast he has loosed upon the world is the embodiment of his own failings, notably pride; in Lewis' *The Magician's Nephew* (1955), Digory realizes that he is responsible for introducing evil, in the person of Jadis, into Narnia. However, except where the traditional pattern of the legendary material imposes a tragic form, as in the story of King Arthur's death in Malory's *Le Morte D'Arthur* and White's *The Once and Future King,* the sorrow of disillusionment and loss is balanced by the joy of real achievement and victory, and this is marked by celebrations, weddings, the triumphant installation of rightful monarchs, and by signal honors in gratitude to returning heroes who have rescued ladies in distress or have saved their lands from chaos and repression—Tolkien's "Eucatastrophe."[25]

In summary, then, the parallels between medieval romance and modern fantasy, particularly that branch known as heroic fantasy, are indeed close. The central theme of both is self-realization, the proving of a particular set of values: in romance the values are those of chivalry, in fantasy the concept of heroism is not thus limited; yet in both beneath the apparently wide variation in values lies a shared basis of admired traits, notably prowess or strength (be it of arm or of will), courage, loyalty, consideration for others (often associated with preserving freedom from oppression), and wisdom. In medieval romance the subject is set in a medieval cultural environment to explore the chivalric ideal, a topic of particular interest to the Middle Ages; in modern fantasy, although the setting is frequently quasi-medieval, concepts such as the problems of power, the conflict between individual freedom and social responsibility, the upheavals of change, which are explored therein, retain a special relevance to the modern era. Both medieval romance and modern fantasy heighten setting, characters and action to examine their themes most effectively, and both have a weakness for exaggeration and a fondness for happy endings.

However, there are two areas of difference. First of all, the element of the marvellous, which is incidental in medieval romance, is central in modern fantasy. Second of all, modern fantasy takes greater care over plausibility of its secondary world than medieval romance appears to, notably in that its concern does extend to "ordinary" people and to topographical detail. However, this difference is more apparent than real and can largely be explained by the greater credulity of the medieval audience, which was readier to accept the marvellous than its modern equivalent.[26] These variations support the views of those theorists who contend that two vital elements in fantasy are apparently contradictory: that it deals with events that violate the laws of our universe, yet "bear an intelligible relationship to the real world, hence, serve some reality-function."[27]

Nevertheless, the closeness of the two genres argues that they can and should be measured by similar criteria. The pattern of events should be scrutinized carefully to discern the standards of behavior that are being tested, and a work should be judged by its success in probing the standards meaningfully.

I should like to conclude by returning to my original question: is it legitimate to expect realistic characterization in fantasy? The answer is no. Waggoner's objection that Morris' characters are "mere representatives, in human form of unhumanly ideal behavior, puppets without personality to be analyzed" misunderstands the role of such figures in fantasy. They are deliberately heightened *in order to be* representative rather than realistic. Just as the hero of *Sir Gawain and the Green Knight* rides forth across the Wirral to be tested and found wanting, not as an individual but as a representative of what is best in mankind, so Ged must confront and acknowledge the Shadow of evil that lies within each one of us, not just himself, in the Earthsea trilogy. All ideals are "unhuman," beyond our reach. And yet like medieval romance, fantasy teaches us to keep trying. "A man's reach should exceed his grasp, or what's a heaven for?"

NOTES

1. Diana Waggoner, *The Hills of Faraway: A Guide to Fantasy* (New York: Atheneum, 1978), p. 38.

2. The first to offer a definition was E. M. Forster in his *Aspects of the Novel* (1927; rpt. London: Edward Arnold, 1974); other definitions prior to 1978 are summarized by S. C. Fredericks in "Problems of Fantasy," *Science-Fiction Studies,* 5 (1978), 33–44, especially pp. 33–37.

3. R. E. Foust, "Fabulous Paradigm: Fantasy, Meta-Fantasy, and Peter S. Beagle's *The Last Unicorn,*" *Extrapolation,* 21 (1980), 8.

4. A. C. Gibbs, ed., "Introduction," *Middle English Romances* (London: Edward Arnold, 1966), p. 1.

5. The relationship is posited, for example, by L. Sprague de Camp in his *Literary Swordsmen and Sorcerers: The Makers of Heroic Fantasy* (Sauk City, Wis.: Arkham House, 1976), p. 14, and by Waggoner, p. 36.

6. George Kane, *Middle English Literature: A Critical Study of the Romances, the Religious Lyrics, "Piers Plowman"* (London: Methuen, 1951), pp. 4–6.

7. Gibbs, p. 8; see also Robert W. Hanning, *The Individual in Twelfth-Century Romance* (New Haven and London: Yale University Press, 1977), particularly pp. 1–2.

8. Charles Muscatine, *Chaucer and the French Tradition* (Berkeley and Los Angeles: University of California Press, 1957), p. 15. Muscatine also observes that "The medieval audience is ready and able to see effortlessly beyond the surface representation of form and image to a higher reality, to see the concrete itself as metaphor and symbol" (p. 14).

9. Hanning, p. 5.

10. For a study of the major types of heroic ideal in medieval literature, see Sidney Painter, *French Chivalry* (1940; rpt. Ithaca: Cornell University Press, 1964).

11. Ursula K. Le Guin, *The Farthest Shore* (Harmondsworth: Penguin, 1974), p. 77.

12. Waggoner, p. 47.

13. Its limitations are ill-humoredly castigated by Hans Joachim Alpers, "Loincloth, Double Ax, and Magic: 'Heroic Fantasy' and Re-

lated Genres," *Science-Fiction Studies*, 5 (1978), 19–32. Waggoner describes it as "an unambitious form of heroic fantasy" (p. 36). Cf. de Camp, *Literary Swordsmen and Sorcerers*, and Lin Carter, *Imaginary Worlds* (New York: Ballantine, 1973).

14. See Roger C. Schlobin's Introduction to *The Literature of Fantasy: A Comprehensive, Annotated Bibliography of Modern Fantasy Fiction* (New York and London: Garland, 1979), p. xxix.

15. See Randel Helms, *Tolkien's World* (Boston: Houghton Mifflin, 1974), pp. 82–89; see also chap. 4, "Frodo Anti-Faust."

16. See "The Child and the Shadow," collected in Le Guin, *The Languages of the Night*, ed. Susan Wood (New York: Putnam's, 1979), pp. 59–71.

17. See Stith Thompson, *Motif-Index of Folk Literature* (Bloomington and London: Indiana University Press, 1956), III, H71.10.6; cf. H41.9.

18. Collected in *The Mabinogion*. The cauldron reappears in fantasies based upon this tale, notably Walton's *The Children of Llyr* (1971) and Alexander's *The Black Cauldron* (1965).

19. See Tolkien, "On Fairy-Stories," in *Tree and Leaf* (London: Unwin, 1964), pp. 50–61.

20. Gary K. Wolfe, "Symbolic Fantasy," *Genre*, 8 (1975), 201; see also Schlobin, p. xxviii.

21. Northrop Frye, *Anatomy of Criticism: Four Essays* (Princeton: Princeton University Press, 1957), p. 33; cf. Dorothy Everett, "A Characterization of the English Medieval Romances," in *Essays on Middle English Literature* (Oxford: Oxford University Press, 1955), p. 9.

22. Jirel's relationship with men is perceptively analyzed by Susan Gubar, "C. L. Moore and the Conventions of Women's SF," *Science-Fiction Studies*, 7 (1980), 22–23.

23. For a discussion of the treatment of the marvellous in medieval romance, see Everett, pp. 9–12.

24. Schlobin, pp. xxv–xxvi; see also Fredericks, 37–39.

25. Tolkien, pp. 60–61.

26. Gibbs observes, "If poet and audience share a belief in the supernatural, there is no great need for an effort of persuasion on the poet's part" (p. 9).

27. Fredericks, p. 39.

Heroic Fantasy and Social Reality: *ex nihilo nihil fit*

Jules Zanger

EACH KIND OF LITERATURE retains for its own purposes certain aspects of reality and denies certain others. Realism and naturalism, for example, are defined by those elements of the real world they retain; fantasy, on the other hand, is defined by those aspects of reality it denies, by representations that are not merely improbable or untrue, as are common to all fictions, but patently false.

That reality, both the physical reality of experience and the conventionalized reality of literature, provides the foil against which fantasy defines itself. Unlike other literary modes which, to be effective, traditionally require the "suspension of disbelief," fantasy requires the reader's disbelief, his recognition that the fiction is not real, to achieve its nature as fantasy.

The base line of reality, therefore, is always implicit in even the most errant fantasy, and in the tension between those solid, familiar, unalterable givens of experience and the particular denials of them that constitute the fiction is generated the special delight that fantasy affords us.

The airiest of fantasies created by the writer's imagination is always firmly staked to the bedrock provided by the reader's knowledge and experience of reality. Each fantasy takes its distinctive shape from those aspects of the real world it most strongly rejects. The roots of fantasy are to be found, then, not mainly in myth nor in the collective unconscious nor the spillage of a frustrated psyche, but in the denial of real human experience taking place in real historical time.

Fantasy offers an alternative vision, a critique, and the basis of opposition to that real world. The author's private vision, when written, becomes public and socialized, contrived to embody and reinforce the private fantasies of its readers. To the extent that those private fantasies are conformable into the literary fantasy—and that the literary fantasy succeeds in crystallizing and giving hard artifactual shape to the daydreams and undisciplined imaginings of the public—that fantasy is rooted in the social experience of the real world. Fantasy, consequently, always exists in a symbiotic relationship with reality and its conventionalized representation, depending on it for its existence and at the same time commenting upon it, criticizing it, and illuminating it.

Since fantasy springs (but not very far) from the denial of aspects of the real world, the distance between that real world and the world created by the fantasist reveals those stress points at which the real world chafes the writer and reader, and chafing, generates the imaginative alternative, as the grain of sand generates the baroque pearl.

Loren Eiseley suggests in his essay, "The Lethal Factor," that this ability to create the imaginative alternative is one of the quantum steps that distinguishes human beings from beasts: "The *mundus alter*—this other intangible, faery world of dreams, fantasies, inventions—has been flowing through the heads of men since the first ape-man succeeded in cutting out a portion of his environment and delineating it in a transmissible word."[1] The human mind, that is, in its ability to imagine an existence other than the one which it experiences, is permitted to perceive, as if from the outside, the existence in which it actually is immersed. The ability to create fantasy permits us to create history. But fantasy is not merely the creation of a "*mundus alter*," an alternative to the real world; any reality can have an almost infinite number of alternatives. Fantasy is a response to a particular combination of historical conditions. When, however, we have a significant number of literary works that share as their primary characteristic similar violations of the limits of possible experience, we have a literary convention, a genre of fantasy which itself shapes subsequent fantasies. The particular fantasy, then, at one time violates the known and shared parameters of reality, and observes and reinforces the expectations established by the genre.

To suggest, as does W. R. Irwin,[2] that fantasies violate norms is only half the story; fantasies also perpetuate norms. Eric Rabkin suggests that fantasies involve the reversals of expectation,[3] but that reversal in fantasy is precisely what is the expected. The magical apparition that turns out to have been produced by real trapdoors and mirrors is as inappropriate a reversal in a fantasy as a solution to a locked door mystery of John Dickson Carr's that depends on the villain passing through the keyhole in a puff of smoke.[4]

Fantasy's denials, violations, or reversals all occur within the circumscribed limits of the genre; they must be considered not only in terms of what reality leads us to expect, but, more significantly, in terms of what the genre leads us to expect. To treat each fantasy as if it were the first of its kind is to ignore the highly conventionalized nature of its form and content. The one expectation that cannot be negated is that some expectation will be negated. If this expectation is denied, we have realism, not fantasy.

Though these denials of reality define the fiction as fantasy, they normally constitute only a small portion of the total fiction, embedded in it like plums in the pudding of the familiar. Once we accept the denial of the real world implicit in magic that works, or the existence of elves, or the possibility of talking flowers, we find ourselves on otherwise familiar turf: conflict and resolution, psychological characterization, and motivation all seem relatively undistinguishable from that found in the historical romance. Good and evil remain definable and familiar. George MacDonald, writing of this retained ground base of fantasy, was essentially correct when he observed, "In physical things a man may invent; in moral things he must obey—and take their laws with him into his invented world as well."[5]

Fantasies consist, then, of retentions as well as denials, taken from the context of familiar experience and from a literary convention which is part of that familiar experience.

A number of important forms of fantasy emerge from this experience. One is that kind in which the reader is intended to read the fiction as a more or less thinly disguised commentary on the social situation in which he lives. We immediately think of that whole class of utopian or satiric fantasy—from Aristophanes' *The Birds,* to Swift's *Gulliver's Travels,* to Orwell's *Animal Farm* —that invites the reader to read with a kind of double vision, recording the details of the fantasy world and decoding them into their recognizable real world equivalents. Other forms of fantasy have no such programmatic, conscious, organizing principle. Instead, they rely more heavily on literary models, or variations, which appear to have little systematic relationship to reality. Nevertheless, even in those fantasies least clearly linked to the familiar world of experience or to existing models, the careful reader can discover in the value structure, in the characterizations, even in the imagery and metaphor, evidence of the social situation that the fantasy retains and transforms. The different values placed on chastity—for example, in Spenser's *Faerie Queene* where it is the *sine qua non* of femininity and in Michael Moorcock's *Gloriana* where the same chaste queen that Spenser celebrated couples frequently, casually, and innocently with men, women, and beasts—tell us a great deal about the respective societies that generated them. Fantasy's roots in social reality are to be discovered, then, in both its denials and its retentions.

The possible variations of fantasy in terms of denials and retentions are immense. Unlike lyric poetry or tragedy or the detective story, fantasy is not a self-contained literary type. Because it skirts between high art and pulp fiction, because it emerged and flourishes without the significant benefits of academic commentary, and because its efflorescence has been so wild and gorgeous, it invites and resists the most painstaking classifications.

The relationships of fantasy to social reality are best illustrated in that body of writing popularly called fantasy that emerged in the latter part of the nineteenth century, experienced an astonishing rebirth in the 1950s with the appearance of the Tolkien trilogy, and proliferated into the present. This continuing literary type, though it by no means employs all the possibilities of fantastic writing, represents perhaps the greatest number of the fantasies that have been written and read, and the greatest part of those works customarily identified as fantasies in the checklists and bibliographies of the genre. I am referring, of course, to that type of writing normally designated "heroic fantasy" or "high fantasy," which contains not only the pulp extravaganzas of the "sword-and-sorcery" school but also most of the great familiar classics of fantasy writing from George MacDonald, William Morris, and Lord Dunsany to such contemporary masters as J. R. R. Tolkien and Michael Moorcock. Despite the variety of differences we can find even within this limited type, the great body of heroic fantasy reveals a shared set of romantic characteristics that suggest the highly conventional nature of this form.

Primary among these is the locating of the narrative in a setting that is vaguely medieval, combining the matter of chivalry and of the fairy tale to produce the representative temporal and geographical locus of heroic fantasy. Drawing on the romantic impulses that so infused the work of Sir Walter Scott and John Keats and the contemporary Pre-Raphaelite Brotherhood and on the remarkably pervasive Fairy Books of Andrew Lang, heroic fantasy emerged in the writing of William Morris and George MacDonald, combining romantic adventure, innocent eroticism, and a sense of wonder. Its world was pre-industrial, pre-national, and pre-technological, fixed roughly by its swords and castle-keeps and costumes in the Middle Ages. This model of fantasy offered a society of aristocratic, hierarchical order, but it is such an order at a time of emergence or close to breakdown. It resembles the American frontier world in that at very short distances from its civil centers, chaos and wonder and danger await or intrude. Threatened as it is by forces of evil, it is frequently also only a short temporal distance from chaos and old night. It is neither a peaceful nor a secure world, and the representative fantasy customarily involves the overcoming of the threat of evil and the establishment of order through acts of individual confrontation and personal courage.

One significant characteristic that distinguishes the world of heroic fantasy from that of the historic Middle Ages is the absence of the Church as an institution of power and significance. When C. S. Lewis, in The Chronicles of Narnia, chose to write Christian allegory in the mode of heroic fantasy, he was constrained to substitute pagan elements for those Christian elements that would have been inappropriate to the mode. Heroic fantasy exists in an essentially pagan world within which only minor and local rulers and deities preside, a state strikingly illustrated by Fritz Leiber's highly popular Fafhrd and the Gray Mouser series.

It is a fragmented world of many boundaries and frontiers, the crossing of which seems to be as inevitable for its protagonists as it is dangerous. For this reason, maps have become standard accompaniments to heroic fantasies, not because they impart any versimilitude, since that is never the intention of fantasy, but rather because they illustrate graphically the fragmentation of the fantastic world, and the binding, base-touching aspect of the quest the protagonists customarily pursue. Each frontier offers a new landscape, a new folk, a new testing, or a new alliance. Heroic fantasies demand borders and frontiers because the heroic action customarily begins with the crossing of borders, the violation of the limits of the familiar to enter that *mundus alter* that is just over the mountain or across the running brook. For example, the world-wide meanderings of Robert E. Howard's barbarian Conan through the varied locales of the Hyborian Age are limited only by his vague goal of discovering a fabled golden city.

The most representative denial of the real world that takes place in heroic fantasy is the presence of magic that works, and with such magic, all of its extensions: demons, wizards, elves, goblins, trolls, dragons, and supernatural creatures from traditional folk and fairy tales or transformed versions of them—all of those things, that is, that science and normal experience deny existence to. Without this particular denial, heroic fantasy becomes merely historical romance, a literary type that offers its own particular denials of reality, but never as forthrightly as does fantasy. The presence of magic is most often one of the givens of the fantastic world, so that elves and wizards are as strange as, but no stranger than, Roumanians, for example, or native-born New Yorkers. The protagonists may be astonished at encountering them, but not at their existence. Magic distinguishes heroic fantasy from historical romance, but its function in the fantasy is frequently to be defeated. "Good" magic rarely defeats "bad" magic. Good magicians are frequently—like Gandalf imprisoned in Moria, or Merlin under Nimue's spell, or Schmendrick in Peter Beagle's *The Last Unicorn* (and even, most memorably, the Wizard of Oz)—unavailable, preoccupied, or simply inept. Evil magic is defeated finally by human virtues: courage, skill, innocence, or love.

In fairy tales, magic is part of the natural order. Oberon's realm only incidentally coincides with the world of human affairs and has its own purposes and its own bounds. Magic in heroic fantasy, however, frequently involves a disbalancing of the natural order; the evil magician is employing abilities not properly human in the service of an all-too-human appetite for power, which exercises itself primarily in destroying the human community. In this sense, magic in the heroic fantasy, unlike magic in the folk or fairy tale, which usually involves personal and discrete encounters, has a political and social dimension, concerning itself with kingdoms today and the world tomorrow. It is appropriate, then, that the defeat of evil magic is accomplished by human characters or their representatives in the fantasy. Seen this way, high fantasy dramatizes the successful resistance of heroic individuals to faceless power, the successful resistance of the familiar, personal world to the impersonal forces that would alter or destroy it. In this regard, G. K. Chesterton observed, "Magic was the abuse of preternatural powers by lower agents whose work was preternatural but not supernatural; it was founded on the profound maxim of *diabolus simius Dei*; the Devil is the ape of God. . . . There is in enchantment almost always an idea of captivity. In contrast with this it will be noted that the good miracles, the acts of saints and heroes, are always acts of restoration."[6] This emphasis on restoration or retention of a cherished past is particularly important in heroic fantasy, which always seeks its Golden Age in some earlier time. For this reason, the quest for the True King, the concern for legitimacy, which is nothing more than consonance with the past, emerges as a dominant theme in fantasy. This pattern reveals itself in the confirmatory ceremony of *The Sword in the Stone,* in all the paraphernalia of the past fleshing out the Tolkien trilogy and culminating in *The Return of the King*, and, at its most elaborate, the Ritual of the Investiture of the seventy-seventh Earl of Groan in Mervyn Peake's *Titus Groan.*

This pattern of fantasy, though it had earlier analogs, emerges in the last decades of the nineteenth century and is almost exactly contemporaneous with naturalism, which affirmed the inability of men and women to shape their destinies. In a sense, high fantasy can be regarded as the mirror image of naturalism, celebrating the triumph of human imagination over brutalizing fact. Naturalism regarded humanity in the aggregate, as controlled by huge, impersonal forces that finally could not be resisted. High fantasy offered a uniquely personal world in which individuals could triumph over incredible odds, in which the traditional virtues—love, decency, courage, innocence—were somehow adequate to maintain the balance of Victorian values against a rapidly tilting universe. In an industrial, urbanized age in which individuality seemed endangered and human centrality lost in the infinite universe revealed by science, fantasy reduced the world to a conceivable dimension. Fantasy restored the primacy of the romantic imagination, providing a world which, if not man-centered, was at least confrontable.

This traditional world of heroic fantasy, rich in the conventional signs of its kind—castle keeps, desolate wastes, princesses, supernatural evils and, of course, heroes—emerged as a popular English literary mode in the work of George MacDonald and William Morris, both of whom represent Victorian sensibility at its most divided. Each was an intensely public man—Morris an extremely successful manufacturer, craftsman/artist, and energetic advocate of Socialism, and MacDonald a popular novelist and popular lecturer on subjects as diverse as chemistry, English literature, physics, and Christianity. Both turned to fantasy as it offered imaginative alternatives to the utilitarian world of hard fact and to Victorian bourgeois commodity culture. In a society in which rampant economic individualism prevailed, they created a past in which they could discover fragmented worlds achieving community through transcendent rather than material goals, communities linked together by what Thomas Carlyle called "organic filaments." They constructed this world of elements taken from Spenser and Malory, from the Arthurian cycle, from the idealized medievalism of the literary past, precisely as Spenser and Malory had turned to the idealized medievalism of still earlier writers. High fantasy offered a universe of imaginative possibility rather than of limiting fact, of a green and rural England rather than one of festering urban slums, of a hierarchical, ordered society rather than one racked by the profound social disorders created by an industrial revolution for which there existed no precedent. Fantasy permitted the laissez-faire individualism of the period to be retained but transformed it into a heroic idealism. The goal of Disraeli and the "Young England" party to establish a coalition of aristocracy and the lower classes against the middle class bourgeoisie was achieved in heroic fantasy by the simple device of creating a world in which the middle class had never emerged as an important force. A significant exception to this occurs in William Morris' *The Well at the World's End,* where the focus of villainy is precisely the burghers, who are cold, grasping, and "devil-led."

Lionel Trilling, writing of another eminent Victorian, Matthew Arnold, observed that "much of what man does for himself depends upon what society permits him to do." Fantasy envisioned a world in which the individual was permitted to act with a directness and immediacy denied him in the conventional bureaucratic structures of commercial, industrial society. The same impulses that led to the mass adulation of such public personalities as mountain climbers, cricket stars, and explorers brought readers to heroic fantasy, that afforded an imaginative release from the drab, gradgrind world of the Victorians.

In its reifying of a magical world, heroic fantasy moved its readers back to their own childhoods, to nursery stories and fairy tales and the innocent wonder they provided, and to the satisfying vision of innocence they made briefly possible. But on another level, magic in heroic fantasy is presented as power that decrees rather than petitions, that is opaque and incomprehensible, and that is as threatening to traditional values as the technological, industrial, and social changes England was undergoing. The defeat of such magic in heroic fantasy can be understood, then, as the symbolic expression of Victorian ambivalence toward progress and change. The Crystal Palace, raised as it were by magic and filled with the mechanical wonders of the age, was as seductive and alluring as Spenser's Castle Joyeuse, but to the discerning eye, as false and as ultimately evil.

Another indication of this unease in the presence of social change is illustrated vividly in one particular pattern of imagery that emerges repeatedly in heroic fantasy. The forces of evil—from George MacDonald's Goblins in *The Princess and the Goblin* to Alan Garner's bodachs in *The Moon of Gomrath,* from Tolkien's Orcs in the Ring trilogy to such more recent versions as Joy Chant's trolls in *Red Moon and Black Mountain* and Marion Zimmer Bradley's Ironfolk in *The House Between the Worlds*—take the shape of deformed dwellers underground who emerge into the world of sunlight to overthrow established order. In all of these works, the reader's sympathy is won to support an aristocratic, pastoral world whose rulers are benevolent and supernaturally supported over and beyond the forces of dark magic arrayed against them. This pattern of imagery is not confined to heroic fantasy, of course. It is to be found in this period in fantasies as diverse as H. G. Wells's *The Time Machine* and Arthur Machen's "The Novel of the Black Seal" and Kenneth Grahame's *The Wind in the Willows.* These deformed subterranean dwellers may have had their origins in the legends of such aboriginal dwellers in the land as the Daione Sidhe of Ireland or the Tylwyth Teg of Wales, but their contemporary application was made clear and fixed by George MacDonald when he described his Goblins as follows:

> There was a legend current in the country, that at one time they lived above ground, and were very like other people. But for some reason or other, concerning which there were very different legendary theories, the king had laid what they thought too severe taxes upon them, or had required observances of them they didn't like, or had begun to treat them with more severity, in some way or other, and impose stricter laws, and the consequence was that they had all disappeared from the face of the country. According to the legend, how-

> ever, instead of going to some other country, they had all taken refuge in the subterranean caverns. . . . Those who had caught sight of them said that they had greatly altered in the course of generations: and no wonder, seeing they had lived away from the sun, in wet and dark places. They were now, not ordinarily ugly, but either absolutely hideous, or ludicrously grotesque both in face and form.[7]

H. G. Wells was to describe the origins of his underground dwellers, the Morlocks, less romantically, but in essentially the same terms: "So, in the end, above ground you must have the Haves, pursuing pleasure and comfort and beauty, and below ground the Have-Nots, the Workers getting continually adapted to the conditions of their labour."[8] Emerging as it did following half a century of economic unrest and class violence, heroic fantasy offered the images of evil in shapes that resonated with the nightmares of the middle-class audience for which it was written as well as of its middle-class creators.

When Thomas Carlyle described the Chartist rioters in the Manchester insurrection as "a million-headed hydra" driven by cavalry back "into its subterranean settlements again,"[9] he was anticipating the imagery of almost a century of fantasy to follow. The pale and stunted miners and mill operatives were finally suppressed by armed force, but they still rise to haunt the fantasies we read.

The creators of high fantasy offered to their readers a *mundus alter* that resolutely denied the most pressing and problematical aspects of their real world, but never forgot any of them. These denials of reality were rooted in an acute sensitivity to that world's failure to provide beauty, order, and community. This disappointment generated fantasies that at their worst were sentimental escapism combined with a strong absence of any democratic feeling; at their best they offered imaginative alternatives to reality that embody ideal solutions to problems that are otherwise uncontrollable. Their banalities and their excellences are, of course, the products of individual authors who bring to the form their own particular impress, who make it, for worse or better, their own. The matter they work on, however, is the social reality they share with their readers. Lord Dunsany was aware of this, of course, when he wrote the following preface to *The King of Elfland's Daughter*:

I hope that no suggestion of any strange land that may be conveyed by the title will scare readers away from this book; for, though some chapters do indeed tell of Elfland, in the greater part of them there is no more to be shown than the face of the fields we know, and ordinary English woods and a common village and valley, a good twenty or twenty-five miles from the border of Elfland.[10]

NOTES

1. Loren Eiseley, "The Lethal Factor," in *The Star Thrower* (New York: Harcourt Brace Jovanovich, 1978), p. 256.
2. W. R. Irwin, *The Game of the Impossible* (Urbana: University of Illinois Press, 1976), pp. 9–10.
3. Eric S. Rabkin, *The Fantastic in Literature* (Princeton: Princeton University Press, 1976), p. 12.
4. This, of course, is what Carr does in *The Burning Court* when in the last chapter he transforms a locked-door mystery pretending to be a fantasy into a genuine fantasy that has been pretending to be a locked-door mystery. Also see Tzvetan Todorov's *The Fantastic*, trans. Richard Howard (Cleveland and London: The Press of Case Western Reserve University, 1973), pp. 50–51, for further discussion of *The Burning Court.*
5. George MacDonald, *A Dish of Orts* (London: Sampson, Low, 1893), p. 316.
6. G. K. Chesterton, "Magic and Fantasy in Fiction," *The Bookman,* March 1930, p. 27.
7. George MacDonald, *The Princess and the Goblin* (New York: Grosset and Dunlap, 1907), pp. 14–15.
8. H. G. Wells, *The Time Machine* (New York: Heinemann, 1963), p. 40.
9. Thomas Carlyle, *Works* (Boston: Estes and Laurant, 1884), IV, 16.
10. Lord Dunsany, *The King of Elfland's Daughter* (New York: Ballantine, 1969), p. ix.

Recent Developments in the Theory of Spell Construction

William M. Schuyler, Jr.

INITIALLY WE MUST stipulate that the scope of this essay is limited to those aspects of the Sorcerous Art that may be practiced by all, not only by those adepts who have special, inherent powers. Yet we hope that our findings may be of interest even to these august personages, since it is clearly recorded in Roger Zelazny and elsewhere that adepts use the Art as well as their powers. By the same token, we point out that the results reported here can be applied to every aspect of the Art. To give this essay as broad an interest as possible, we have chosen not to deal here with those areas open only to men and changelings that Poul Anderson so succinctly summarized.[1]

The pioneering works of Fritz Leiber, L. Sprague de Camp, and Fletcher Pratt in the application of symbolic logic to magic lead to remarkable discoveries about the logical form of spells. The applications were immediate and spectacular. Serious research has continued, notably by Randall Garrett, with some gratifying results. It is clear from Jack Vance's reports that the work of Phandaal also falls in this category, but the results of his investigations are not well understood at this time. However, much work was stymied by limitations whose importance has only recently been recognized.[2]

One serious difficulty was the failure of material implication to reflect any kind of relevance or necessity. Anderson and Belnap have reformulated the notion of logical implication in such a way as to resolve the problem.[3] Their system, though more difficult to work with than standard logic, has the advantage of not permitting certain dangerous, even fatal, inferences and constructions, as well as further illuminating the true logical structure of spells. The importance of structure cannot be overemphasized. An imperfect or incomplete structure will break up with a catastrophic release of energy. The shattering of Carcë was an omen to us all in E. R. Eddison's *The Worm Ouroboros*.[4]

Yet it is semantics and phonology that have proved most fruitful for students of magic in the past few years. In this paper I propose to examine three areas in which progress has been made: the theory of magically proper names, the application of generative semantics to word choice in spell formation, and the use of literary criticism in the construction of the theory of phonetically proper sounds, which in turn is applied to the problems of word choice.

Proper names are an important part of many spells. The reason is clear. If a correct proper name is used, the spell will act on the right individual. Someone or something else's proper name will cause the action of the spell to be misdirected. Results of this kind are quite unpredictable and usually distressing to those whose spells go astray. This is amply documented in a case study by R. A. Lafferty.[5] Alternatively, use of a "proper name" that does not name anything may well cause a backlash of the unleashed energies on the unfortunate individual who cast the spell.

Bertrand Russell's theory of logically proper names was prompted by similar considerations; i.e., he wanted to be sure that when a proper name was applied that there would be something it applied to. One of his most acute observations was that what seem to be proper names are actually concealed descriptions. Thus, in the sentence "The author of *Waverley* is Scott," "Scott" actually functions not as a name but as an abbreviation for the description "the man who is called 'Scott,'" which is a predicate. Such a description can also appear in the subject position in a sentence of ordinary language.[6]

Descriptions, however, cannot be the *logical* subjects of sentences because by their form they must be predicates. Only true proper names and variables have the correct logical form to fill the subject position. Hence a description cannot *mean* an individual at all. Only a name can do that.[7] We now see the theoretical basis for concealing one's real name and being called something else. As "Mr. Underhill" so aptly put it, "'. . . the name is the thing . . . and the true name is the true thing. To speak the name is to control the thing.'"[8] The other "name" is not yours. Spells using it will not affect you. In fact, since it is not a name at all but a description, the spell is formally incorrect and will rebound against its maker.

From our point of view, one problem with Russell's theory is that the things we want to cast spells on do not have proper names at all in his sense. People, etc., turn out to be no more than collections of sense data, which turn out to be the only things that can have proper names.[9] But in that case, all our spells based on the use of what we have always thought were proper names are founded on theoretical quicksand. Though Russell would assent to this, I find the conclusion dubious.

Saul Kripke has a better idea. To introduce it, I need to talk a little about possible world semantics. These possible worlds are not the ones we are used to in science fiction, where travel between them is possible. Rather it is built into the mathematics, in terms of which the theory is formulated that no interaction between possible worlds can take place.[10]

Virgil was a great magician. Is it possible that he might not have been? Could his life have been so different that none of the descriptions we apply to him would be true? If so, would he still, in this other possible world, be Virgil? Yes, says Kripke, because a name is a *rigid designator*. It applies to the same individual in every possible world where he or she exists, regardless of what changes we would have to make in our descriptions of the individual. (There are some possible worlds in which Virgil was a bucolic poet, and ones in which Sherlock Holmes is a fictional character.)[11]

What a rigid designator designates is the essence of the individual it names. This is a very Aristotelian point of view, which will also be familiar to students of the theory of magic. Language cannot describe essence, but if you think of your essence as the unchanging center of your being, you won't be too far off.[12]

We can now see why proper names are so effective in spells. The Principle of Contagion says that when two things have been brought together, one can be used to influence the other forever after because of this temporary connection. But names, being rigid designators, remain connected with what they name. Indeed, the connection between name and named is closely related to the connection between soul and body, which, as Lee puts it, is a "magic cord" that one must be careful not to sever lest the body die of the soul's absence. Thus the effect of the Principle of Contagion is multiplied, just as prolonged and continuous exposure to a disease increases the chances of catching it.[13]

However, not all spells involve proper names. Sometimes names are not known. Sometimes they are unpronounceable, and mispronunciation invites a backlash. And of course not everything on which we might want to cast a spell has a name.

Hence there are places in our spells where descriptions must suffice. But if Russell is correct, descriptions simply call attention to things by mentioning their properties. This would be a tenuous basis, indeed, on which to release the energy of a spell. Kripke once again provides the basis for a sound theoretical treatment of this problem. He argues convincingly that there are essences of kinds as well as of individuals. The essences of the different kinds invoked in an adequate description in combination resemble uniquely that which is described, because sentences mean in the same way that pictures depict.[14]

Thus do we invoke the Principle of Sympathy, i.e., that if one thing is like another, we can use each to influence the other. This, as Patricia A. McKillip argues, is the basis of shape-changing in which the changer deliberately enhances the similarity of what is to be changed to the desired form. Here it is the picturing relation of a precise description to what it describes that provides the resemblance permitting the Principle of Sympathy to operate.[15]

It is easy to see why spells that depend heavily on descriptions are not as compelling as those solidly based on proper names. Descriptions do not touch the essence of the individual, so they cannot expend their full power in achieving their effect. Instead, the eccentric application of their force requires that some of their power be used to stabilize the transfer of force. Here is an analogy: two slender rods pressed end to end with equal force are in equilibrium, albeit an unstable one. But if the rods are not centered on each other, force must be expended to keep them aligned. A description that is ambiguous or lacking in precise detail is therefore an invitation to disaster since the forces called up can easily get out of control. James Blish records an especially sobering case of this type.[16]

With this groundwork laid, we can turn to the criteria by which words are to be chosen for spells. The first thing to note is that symbolic logic does not give a completely adequate characterization of the form of a spell. There are several reasons for this.

Effective spells must be good poetry. This is clear on empirical grounds; there are also strong theoretical reasons. The logical form of a spell acts on the deepest structures that the spell reaches. But the phonetic expression of the logical form may not resemble the logical form very closely,[17] and it is the phonetic expression of the spell that is responsible for superficial side effects. For example, jaundice is the superficial effect of an underlying liver problem. The logical form of a spell against jaundice should work on the liver, not the color. At the same time, we must take care that the phonetic expression, which is what will affect the color, does not work at odds with the logical form and, say, turn the patient purple. It is poetic form that imposes the necessary discipline on linguistic expression.

To those who have some slight acquaintance with linguistics, this should begin to sound familiar. The model, it should be emphasized, is that of McCawley and Fillmore rather than Chomsky. Chomsky's key suggestion was that underlying structures undergo a series of rule-governed transformations on their way to becoming the surface structures to which we give phonetic expression. These rules can be cast into logistic (i.e., formal) systems. Some of the rules govern syntax; others govern phonology, the study of the combination of sounds in language. The rules governing meaning, grammar, and phonology are completely separate from each other in his system.[18]

This separation is unsatisfactory on empirical and theoretical grounds, which I will not go into here. McCawley, Fillmore, and others have proposed instead that the rules governing semantics, syntax, and phonology are interlocked and interdependent. One of their most striking innovations is the idea that a single word in surface structures might be the result of transformations of underlying structures having the form of phrases, clauses, or sentences. Thus the word "persuade" is provisionally analyzed as a transform of a structure that could also reach the surface more or less in its original state as "do cause become intend."[19]

Now it turns out that underlying structure is logical form.[20] The logical form of your utterances is going to depend on what you want to say, but this is not enough to determine surface structure completely, because some transformations are optional. More than logic is needed to characterize the form of any utterance, let alone a spell.

However, these same considerations give deep insight into

the systematic construction of spells. Having decided what we want to do, we choose our semantic information and our logical form accordingly. Moving from this underlying structure by one transformation after another, we use the optional transformations to mold the emergent surface structure into suitable poetic form.

As we have seen, syntactical transformations can determine what words ultimately appear in the surface structure. And of course a given word will be more desirable in some kinds of spells than in others for a variety of reasons, some of which I shall discuss presently. Knowledge of the optional transformations and underlying forms gives us increased ability to work desirable words into our spells while avoiding undesirable ones. At the same time it permits us to do this in a way that conforms to the appropriate poetic form by using the transformations to find locutions that fit.

Here I should point out that poetic form is to be taken very broadly. Following Coleridge, we may say that prose is words in their best order and poetry the best words in their best order.[21] In general, it is not required that poetry for spells adhere strictly to a metric pattern or a rhyme scheme, or even that it rhyme at all. But as any poet will tell you, irregular forms make demands as stringent, if not more so than regular ones.

Since language in general and spells in particular are representational,[22] it is clear that the choice of poetic form is crucial to a successful spell. Thus spells of regular form concerning fire must have, at least in the crucial places, lines of three feet. An even number will not work; it would be too stable. Five feet would be too many; the quickness of fire would be lost. Moreover, the feet must be iambs or trochees; spondees and dactyls glide rather than leap.

Having examined some of the formal requirements laid on words in spells, we now turn to phonetic requirements. Onomatopoeia is always helpful in invoking the Principle of Sympathy, but theory takes us far beyond such simple devices, even to an analysis of the foundation of the resemblance between name and named. "Vowels play the part of light or of darkness," says Dame Edith Sitwell,

> and consonants that of matter—having the most universal qualities of matter . . . such as gravity, cohesion, rigidity, sensitiveness to light. Consonants therefore seem, often, to be soaked with light or with darkness. . . .

> Again, with regard to the relationship of consonants and vowels, it might perhaps be said that the vowels are the spirit, the consonants and labials the physical identity, with all the variations of harshness, hairiness, coldness, roughness, smoothness, etc. . . . Consonants shape; they do not affect time as do vowels. Although vowels have also their place, position, depth and height, they do not give body.[23]

Indeed, each phoneme has its own character, which combines with those of the other phonemes of a word to make it shaggy or buttered or combed, or whatever other quality it exemplifies. Thus, in Japanese, repeated *G's* give an effect of dullness, obscurity, or profundity; repeated *K's* are melancholic; *S's* soft or tender. Similar effects may be noted in English, but the situation there is more complex because of the larger number of phonemes, which are often closely related without being identical.[24]

This brings us back to proper names. It may be true from a syntactic or a semantic view that proper names have no connotation, but phonetically it is false. For a name to be a true proper name, it must be an accurate phonetic representation of that which is named. Here is another source of the power of proper names: since proper names are representatives, the Principle of Sympathy applies. It also follows that unless you fully understand your own nature, you yourself will not know your true name.[25]

This is the broad foundation for the phonology of spells and all other poetry. The devices to make use of it are obvious: agreement of consonants to reinforce desired physical properties, dissonance to cancel unwanted ones against each other, choice of vowels to set timing, and agreement of vowels to enforce timing.

Research on the relative effectiveness of different languages for various kinds of spells has lagged, but it may be expected that there will be differences based on surface structure, phonology, and the nature of indigenous poetic form. For example, an unstressed language like French should be most effective in spells designed to maintain the status quo, but perhaps less easy to use for spells that bring about major changes. Certainly the fact that there are different words with different sounds for the same thing in various languages would make a difference. One would prefer to cast each spell in the language whose sounds best expressed one's immediate purpose.

It remains only to illustrate some of our more recherché points.

First, we were not speaking metaphorically when we spoke of the energies unleashed by spells. They must be controlled. Even though these are not drawn from the spell caster, the energy to control them is. That is why, as Alexei and Cory Panshin and others report, magic is painful and exhausting to those who practice it.[26]

Second, Diane Duane's fine history of the Middle Kingdoms, *The Door Into Fire,* supplies the remaining examples. It is especially valuable for the understanding she brings to her discussions of the Science of Magic. Her grasp of detail and her use of it give us a sure sense of how things really happen, unlike those dry tomes which simply tell us that magic is done or callow fantasies about a mysterious electro-magnetic force that is supposed to be able to do everything from make light to perform complex calculations. Describing a spell being cast, Duane says:

> The spells had to be built, word by cautious word, each word placed delicately on edge against another, stressed and counter-stressed, pronunciations clean and careful, intentions plain. The words were sharp as knives, and could cut deeper than any sword if they were dropped or broken. A word here, and another one there: this one placed with care atop two others, taking care always to keep the whole structure in mind—too much attention to one part could collapse others. Here a jagged word like cutting crystal, with a history to it—don't pause too long to admire the glitter of it, the others will resent the partiality and turn on you. There a word fragile as a butterfly's wing. . . .
>
> The balance was perilous to maintain, and once or twice, he almost lost it as a word shifted under another's weight. Another one turned on the word next to it—they were too much alike—and savaged it before Herewiss could remove the offender and put another, less violent, but also less effective, in its place. He had to make up for the loss of power elsewhere, at the top of the structure. He wasn't sure whether it would stand the strain or not. . . .[27]

The richness of this passage is typical of Duane and remarkable in anyone. Here is a sense of structure, of the relations of the words that make it up and of the nature of the words themselves. She does not speak metaphorically, as an example or two will show—not from spells, of course, but from poetry, such as Swinburne's "A Ballad of Dreamland":

> I hid my heart in a nest of roses,
> Out of the sun's way, hidden apart.
> On a softer bed than the soft white snow's is,
> Under the roses I hid my heart.

The rhyme in the first and third lines is disastrous. "Roses" shifts under the weight of the bad rhyme. Yet the sounds of the third line do evoke the softness of which they speak. The stanza continues

> Why would it sleep not? Why should it start?
> When never a leaf of the rose tree stirred?
> What made sleep flutter its wings and part?
> Only the song of a secret bird.

The staccato of the first line here does "start," particularly in comparison with the smooth glide of the second. And who can deny that T's and the lax vowels of the third line flutter?[28]

These are phonetic flaws and triumphs. Structural flaws, in much the same way, are not always simply the result of broken rules of poetic form. The Japanese *tanka* is a thirty-one syllable form with a 5-7-5-7-7 pattern. Early *tanka* are "divisible into units of five and seven (twelve), five and seven (twelve), and seven, a top-heavy pattern which . . . tends to lose its force in the final short unit." In later *tanka*, "the caesuras often fall at the end of the first and third lines, thus dividing the poem into three units of . . . five, twelve and fourteen syllables. . . . It is not simply that this pattern of growth is more pleasing and powerful in itself," it also leads to greater flexibility. If they were buildings, both kinds of structure would be able to stand up, but structures of the first type would have a tendency to collapse under their own weight. Structures of the same shape may be based on entirely different engineering principles.[29]

It may seem that the foundation of a poem should be its beginning, so that the word "top-heavy" has been misapplied, but this need not be the case. "The origin, the germ of ['A Ballad of Dreamland'] was, Swinburne said, the line 'Only the song of a secret bird,' by which he was haunted."[30] Deep structure is not immediately obvious in poetic form.

Nowhere is the importance of the relation of deep structure to surface structure more apparent than it is here. Clearly the older and newer *tanka* must have different deep structures. Equally clear is the fact that although both types of deep structures can be made to fit the poetic form, one works better than the other.

Many more examples come to mind, and the finer points of theory cry out for discussion. Unfortunately, our space is limited, so we must stop, which we have never liked to do. Next year, however, this problem will not arise. The final development which we have to report is that we have nearly perfected a spell which not only guarantees that whatever we write will be accepted for publication but also adjusts the measure of space so that no matter how much we write, it takes up less than twenty pages. We're sure you will enjoy it. The spell guarantees that, too.

NOTES

1. Roger Zelazny, "Jack of Shadows, Part I," *The Magazine of Fantasy and Science Fiction,* July 1966, chap. 3 (p. 23); chap. 5 (p. 41). Poul Anderson, *The Broken Sword,* rev. ed. (New York: Ballantine, 1971), chap. 5 (pp. 17, 22).

2. Fritz Leiber, "Conjure Wife," in *Witches Three* (1943; rpt. as a separate book New York: Twayne, 1952), chap. 16 (pp. 129–31); chap. 18 (pp. 141–43). L. Sprague de Camp and Fletcher Pratt, *The Incomplete Enchanter* (1941; rpt. New York: Pyramid, 1962), chap. 15 (p. 134). Randall Garrett, "Too Many Magicians, Part II," *Analog,* September 1966, chap. 6 (p. 113); chap. 8 (pp. 124–25). Jack Vance, "Turjan of Miir," in *The Dying Earth* (1950; rpt. New York: Lancer, 1962), pp. 16–17.

3. Alan Ross Anderson and Nuel D. Belnap, Jr., *Entailment: The Logic of Relevance and Necessity* (Princeton: Princeton University Press, 1975), I, 13–30, 230–32.

4. E. R. Eddison, *The Worm Ouroboros* (1926; rpt. New York: E. P. Dutton, 1952), chap. 32 (pp. 413–14).

5. R. A. Lafferty, *Fourth Mansions* (New York: Ace, 1969), chap. 1 (pp. 20–21); chap. 2 (p. 34); chap. 4 (p. 76).

6. Bertrand Russell, "Descriptions," in *Introduction to Mathematical Philosophy* (London: George Allen & Unwin, 1919), chap. 16; rpt. in *Twentieth Century Philosophy: The Analytic Tradition,* ed. Morris Weitz (New York: The Free Press, 1966), pp. 147–48. Also see p. 151.

7. Ibid., pp. 150–53.

8. Ursula K. Le Guin, "The Rule of Names," in *The Wind's Twelve Quarters* (New York: Harper & Row, 1975), p. 67.

9. Bertrand Russell, "The Relationship of Sense Data to Physics," in *Mysticism and Logic* (London: Longmans, Green, 1918), chap. 8; rpt. in Weitz, p. 158.

10. Saul Kripke, "Naming and Necessity," in *Semantics of Natural Language,* 2nd ed., ed. Donald Davidson and Gilbert Harman (Dordrecht, Holland: D. Reidel, 1972), pp. 266–67.

11. Avram Davidson, *The Phoenix and the Mirror* (New York: Ace, 1969), author's note, p. 6. Kripke, p. 269.

12. Kripke, pp. 269–73. This is, of course, a little misleading. The problem with language here is that descriptions mention qualities, and essences have no qualities.

13. Tanith Lee, *Volkhavaar* (New York: DAW, 1977), chap. 14 (p. 127). DeCamp and Pratt, chap. 1 (p. 9).

14. Kripke, pp. 314–31. DeCamp and Pratt, chap. 1 (pp. 8–9), where it is called the "Principle of Similarity."

15. Patricia A. McKillip, *The Riddle Master of Hed* (New York: Ballantine, 1976), chap. 11 (pp. 207–9). Conversely, failure to depict properly, e.g., by getting the elements of the spell in the wrong place, can have disastrous results. Jack Vance, *The Eyes of the Overworld* (1966; rpt. New York: Pocket Books, 1977), chap. 7 (pp. 188–90).

16. James Blish, *Black Easter* (1968; rpt. New York: Avon, 1977), chap. 15 (p. 137), chap. 17 (pp. 162–65).

17. This is easily seen from Noam Chomsky's famous example, the pair of sentences "John is easy to please" and "John is eager to please." They both have the same surface structure, but they must have different underlying structures because "John" is the object of the former and the subject in the latter. But as Gilbert Harman has pointed out ("Deep Structure as Logical Form," in Davidson and Harman, p. 35), deep structure is logical form.

18. Noam Chomsky, "Form and Meaning in Natural Languages," in *Language and Mind,* enlarged ed. (New York: Harcourt Brace Jovanovich, 1972), pp. 103–111.

19. James D. McCawley, "Pre-Lexical Syntax," in *Semantic Syntax,* ed. Pieter A. M. Seuren (London: Oxford University Press, 1974), pp. 29–31; and Charles J. Fillmore, "Subjects, Speakers, and Rules," in Davidson and Harman, pp. 3–4. McCawley, p. 30.

20. Harman, p. 35.

21. Quoted in John Bartlett, ed., *Familiar Quotations,* 13th ed. (Boston: Little, Brown, 1955), p. 424a.

22. Wittgenstein, Prop. 2.1. There are those who question the picture theory of meaning. It is kindest to ignore them. However, see my paper, "Could Anyone Here Speak Babel-17?" in *Philosophers Look at Science Fiction,* ed. Nicholas D. Smith (Chicago: Nelson-Hall, forthcoming).

23. Dame Edith Sitwell, ed., Intro., *Swinburne: A Selection* (New York: Harcourt, Brace, 1960), p. 6.

24. Ibid., p. 6. Geoffrey Bownas and Anthony Thwaite, trans., Intro., *The Penguin Book of Japanese Verse* (Baltimore: Penguin Books, 1964), p. liii.

25. Kripke, p. 255, takes this position and credits it to Mill. Diane Duane, *The Door into Fire* (New York: Dell, 1979), pp. 284–87. If a spell were not an adequate phonetic representation, it would clash with the denotations of the names in it and miscarry.

26. Alexei and Cory Panshin, *Earth Magic* (New York: Ace, 1978), pp. 93, 131.

27. Duane, pp. 284–87, 110–12.

28. Algernon Charles Swinburne, quoted in Sitwell, p. 28.

29. Bownas and Thwaite, pp. li–liii. Sitwell, p. 29.

30. Sitwell, p. 29.

Modern Fantasy Fiction: A Checklist

Roger C. Schlobin

THE FOLLOWING CHECKLIST is offered solely to support references in the preceding essays. All citations are to first editions, and series are labeled and listed in reading order. Readers interested in a more extensive list, with annotations, should consult this author's *The Literature of Fantasy: A Comprehensive, Annotated Bibliography of Modern Fantasy Fiction* (New York: Garland, 1979).

ADAMS, RICHARD.
Watership Down. London: Rex Collings, 1972.

ALEXANDER, LLOYD
The Chronicles of Prydain.
The Book of Three. New York: Henry Holt, 1964.
The Black Cauldron. New York: Henry Holt, 1965.
The Castle of Llyr. New York: Henry Holt, 1966.
Taran Wandered. New York: Henry Holt, 1967.
The High King. New York: Henry Holt, 1968.

ANDERSON, POUL.
The Broken Sword. New York: Abelard-Schuman, 1954. Rev. ed. New York: Ballantine, 1971 [paper].
A Midsummer Tempest. Garden City, N.Y.: Doubleday, 1974.
Three Hearts and Three Lions. Garden City, N.Y.: Doubleday, 1961.

ANTHONY, PIERS [pseud.]. See JACOB, PIERS ANTHONY DILLINGHAM.

BEAGLE, PETER S.
A Fine and Private Place. New York: Viking, 1960.
The Last Unicorn. New York: Viking, 1968.

BECKFORD, WILLIAM.
An Arabian Tale from an Unpublished Manuscript with Notes Critical and Explanatory. London: J. Johnson, 1786 [1st English ed.]. Later title: *Vathek*.

BEERBOHM, MAX.
Zuleika Dobson; or, An Oxford Love Story. London: Heinemann, 1911.

BLISH, JAMES.
The After Such Knowledge Tetralogy
Doctor Mirabilis. New York: Dodd, Mead, 1971.
Black Easter or Faust Aleph-Null. Garden City, N.Y.: Doubleday, 1968.
The Day After Judgment. Garden City, N.Y.: Doubleday, 1971.
A Case of Conscience. New York: Ballantine, 1958 [paper].

BRAHAM, ERNEST [pseud.]. See SMITH, ERNEST BRAHAM.

BROOKS, TERRY.
The Sword of Shannara. New York: Ballantine [paper]; New York: Random House, 1977.

CARROLL, LEWIS [pseud.]. See DODGSON, CHARLES LUTWIDGE.

CHANT, JOY.
Red Moon and Black Mountain: The End of the House of Kendreth. London: Allen & Unwin, 1970.

CHAPMAN, VERA.
The Three Damosels Trilogy
The Green Knight. London: Rex Collings, 1975.
The King's Damosel. London: Rex Collings, 1976.
King Arthur's Daughter. London: Rex Collings, 1976.

COOPER, SUSAN.
The Dark Is Rising Series
Over Sea, Under Stone. London: J. Cape, 1965.

The Dark Is Rising. New York: Atheneum, 1973.
Greenwitch. New York: Atheneum, 1975.
The Grey King. New York: Atheneum, 1975.
Silver on the Tree. New York: Atheneum, 1977.

CURRY, JANE LOUISE.
Beneath the Hill. New York: Harcourt, Brace & World, 1967.
The Sleepers. New York: Harcourt, Brace & World, 1968.

DAVIDSON, AVRAM.
The Phoenix and the Mirror [*or the Enigmatic Speculum*]. Garden City, N.Y.: Doubleday, 1969.

DE CAMP, L. SPRAGUE, and FLETCHER PRATT.
The Incomplete Enchanter Series
The Incomplete Enchanter. New York: Henry Holt, 1941.
The Castle of Iron: A Science Fantasy Adventure. New York: Gnome, 1950.
The Wall of Serpents. New York: Avalon, 1960.

DICKINSON, PETER.
The Blue Hawk. London: Gollancz, 1976.

DICKSON, GORDON R.
The Dragon and the George. Garden City, N.Y.: Nelson Doubleday [Science Fiction Book Club], 1976.

DODGSON, CHARLES LUTWIDGE.
The Alice Books
Carroll, Lewis [pseud.]. *Alice's Adventures in Wonderland*. London: Macmillan, 1865.
———. *Through the Looking Glass, and What Alice Found There*. London: Macmillan, 1972 [issued in 1871].
———. *The Wasp in the Wig: A "Suppressed" Episode of Through the Looking Glass and What Alice Found There*. Ed. Martin Gardner. Carroll Studies No. 2. New York: The Lewis Carroll Society of North America, 1977.

DONALDSON, STEPHEN R.
The Chronicles of Thomas Covenant
Lord Foul's Bane: The Chronicles of Thomas Covenant, the Un-

believer. Book One. Garden City, N.Y.: Nelson Doubleday [Science Fiction Book Club], 1977.

The Chronicles of Thomas Covenant, the Unbeliever: The Illearth War. New York: Holt, Rinehart and Winston, 1977.

The Chronicles of Thomas Covenant, the Unbeliever: The Power That Preserves. New York: Holt, Rinehart and Winston, 1977.

Book One of the Second Chronicles of Thomas Covenant: The Wounded Land. New York: Ballantine, 1980.

DOUGLAS, NORMAN.

South Wind. London: Martin Secker, 1917.

DUANE, DIANE.

The Door Into Fire. New York: Dell, 1979 [paper].

DUNSANY, LORD. See PLUNKETT, EDWARD JOHN MORETON DRAX.

EDDISON, E. R.

The Worm Ouroboros: A Romance. London: J. Cape, 1922.

The Zimiamvian Trilogy

Mezentian Gate. Plaistow, England: Curwen Press, 1958.

A Fish Dinner in Memison. New York: E. P. Dutton, 1941.

Mistress of Mistresses. New York: E. P. Dutton, 1935.

ENSLEY, EVANGELINE WALTON.

The Mabinogion Series

Walton, Evangeline [pseud.]. *Prince of Annwn: The First Branch of the Mabinogion.* New York: Ballantine, 1974 [paper].

———. *The Children of Llyr: The Second Branch of the Mabinogion.* New York: Ballantine, 1971 [paper].

———. *The Song of Rhiannon: The Third Branch of the Mabinogion.* New York: Ballantine, 1972 [paper].

———. *The Virgin and the Swine: The Fourth Branch of the Mabinogion.* Chicago and New York: Willet, Clark, 1936. Rpt. as *The Island of the Mighty: The Fourth Branch of the Mabinogion.* New York: Ballantine, 1970 [paper].

GARNER, ALAN.

The Moon of Gomrath. London: William Collins, 1963.

The Owl Service. London: William Collins, 1967.

The Weirdstone of Brisingamen: A Tale of Alderley. London: William Collins, 1960. Rev. ed. London: Penguin, 1963.

GARRETT, RANDALL.
Murder and Magic. New York: Ace Books, 1979 [paper].
Too Many Magicians. New York: Doubleday, 1966.

GORDON, JOHN.
The Giant Under the Snow. London: Hutchinson Junior Books, 1968.

GRAHAME, KENNETH.
The Wind in the Willows. London: Methuen, 1908.

GREGORIAN, JOYCE BALLOU.
The Broken Citadel. New York: Atheneum, 1975.

HAGGARD, H. RIDER.

The She Series

Wisdom's Daughter: The Life and Love Story of She-Who-Must-Be-Obeyed. London: Hutchinson, [1923].
She: A History of Adventure. Harper's Franklin Square Library No. 558. New York: Harper & Brothers, 1886 [paper].
Ayesha: The Return of She. London: Ward Lock, 1905.
She and Allan. New York: Longmans, Green, 1921.

HAGGARD, H. RIDER, and ANDREW LANG.
The World's Desire. London and New York: Longmans, Green, 1890.

HILTON, JAMES.
Lost Horizon. New York: William Morrow; London: Macmillan, 1933.

HODGSON, WILLIAM HOPE.
The Boats of the 'Glen Carrig': Being an Account of Their Adventures in the Strange Places of the Earth, After the Foundering of the Good Ship Glen Carrig Through the Striking Upon a Hidden Rock in the Unknown Sea to the Southward. As Told by John Winterstraw, Gent., to His Son James Winterstraw, in the Year 1757, and by Him Commited Very Properly to Manuscript. London: Chapman & Hall, 1907.
The House on the Borderland, from the Manuscript, discovered in 1877 by Mesors. Tonnison and Berroggnog, in the Ruins That Lie to the South of the Village of Kraighten in the West of Ireland. London: Chapman & Hall, 1908.
The Nightland: A Love Tale. London: Nash, 1912.

HOWARD, ROBERT E.

The Conan Series

Conan the Conquerer: The Hyborean Age. New York: Gnome, 1950.
The Sword of Conan. New York: Gnome, 1952.
King Conan. New York: Gnome, 1953.
The Coming of Conan. New York: Gnome, 1953.
Conan the Barbarian. New York: Gnome Press, 1954.
Tales of Conan, with L. Sprague de Camp. New York: Gnome, 1955.
Conan, with L. Sprague de Camp and Lin Carter. New York: Lancer, 1967 [paper].
Conan of Cimmeria, with L. Sprague de Camp and Lin Carter. New York: Lancer, 1969 [paper].
Conan the Freebooter, with L. Sprague de Camp. New York: Lancer, 1968 [paper].
Conan the Wanderer, with L. Sprague de Camp and Lin Carter. New York: Lancer, 1968 [paper].
Conan the Adventurer, with L. Sprague de Camp. New York: Lancer, 1966 [paper].
Conan the Buccaneer, by L. Sprague de Camp and Lin Carter. New York: Lancer, 1971 [paper].
Conan the Warrior. Ed. L. Sprague de Camp. New York: Lancer, 1967 [paper].
Conan the Usurper, with L. Sprague de Camp. New York: Lancer, 1967 [paper].
Conan the Conqueror. Ed. L. Sprague de Camp. New York: Lancer, 1967 [paper].
Conan: The Hour of the Dragon. Ed. Karl Edward Wagner. New York: Berkley, 1977 [paper].
Conan: The People of the Black Circle. Ed. Karl Edward Wagner. New York: Berkley, 1977 [paper].
Conan: Red Nails. Ed. Karl Edward Wagner. New York: Berkley, 1977 [paper].

The Kane Series

The Moon of Skulls. New York: Centaur, 1969 [paper].
The Hand of Kane. New York: Centaur, 1970 [paper].
Solomon Kane. New York: Centaur, 1971 [paper].

HYNE, C. J. CUTCLIFFE.
The Lost Continent. New York: Harper; London: Hutchinson, 1900.

JACOB, PIERS ANTHONY DILLINGHAM.

The Chameleon Series

Anthony, Piers [pseud.]. *A Spell for Chameleon.* New York: Ballantine, 1977 [paper].

———. *The Source of Magic*. New York: Ballantine, 1979 [paper].
———. *Castle Roogna*. New York: Ballantine, 1979 [paper].

JONES, DIANA WYNNE.
The Dalemark Series
Cart and Cwidder. London: Macmillan, 1975.
Drowned Ammet. London: Macmillan, 1977.
The Spellcoats. New York: Atheneum, 1979 [1st American edition].

KINGSLEY, CHARLES.
The Water Babies: A Fairy Tale for a Land Baby. London: Macmillan, 1863.

LAFFERTY, R. A.
The Devil is Dead. New York: Avon, 1971 [paper].
Fourth Mansions. New York: Ace, 1969 [paper].

LAUBENTHAL, SANDERS ANNE.
Excalibur. New York: Ballantine, 1973 [paper].

LE GUIN, URSULA K.
The Earthsea Trilogy
A Wizard of Earthsea. Berkeley: Parnassus, 1968.
The Tombs of Atuan. New York: Atheneum, 1971.
The Farthest Shore. New York: Atheneum, 1972. Rev. ed. London: Gollancz, 1973.

LEIBER, FRITZ.
"Conjure Wife." In *Witches Three*. New York: Twayne, 1952, pp. 19–168. First separate book publication: New York: Twayne, 1953.
The Fafhrd and Gray Mouser Series
Two Sought Adventure: Exploits of Fafhrd and the Gray Mouser. New York: Gnome, 1957. Expanded edition: see *Swords Against Death* (below).
Swords and Deviltry. New York: Ace, 1970 [paper].
Swords Aganist Death. New York: Ace, 1970 [paper]. An expansion of *Two Sought Adventure* (see above).
Swords in the Mist. New York: Ace, 1968 [paper].
Swords Against Wizardry. New York: Ace, 1968 [paper].
The Swords of Lankhmar. New York: Ace, 1968 [paper].
Swords and Ice Magic. New York: Ace, 1977 [paper].
Rime Isle. Chapel Hill, N.C.: Whispers Press, 1977.
Bazaar of the Bizarre. West Kingston, R.I.: Donald M. Grant, 1978.

L'Engle, Madeleine.

The Unicorn Trilogy.

A Wrinkle in Time. New York: Farrar, Straus and Cudahy, 1962.
A Wind in the Door. New York: Farrar, Straus & Giroux, 1973.
A Swiftly Tilting Planet. New York: Farrar, Straus & Giroux, 1978.

Lewis, C. S.

The Chronicles of Narnia

The Lion, the Witch, and the Wardrobe. London: Geoffrey Bles, 1950.
Prince Caspian. London: Geoffrey Bles, 1951.
The Voyage of the "Dawn Treader." London: Geoffrey Bles, 1952.
The Silver Chair. London: Geoffrey Bles, 1953.
The Magician's Nephew. London: Bodley Head, 1955.
The Horse and His Boy. London: Geoffrey Bles, 1954.
The Last Battle: A Story for Children. London: Bodley Head, 1956.

The Space Trilogy

Out of the Silent Planet. London: Lane, 1938.
Perelandra [occasionally titled *Voyage to Venus: Perelandra* in later editions]. London: Lane, 1943.
That Hideous Strength: A Modern Fairy-Tale for Grown-Ups. London: Lane, 1945. Abridged edition as *The Tortured Planet.* New York: Avon, [1958] [paper].

Lindsay, David.

Devil's Tor. London: G. P. Putnam's Sons, 1932.
A Voyage to Arcturus. London: Methuen, 1920.

Lively, Penelope.

The Whispering Knights. London: Heinemann, 1971.

Lupoff, Richard A.

Sword of the Demon. New York: Harper & Row, 1977.

MacDonald, George

At the Back of the North Wind. London: Strahan, 1871 [issued in 1870].
Lilith: A Romance. London: Chatto & Windus; New York: Dodd, Mead, 1895.
Phantastes: A Faerie Romance for Men and Women. London: Smith Elder, 1858.
The Princess and Curdie. London: Chatto & Windus, 1883 [issued in 1882].

The Princess and the Goblin. London: [Strahan], 1872 [issued in 1871].

McKillip, Patricia A.
The Forgotten Beasts of Eld. New York: Atheneum, 1974.
The Hed Trilogy
The Riddle-Master of Hed. New York: Atheneum, 1976.
Heir of Sea and Fire. New York: Atheneum, 1977.
Harpist in the Wind. New York: Atheneum, 1979.

Meredith, George.
The Shaving of Shagpat: An Arabian Adventure. London: Chapman and Hall, 1856. Rev. ed. Westminster: Archibald Constable, 1898.

Merritt, A.
Dwellers in the Mirage. New York: Liveright, 1932.
The Moon Pool. New York and London: G. P. Putnam's Sons, 1919.
Ship of Ishtar. New York: G. P. Putnam's Sons, 1926.

Moorcock, Michael.
Gloriana, or the Unfulfill'd Queen: Being a Romance. London: Allison & Busby, 1978.

Morris, Kenneth.
The Book of Three Dragons. New York and Toronto: Longmans, Green, 1930.
Morus, Cenydd [Welsh for Kenneth Morris]. *The Fates of the Princes of Dyfed.* Point Loma, Calif.: Aryan Theosophical Press, 1914.

Morris, William.
The Dream of John Ball; and, A King's Lesson. London: Reeves & Turner, 1888.
The Story of the Glittering Plain Which Has Been Also Called the Land of Living Men or the Acre of the Undying. Hammersmith, England: Kelmscott Press, 1891.
The Water of the Wondrous Isles. Hammersmith, England: Kelmscott Press, 1897.
The Well at the World's End. Hammersmith, England: Kelmscott Press, 1896.
The Wood Beyond the World. Hammersmith, England: Kelmscott Press, 1894.

MUNDY, TALBOT.

The Jimgrim Series

The Nine Unknown. Indianapolis: Bobbs-Merrill, 1924.

The Devil's Guard. Indianapolis: Bobbs-Merrill, 1926. British edition: *Ramsden.* London: Hutchinson, 1926.

Jimgrim. New York: Century, 1931.

NICHOLS, RUTH.

The Marrow of the World. New York: Atheneum, 1972.

NORTON, ANDRE.

Steel Magic. Cleveland: World, 1965.

The Witch World Series: Simon Tregarth and Family

Horn Crown. New York: DAW, 1981 [paper].

Witch World. New York: Ace, 1963 [paper].

Web of the Witch World. New York: Ace, 1964 [paper].

Three Against the Witch World: [Beyond the Mind Barrier]. New York: Ace, 1965 [paper].

Warlock of the Witch World. New York: Ace, 1967 [paper].

Sorceress of the Witch World. New York: Ace, 1968 [paper].

The Witch World Series: Wereriders

The Crystal Gryphon. New York: Atheneum, 1972.

Gryphon in Glory. New York: Atheneum, 1981.

The Year of the Unicorn. New York: Ace, 1965 [paper].

The Jargoon Pard. New York: Atheneum, 1974.

The Witch World Series: Miscellaneous

Spell of the Witch World. New York: DAW, 1972 [paper].

Trey of Swords. New York: Crosset and Dunlap, 1977.

Zarsthor's Bane. New York: Ace, 1978 [paper].

Lore of the Witch World. New York: DAW, 1980 [paper].

OFFUTT, ANDREW J., and RICHARD K. LYON.

Demon in the Mirror. New York: Pocket Books, 1978 [paper].

PAGE, NORVELL W.

Flame Winds. New York: Berkley, 1969 [paper].

Sons of the Bear-God. New York: Berkley, 1969 [paper].

PANSHIN, ALEXEI and CORY.

Earth Magic. New York: Ace, 1978 [paper].

PEAKE, MERVYN.

The Gormenghast Trilogy

Titus Groan. London: Eyre and Spottiswoode, 1946.
Gormenghast. London: Eyre and Spottiswoode, 1950.
Titus Alone. London: Eyre and Spottiswoode, 1959.

PLUNKETT, EDWARD JOHN MORETON DRAX.

Lord Dunsany. *The Charwoman's Shadow*. London and New York: G. P. Putnam's Sons, 1926.
_______. *The Gods of Pegãna*. London: Elkin Mathews, 1905.
_______. *The King of Elfland's Daughter*. London: G. P. Putnam's Sons, 1924.
_______. *The Sword of Welleran and Other Stories*. London: George Allen and Sons, 1908.

SHAVER, RICHARD S

I Remember Lemuria and The Return of Sathanas. Evanston, Ill.: Venture Books, 1948.

SIMAK, CLIFFORD.

The Enchanted Pilgrimage. New York: Berkley, 1975.

SMITH, ERNEST BRAHAM.

The Kai Lung Series

Bramah, Ernest [pseud.]. *The Wallet of Kai Lung*. London: Grant Richards, 1900.
_______. *Kai Lung's Golden Hours*. London: Grant Richards, 1922.
_______. *Kai Lung Unrolls His Mat*. London: Grant Richards, 1928.
_______. *Moon of Much Gladness: Related by Kai Lung*. London: Cassell, 1932; later title: *The Return of Kai Lung* (1937).
_______. *Kai Lung Beneath the Mulberry-Tree*. London: Grant Richards, 1940.
_______. *Kai Lung: Six: Uncollected Tales from Punch*. Ed. William While. Tacoma, Wash.: Non-Profit Press, 1974.

SWANN, THOMAS BURNETT.

Aeneas Trilogy

Queens Walk in the Dusk. Forest Park, Ga.: Heritage Press, 1977.
Lady of the Bees. New York: Ace, 1976 [paper].
Green Phoenix. New York: DAW, 1972 [paper].

The Minotaur Trilogy

Cry Silver Bells. New York: DAW Books, 1977 [paper].

The Forest of Forever. New York: Ace Books, 1971 [paper].
Days of the Minotaur. New York: Ace, 1966 [paper].

TOLKIEN, J. R. R.

The Lord of the Rings

The Hobbit or There and Back Again. London: Allen and Unwin, 1937. Rev. ed London: Allen and Unwin, 1951. 2nd rev. ed. London: Allen and Unwin, 1966.
The Fellowship of the Ring: Being the First Part of the Lord of the Rings. London: Allen and Unwin, 1954. Rev. ed. New York: Ballantine, 1965 [paper].
The Two Towers: Being the Second Part of the Lord of the Rings. London: Allen and Unwin, 1954. Rev. ed. New York: Ballantine, 1965 [paper].
The Return of the King: Being the Third Part of the Lord of the Rings. London: Allen and Unwin, 1955. Rev. ed. New York: Ballantine, 1965 [paper].

VANCE, JACK.

The Dying Earth Series

The Dying Earth. New York: [Hillman Periodicals], 1950 [paper]. In this edition, the first two chapters are reversed. This is corrected in the 1962 Lancer and later editions.
The Eyes of the Overworld. New York: Ace Books, 1966.
Morreion: A Tale of Dying Earth. San Francisco and Columbia, Pa. Underwood/Miller, 1979.

WALTON, EVANGELINE [pseud.]. See ENSLEY, EVANGELINE WALTON.

WHITE, T. H.
The Elephant and the Kangaroo. New York: G. P. Putnam's Sons, 1947.

The Once and Future King Novels

The Sword in the Stone. New York: G. P. Putnam's Sons, 1938.
The Witch in the Wood [retitled "The Queen of Air and Darkness" in *The Once and Future King*]. New York: G. P. Putnam's Sons, 1939.
The Ill-Made Knight. New York: G. P. Putnam's Sons, 1940.
The Once and Future King. London: Collins, 1958.
The Book of Merlyn: The Unpublished Conclusion to "The Once and Future King." Austin: University of Texas Press, 1977.

WILLIAMS, CHARLES W. S.
All Hallows' Eve. London: Faber & Faber, 1945.
War in Heaven. London: Victor Gollancz, 1930.

WILLIAMS, JAY.
The Hero from Otherwhere. New York: Dell, 1972 [paper].

ZELAZNY, ROGER.

The "Amber" Series

Nine Princes in Amber. Garden City, N.Y.: Doubleday, 1970.
The Guns of Avalon. Garden City, N.Y.: Doubleday, 1972.
The Sign of the Unicorn. Garden City, N.Y.: Doubleday, 1975.
The Hand of Oberon. Garden City, N.Y.: Doubleday, 1976.
The Courts of Chaos. Garden City, N.Y.: Doubleday, 1978.

Modern Critical Studies and Reference Works on Fantasy

Marshall B. Tymn

THIS BIBLIOGRAPHY lists the major works of criticism and reference published during the last few years. Sections 1 to 3 are complete, while sections 4 and 5 are highly selective. For a comprehensive, annotated listing of fantasy scholarship published in the 1970s, as well as material on periodicals, organizations, awards, and library fantasy collections, see my *Fantasy Literature: A Core Collection and Reference Guide* (New York: R. R. Bowker Co., 1979).

1. BIBLIOGRAPHIES OF BIBLIOGRAPHIES

Briney, Robert E., and Edward Wood. *SF Bibliographies: An Annotated Bibliography of Bibliographical Works on Science Fiction and Fantasy Fiction.* Chicago: Advent, 1972.
The first attempt to publish information on early bibliographic work in the field. This book supplies exhaustive coverage of bibliographical reference tools, listing and annotating approximately 100 bibliographies, indexes, and checklists published as separate books or pamphlets. Advent reports that an enlarged edition of this work is in preparation.

Tymn, Marshall B., and Roger C. Schlobin. *The Year's Scholarship in Science Fiction and Fantasy: 1972–1975.* See Section 3.

Tymn, Marshall B., Roger C. Schlobin, and L. W. Currey. *A Research Guide to Science Fiction Studies: An Annotated Checklist of Primary and Secondary Sources for Fantasy and Science Fiction*. New York: Garland, 1977.
Supplements and in some cases supersedes citations in Briney and Wood. This reference work remains the current summary of science fiction and fantasy scholarship in pamphlet and book form. Designed as a handbook for researchers, it provides the reader with a comprehensive listing of the important research tools published in the United States and England through 1976. The volume contains over 400 annotated entries that span the entire range of fantasy and science fiction scholarship, including general surveys, histories, genre studies, author studies, bibliographies and indexes, book reviews, and Ph.D. dissertations.

2. PRIMARY BIBLIOGRAPHIES

Derleth, August. *Thirty Years of Arkham House 1939–1969: A History and Bibliography*. Sauk City, Wis.: Arkham House, 1970.
Contains a history of the firm and a bibliography of publications through 1969 issued under the imprints of Arkham House, Mycroft & Moran, and Stanton & Lee. Now the best-known of the specialist fantasy publishers, Arkham House was originally founded by Derleth for the express purpose of publishing the works of H. P. Lovecraft. Derleth soon discovered a distinct but small market for the fantasy short story and published collections by writers other than Lovecraft, providing a forum for new writers in the genre. A key historical document.

Lewis, Naomi. *Fantasy Books for Children*. London: National Book League, 1977.
A useful guide to children's fantasy, with detailed and often lengthy critical annotations of about 200 works. Emphasis is on British imprints. Includes only books currently in print at the time the listing was compiled.

Lynn, Ruth Nadelman. *Fantasy for Children: An Annotated Checklist*. New York: R. R. Bowker, 1979.
A bibliography of about 1,200 works arranged into subject categories. Brief annotations provide a description of the book and information on reading level; only about half of the titles are annotated. The problem with this work is the arrangement of

titles into types of fantasy. The categories are not mutually exclusive and in many cases are not categories of fantasy but elements which are common to most fantasy works.

Schlobin, Roger C. *The Literature of Fantasy: A Comprehensive, Annotated Bibliography of Modern Fantasy Fiction.* New York: Garland, 1979.

This work attempts to list and annotate all major modern fantasy works. Over 1,200 novels, collections and anthologies are listed, covering the period 1858–1979. An Introduction, "Fantasy and Its Literature," examines the psychological nature of fantasy and its manifestations in literature. Fills the bibliographic void that previously existed in adult fantasy scholarship, while correcting errors found in previous compilations. Includes citations of author bibliographies.

Tymn, Marshall B., Kenneth J. Zahorski, and Robert H. Boyer. *Fantasy Literature: A Core Collection and Reference Guide.* New York: R. R. Bowker, 1979.

A guide to the major works of high fantasy published since the Victorian era. Designed as an acquisitions tool for libraries and others building core collections, the volume lists 240 seminal works of high fantasy, with lengthy critical evaluations. An introductory essay examines the nature and development of fantasy literature, and a research aids section provides comprehensive coverage of the various scholarly and fan activities in the field. Cited by the American Library Association as an Outstanding Reference Book of 1979.

Waggoner, Diana. *The Hills of Faraway: A Guide to Fantasy.* New York: Atheneum, 1978.

Two chapters on fantasy as a literary form precede a checklist of about 1,000 primary and secondary works. Annotations for each entry vary from a single sentence to a paragraph to no annotation at all. The unevenness of the annotations is no less disturbing than the major errors of fact in the bibliographic citations as well as major omissions among the works listed.

3. SECONDARY BIBLIOGRAPHIES

Clareson, Thomas. *Science Fiction Criticism: An Annotated Checklist.* Kent, Ohio: Kent State University Press, 1972.

A comprehensive guide to the critical literature published in English-language books and periodicals prior to 1972. Contains approximately 800 annotated entries arranged in nine sections:

General Studies; Literary Studies; Book Reviews; The Visual Arts; Futurology; Utopia and Dystopia; Classroom and Library; Publishing; Specialist Bibliographies, Checklists and Indices; and The Contemporary Scene. Indexed by author only. A pioneer work, this volume must be consulted by anyone researching secondary materials in fantasy.

Tymn, Marshall B., and Roger C. Schlobin. *The Year's Scholarship in Science Fiction and Fantasy: 1972–1975*. Kent, Ohio: Kent State University Press, 1979.

The chronological continuation of Clareson's *Science Fiction Criticism* and the first hardcover cumulation of the field's only ongoing secondary bibliography, "The Year's Scholarship in Science Fiction and Fantasy," published annually in *Extrapolation* (1976–). Covers all American and selected British scholarship, and important items from major, established fanzines. Arranged into the following sections: General Studies, Bibliography and Reference, Author Studies and Bibliographies, and Teaching and Visual Aids. Includes books, monographs, articles, Ph.D. dissertations, published M.A. theses, reprints of major scholarship that have been out of print for a significant period, and scholarly or instructional media. Supplements for the period 1976–78 have been published in *Extrapolation*.

4. HISTORY AND CRITICISM

Alpers, Hans Joachim. "Loincloth, Double Ax, and Magic: 'Heroic Fantasy' and Related Genres." *Science-Fiction Studies*, 5 (1978), 19–32.

A preliminary attempt at a taxonomy of heroic fantasy contents, using the following main groups as starting points: science fantasy, heroic fantasy with science-fiction elements, heroic fantasy with historic and realistic elements, and hardcore heroic fantasy.

Attebury, Brian. *The Fantasy Tradition in American Literature From Irving to Le Guin*. Bloomington: Indiana University Press, 1980.

An important attempt to define and explore the history and tradition of American fantasy, a departure from the usual Anglo-American approach. Traces the roots of the literature in the magical folk tale and its limitations and parameters, with some consideration of motifs from legend, ballad, and epic. Focuses particularly on the works of L. Frank Baum, Ray Bradbury, Edgar Rice

Burroughs, James Branch Cabell, Nathaniel Hawthorne, Washington Irving, Ursula K. Le Guin, Herman Melville, and James Thurber, with brief treatments of other authors. One of the first studies to examine fantasy from a historical perspective.

Carter, Lin. *Imaginary Worlds: The Art of Fantasy.* New York: Ballantine, 1973.
Includes coverage of major genre authors (Morris, Dunsany, Eddison, Cabell, Hodgson, Howard, Lovecraft, Lewis, and Tolkien) and discusses their contributions to and influence on the field. Some chapters are organized around a specific group, magazine influence, or sub-genre, e.g., the Inklings, the Munsey magazines, *Weird Tales, Unknown,* "sword-and-sorcery." Carter also devotes three chapters to the techniques of writing fantasy. The book, however, is marred by the author's lack of attention to scholarly detail.

Crossley, Robert. "Education and Fantasy." *College English,* 37 (1975), 281–93.
Using undergraduate responses, Crossley analyzes the student reaction to fantasy and postulates that fantasy is divided into two types: the fantasy of recovery and the fantasy of revelation. He concludes that fantasy as a genre and as a teaching tool is irreducible, educational, evocative, thought-provoking, and psychedelic.

Eichner, Henry M. *Atlantean Chronicles.* Alhambra, Calif.: Fantasy Publishing Company, 1971.
A study of theories concerning the location of Atlantis. The bibliography, which comprises the final 99 pages of the volume, is the most extensive listing to date of the Atlantis theme in fiction. The core is an annotated listing of over 130 English-language novels. In addition, there are non-annotated checklists of fiction appearing in *Weird Tales* and *Amazing Stories,* foreign-language works, and secondary materials.

Fredericks, S. C. "Problems of Fantasy." *Science-Fiction Studies,* 5 (1978), 33–44.
A survey of fantasy criticism through 1977 in an attempt "(1) to discover what perspectives on fantasy are common to the diverse theorists, (2) to make judgments as to what might be the most or least valuable in the various theories, and (3) to suggest what problem areas might be most productive for future research on Fantasy."

Hunter, Mollie. "One World" [part one]. *Horn Book Magazine,* 51 (1975), 557–63.
Postulates that folklore is a necessary element of fantasy and examines the significance and function of fantasy in children's literature.

———. "One World: Part II." *Horn Book Magazine*, 52 (1976), 32–38.

A continuation of the examination of the function of fantasy in children's literature with a consideration of the role of the supernatural in the related genres of fantasy and the fairy tale.

Irwin, W. R. *The Game of the Impossible: The Rhetoric of Fantasy*. Urbana: University of Illinois Press, 1976.

Examines some of the common characteristics of fantasies written between 1880 and 1957, a period in which, according to Irwin, fantasy existed as a distinct literary mode. Selected works by major fantasists are analyzed for their intrinsic importance and illustrative value.

Jackson, Rosemary. *Fantasy: The Literature of Subversion*. New York and London: Methuen, 1981.

Exploring literary fantasies from the Gothic tale of terror to the twentieth-century dystopia, Jackson locates fantasy between the related romance forms of fairy tale and science fiction. Her study relies on theoretical texts by Vladimir Propp, Tzvetan Todorov, and Louis Vax to analyze recurrent motifs and structures in works by Mary Shelley, James Hogg, E. T. A. Hoffmann, Lewis Carroll, George MacDonald, Edgar Allan Poe, Robert Louis Stevenson, Franz Kafka, Mervyn Peake, and others. Jackson concludes by arguing that fantasy is a distinct form of narrative whose ambiguities are expressions of cultural unease.

Kennard, Jean E. *Number and Nightmare: Forms of Fantasy in Contemporary Fiction*. Hamden, Conn.: Archon Books, 1975.

A discussion of the techniques and devices used by Joseph Heller, John Barth, James Purdy, Kurt Vonnegut, Jr., Anthony Burgess, Iris Murdoch, and William Golding to deal with existentialism, absurdity, and myth. Includes a bibliography of general criticism and a list of primary and secondary works for each author.

Landow, George P. "And the World Became Strange: Realms of Literary Fantasy." In *Fantastic Illustration and Design in Britain, 1850–1930*. By Diane L. Johnson. Providence: Rhode Island School of Design, 1979, pp. 9–43. Rpt. *Georgia Review*, 33 (Spring 1979), 7–42.

Following a survey of critical attitudes toward fantasy, Landow examines a representative literary fantasy by each of five nineteenth-century authors: John Ruskin, George MacDonald, George Meredith, William Morris, and William Hope Hodgson. In addition—and this is the major reason for the importance of this essay—Landow examines the relationships between nineteenth-century fantasy literature and visual art, discussing aesthetic parallels and examining the works of Dante Gabriel Rossetti, Burne-Jones, Arthur Rackham, Richard Doyle, John Simmons, Randolph Caldecott, Ernest Henry Griset, Edward Julius Detmold, Kate Greenway, and Walter Crane. Reprinted in this volume.

Manlove, C. N. *Modern Fantasy: Five Studies*. Cambridge: Cambridge University Press, 1975.

A major literary analysis and evaluation of the achievement of five fantasy authors—Charles Kingsley, George MacDonald, C. S. Lewis, J. R. R. Tolkien, and Mervyn Peake—with an introduction discussing the nature and character of fantasy, which is reprinted and amplified in this volume.

Mobley, Jane. "Toward a Definition of Fantasy Fiction." *Extrapolation,* 15 (1974), 117–28.

An attempt to separate fantasy fiction from other genres within the mode of speculative fiction, operating on the premise that fantasy depends on a conjunction of focus and form peculiar to itself and not readily applicable to other types of speculative fiction. Points to magic as the key informing principle in fantasy, as it delineates both the focus (subject) and form (treatment) of the genre.

Prickett, Stephen. *Victorian Fantasy*. Bloomington: Indiana University Press, 1979.

Traces the evolution of the aesthetics of fantasy from its beginnings into the Victorian era, showing how the fantastic flourished in the popular and comic tradition of the period. Examines in detail the development and influence of six writers: Edward Lear, Lewis Carroll, Charles Kingsley, George MacDonald, Rudyard Kipling, and Edith Nesbit.

Rabkin, Eric S. *The Fantastic in Literature*. Princeton, N.J.: Princeton University Press, 1976.

An exploration of the nature and uses of the fantastic following from the recognition that it is not the unreal by itself that is fantastic but the unreal in a particular context. Each chapter develops this view, using examples from other literary modes. By analyzing different works of literature, Rabkin shows that the fantastic depends on a reversal of the ground rules of a narrative world. This reversal signals most commonly a psychological escape to an unknown world secretly yearned for, whose order, although reversed, bears a precise relation to reality. In the ongoing dialogue among fantasy scholars regarding the nature of the fantastic, this study

Todorov, Tzvetan. *The Fantastic: A Structural Approach to a*

must be regarded as a key work.

Literary Genre. Trans. Richard Howard. Cleveland: Press of Case Western Reserve University, 1973.

A discussion of certain verbal, syntactic, and thematic strategies that recur with frequency in the literature of the fantastic, and an examination of the precise response that a confrontation with the fantastic characteristically evokes in the reader. Speculating on the social and cultural function of the supernatural within the framework of the modern sensibility, Todorov draws upon such thinkers as Buber, Freud, and Sartre.

Wolfe, Gary K. "Symbolic Fantasy." *Genre,* 8 (1975), 194–209.

A well-documented examination of the critical appraisals of fantasy and a description of the genre's narrative, stylistic, structural, and mythical characteristics with illustrations from the works of David Lindsay, George MacDonald, and C. S. Lewis.

5. MAJOR PERIODICALS AND SPECIAL ISSUES

A. *Periodicals*

Anduril. Ed. John Martin, 101 Eskdale, Tanhouse 5, Skelmersdale, Lancaster WN8 6EB, U. K. Irregular; first issue, 1972.

Winner of the British Fantasy Award in 1976, small press category. Contains articles, short fiction, and book reviews.

Dark Fantasy. Ed. Howard E. Day, 204 First St., Box 207, Gananoque, Ontario, Canada K7G 2T7. Quarterly; first issue, July 1973.

Primarily a fiction and poetry magazine that publishes the work of new writers and artists.

Dark Horizons. Ed. Geoffrey N. Smith ,113a High St., Whitstable, Kent CT5 1AY, U. K. Three times yearly; first issue, December 1971. Published by the British Fantasy Society.

Contains poetry, fiction, articles and interviews on all aspects of fantasy in literature.

Fantasy Media. Ed. Jon M. Harvey, 194 Station Rd., Kings Heath, Birmingham, B14 7TE, U. K. Five times yearly; first issue, March 1979.

An information magazine on the fantasy and horror fields, with sections on books and writers, reviews, interviews, small publishers, film, graphics, magazines, and other items of interest. Comprehensive coverage of the field. Now defunct.

Fantasy Newsletter. Ed. Robert Collins, Florida Atlantic Univer-

sity, Boca Raton, Fla. 33431. Monthly; first issue, June 1978.
The newspaper of the fantasy field. Reports on recent and forthcoming events and publications of interest to fantasy readers. Very thorough in its coverage, this attractively illustrated publication nicely complements the fantasy coverage in *Locus*.

The Romantist. Ed. John C. Moran and Don Herron, 3610 Meadowbrook Ave., Nashville, Tenn. 37205. Irregular; first issue, 1977. Published by the F. Marion Crawford Memorial Society.
Serves as a forum for studies about authors and artists representative of the Romantic tradition in literature and the arts.

B. *Special Issues*

Mosaic: A Journal for the Comparative Study of Literature and Ideas. Winnipeg, Canada: University of Manitoba, Winter 1977.
A special issue on "Faerie, Fantasy, and Pseudo-mediaevalia in Twentieth-Century Literature." Essays on George MacDonald, T. H. White, J. R. R. Tolkien, John Cowper Powys, E. Nesbit, Ursula K. Le Guin, and selected fantasy subjects.

The CEA Critic. College Station, Texas: Texas A & M University, January 1978.
A special "Fantasy" issue featuring articles on teaching, selected topics and authors, and bibliographies.

Contributors

ROGER C. SCHLOBIN holds a Ph.D. in medieval literature from Ohio State University and is currently an Associate Professor of English and the Special Assistant to the Chancellor at the North Central Campus of Purdue University. He is the author of *The Literature of Fantasy: A Comprehensive, Annotated Bibliography of Modern Fantasy Fiction* and *Andre Norton: A Primary and Secondary Bibliography* as well as past coeditor of "The Year's Scholarship in Science Fiction and Fantasy," which appears annually in *Extrapolation* and is cumulated in book form by Kent State University Press. He is the editor of *The Garland Library of Fantasy Classics* and *The Starmont Reader's Guides* to contemporary science-fiction and fantasy authors and is a consulting editor for a number of fantasy publications. His essays, articles, bibliographies, and reviews have appeared in a wide variety of periodicals.

ROBERT H. BOYER, Associate Professor of English at St. Norbert College, teaches courses in Chaucer, Arthurian romance, modern poetry, and science fiction and fantasy. He was a National Endowment for the Humanities Junior Fellow, and currently he is a Danforth Associate. He is coeditor of four anthologies of fantasy with Kenneth J. Zahorski (see below) and coauthor of *Fantasy Literature: A Core Collection and Reference Guide*. At present, he is working in the areas of poetry (W. H. Auden) and children's and all-ages' fantasy literature.

ROBERT CROSSLEY was educated at Rockhurst College (A.B.) and the University of Virginia (M.A., Ph.D.). Since 1972, he has been at the University of Massachusetts at Boston, where he is now an Associate Professor of English and Director of the English major. He teaches courses in fantasy and utopia, English epic poetry, eighteenth-century fiction, Wells and Tolkien, introductory literature and composition, and a graduate seminar in the teaching of science fiction and fantasy. His published work—which has appeared in *Genre, College English, The Massachusetts Review, Philological Quarterly,* and the *Journal of General Education*—includes essays on Poe's fiction, the teaching of fantasy, the literature-versus-science controversy, Pope's translation of the *Iliad,* and the autobiographies of John Stuart Mill and Henry Adams. He has also contributed essays to the *Survey of Science-Fiction Literature* and has written a monograph on H. G. Wells for the *Starmont Reader's Guide* series. His current areas of active research are literature and pedagogy, feminist utopian fiction, and the intellectual relationship of H. G. Wells and Olaf Stapledon.

TERRY REECE HACKFORD earned her B.A. in literature from Princeton University in 1974. She then worked on the curatorial staff of the Wadsworth Atheneum in Hartford, Connecticut, prior to earning her M.A. in Art History at Brown University in 1981. She has published in the field of Renaissance art and wrote her M.A. thesis on Frederick Lord Leighton's Arab Hall. She is currently special projects editor for the New York Graphic Society in Boston.

W. R. IRWIN is a Professor of English and Associate Chairman of the department at the University of Iowa. He is the author of *The Game of the Impossible: A Rhetoric of Fantasy* and of studies concerning Swift, Fielding, Frederick Prince of Wales, the literature of mountaineering, C. E. Montague, Victoria Sackville-West, Rose Macaulay, Robert Frost, F. Scott Fitzgerald, Dos Passos, David Garnett, Charles Williams, C. S. Lewis, and J. R. R. Tolkien. He is the coauthor, with J. B. Ratermanis, of *The Comic Style of Beaumarchais.*

George P. Landow, Professor of English at Brown University, has taught at Columbia, Cornell, and Oxford Universities and at the University of Chicago. He has been a Fulbright Scholar and a Fellow of the Woodrow Wilson Foundation, the Cornell University Society for the Humanities, the Guggenheim Foundation, and Brasenose College, Oxford. He has written widely on nineteenth-century art, literature, theology, and critical theory, and his books include *The Aesthetic and Critical Theories of John Ruskin*; *William Holman Hunt and Typological Symbolism*; *Approaches to Victorian Autobiography* (editor); *Victorian Types, Victorian Shadows: Biblical Typology and Victorian Literature, Art, and Thought*; and *Images of Crisis: Literary Iconology, 1750 to the Present.* He was the co-organizer of the international loan exhibition *Fantastic Literature and Design in Britain, 1850–1930*, a project funded by the National Endowment for the Humanities.

Colin N. Manlove has been a lecturer in English Literature at Edinburgh University since 1967. He is the author of *Modern Fantasy: Five Studies*; *Literature and Reality 1600–1800*; *The Gap in Shakespeare: The Motif of Division from Richard II to The Tempest*; and numerous essays and articles, often on fantasy. He has recently completed a further book on fantasy, *Fantasy: The Many Faces of Wonder,* which discusses a variety of authors, and he is currently working on a book for the teaching of literary criticism.

Francis J. Molson, Professor of English at Central Michigan University, is a specialist in nineteenth-century American literature, children's literature, and science fiction and fantasy. He has published on topics as diverse as Emily Dickinson; Francis H. Burnett; Ursula K. Le Guin; Francis Finn, author of American Catholic juveniles; the Tom Swift books; teaching children's literature; and the image of the child-writer in children's fiction. His current research includes children's science fiction and the development of children's fantasy.

William M. Schuyler, Jr., was born in Chicago and spent most of his childhood there. He did his undergraduate work in mathematics at the University of Illinois and graduate work in philosophy and the history of science at Princeton University. He has taught at the University of Louisville since 1963. He and his wife live in a house with a W-shaped floor plan, a hexagonal living room, and a thirteen-sided patio. He has been reading fantasy ever since he could read and now spends much time reading about Art Nouveau and Japanese prints.

RAYMOND H. THOMPSON, B.A. (Queen's, Belfast), M.A. (University of Michigan), and Ph.D. (Alberta), is an Associate Professor of English at Acadia University, Wolfsville, Nova Scotia. His interest in the romance mode of literature spans both medieval literature and modern science fiction and fantasy. He has published articles on the Arthurian legend in medieval literature and on Gordon R. Dickson, creator of the famous Dorsai series. He is currently completing a bibliography of Dickson for G. K. Hall and is working on a treatment of the Arthurian legend in modern fantasy.

MARSHALL B. TYMN, Associate Professor of English at Eastern Michigan University, is Director of the national Workshop on the Teaching of Science Fiction and the author of numerous reference works and articles on science-fiction and fantasy literature. His books include *A Research Guide to Science Fiction Studies* (co-compiler); *Index to Stories in Thematic Anthologies of Science Fiction*; *American Fantasy and Science Fiction: Toward a Bibliography of Works Published in the United States, 1948–1973*; *The Year's Scholarship in Science Fiction and Fantasy, 1972–1975* (co-compiler); *Fantasy Literature: A Core Collection and Reference Guide* (co-compiler); *The Science Reference Book*; and *Horror Literature: A Core Collection and Reference Guide*. He is the editor of the largest projected critical series in the fields of science fiction and fantasy, *Contributions to the Study of Science Fiction and Fantasy*; is advisory acquisitions editor for G. K. Hall's *Masters of Science Fiction and Fantasy* bibliographic series; and bibliographer for Writers of the 21st Century series. He is a former officer of the Science Fiction Research Association and a member of the Science Fiction Writers of America. He holds a Ph.D. in American Culture from the University of

Michigan, and his continuing interest in American literature of the Romantic period is reflected in his *Thomas Cole's Poetry* and *Thomas Cole: The Collected Essays and Prose Sketches.*

SAMUEL H. VASBINDER holds three degrees from Kent State University, including the Ph.D. He has been a John Hay Summer Fellow in the Humanities, is included in *Outstanding Secondary Teachers of America,* served as county-wide department chairman in English for the Canton City Schools from 1975 to 1978, and is a member of Phi Delta Kappa. He currently directs the Humanities program for the Canton City Schools and teaches in the Department of English at the University of Akron.

GARY K. WOLFE, Associate Professor of Humanities at Roosevelt University, received his doctorate from the University of Chicago. In addition to his work in science-fiction and fantasy criticism, he has coauthored (with Carol T. Williams) a textbook on research methods, *Elements of Research*, and published essays in fields from adult education to popular culture. In the science-fiction and fantasy fields, his essays have appeared in *Extrapolation, Science-Fiction Studies, Genres, Studies in Scottish Literature*, and elsewhere, as well as in numerous *festschriften* and reference works, including the *Survey of Science Fiction Literature,* for which he served as a consulting editor. He is the author of the Eaton Award-winning *The Known and the Unknown: The Iconography of Science Fiction* and *David Lindsay: A Starmont Reader's Guide.*

KENNETH J. ZAHORSKI is a Professor of English at St. Norbert College, where he teaches Renaissance literature, Shakespeare, modern drama, and fantasy and science-fiction literature. Active in the Wisconsin Council of Teachers of English, he has served on both its Executive Committee and its College and University Committee. He is the coauthor of *Fantasy Literature: A Core Collection and Reference Guide*, and coeditor (with Robert H. Boyer) of the two-volume *The*

Fantastic Imagination: An Anthology of High Fantasy; *Dark Imaginings: An Anthology of Gothic Fantasy*; and *The Phoenix Tree: An Anthology of Myth Fantasy*. His reviews and articles have appeared in *College English, Wisconsin English Journal, CLA Journal, Choice,* and the *SFRA Newsletter*.

JULES ZANGER was born in New York City in 1927 and received his education in the New York public schools and libraries, at the University of Denver, the University of Chicago, and Washington University, which awarded him a Ph.D. in English in 1954. He spent a couple of years in the army and has taught at Ohio State University, Illinois Institute of Technology, and Southern Illinois University at Edwardsville, where he is now a Professor of English. His critical articles have appeared in a wide variety of journals, including *American Literature, Landscape, William and Mary Quarterly, Children's Literature in Education, American Quarterly,* and *American Studies*.

Index